STECK-VAUGHN

PreGED

Science

REVIEWERS

Robert Christensen
Principal
Handlon Correctional Facility
Michigan Department
of Corrections
Ionia, MI

Linda Correnti
GED Staff Developer
Alternative Schools & Programs
New York City Department
of Education
New York, NY

Dr. Gary A. Eyre
Consultant
GED Testing Service
Advance Associates
and Consultants
Phoenix, AZ

Arnoldo Hinojosa
Senior Director
Community Initiatives
Harris County Department
of Education
Houston, TX

Nancy Lawrence
E-teacher
KC Distance Learning, Inc.
Butler, PA

Charan Lee
Director
Adult Education
Anderson School Districts 1 & 2
Williamston, SC

STECK-VAUGHN
Harcourt Supplemental Publishers

www.steck-vaughn.com

ACKNOWLEDGMENTS

Executive Editor: Ellen Northcutt

Senior Editor: Donna Townsend

Associate Design Director: Joyce Spicer

Senior Designer: Jim Cauthron

Senior Photo Researcher: Alyx Kellington

Editorial Development: Learning Unlimited, Oak Park, IL

Photography credits: p. 14 © John Henley/CORBIS; pp. 17, 19 Courtesy of NASA; p. 23 Courtesy of American Cancer Society; p. 30a,b © Science Photo Library/Photo Researchers, Inc.; p. 35 © Bonnie Kamin/PhotoEdit Inc.; p. 49 © Biophoto Associates/Science Source/Photo Researchers, Inc.; p. 53 © Elliot Dick, Discover Magazine; p. 59 © Michael J. Balick/Peter Arnold, Inc.; p. 71 © E.R. Degginger/Animals Animals; p. 89 © O.Louis Mazzatenta/National Geographic Image Collection; p. 94 © Randy M. Ury/CORBIS; p. 102 © Bob Daemmrich/Stock Boston; p. 105 © SuperStock; p. 111 © Stephen Saks/Photo Researchers, Inc.; p. 117 © Alexander Lowry/Photo Researchers, Inc.; pp. 123,125,129 Courtesy of NASA; p. 134 © Mug Shots/CORBIS; p. 142 © Mary Kate Denny/PhotoEdit Inc.; p. 145, 151b © David Young-Wolff/PhotoEdit Inc; p. 153 © Robert Brenner/PhotoEdit Inc.; p. 157a © Canadian Museum of Civilization, artist Charles Edenshaw, image no.585-3276, catalogue no. VII-B-103a/CORBIS; p. 157b © Tony Freeman/PhotoEdit Inc.; p. 163 © Will & Deni McIntyre/CORBIS; p. 168 © Roy Volkmann /CORBIS SYGMA; p. 176 © Joe McBride/CORBIS; p. 179 © Tom Prettyman/PhotoEdit Inc.; p. 185 © Jonathan Daniel/AllSport/Getty Images; p. 187 © John Swart/AllSport/Getty Images; p. 191 © George Widman/AP/Wide World; p. 197 © Euroaelios/Phototake; p. 208 © SuperStock.
Additional photography by Getty Royalty Free.

ISBN 0-7398-6700-8

11 12 13 14 15 0982 14 13 12
4500371367

CONTENTS

How to Use This Book

The purpose of this book is to help you develop the foundation you need to pass the *GED Science* Test. In this book, you will be introduced to different areas of life science, physical science, and Earth and space science. Throughout the book, you will learn a variety of thinking and reading skills. You will also learn graphic skills, such as interpreting diagrams and drawing conclusions from graphs, that are necessary for success on the GED Science Test.

Units

Unit 1: Life Science Life science is the study of living things, where they live, and how they affect each other. In this unit, you will develop such thinking skills as making inferences and predictions, distinguishing fact from opinion, and comparing and contrasting. The graphic illustrations in this unit also provide practice in skills such as interpreting diagrams and reading maps, timelines, and graphs. You will read articles about the human body, plants, animals, the environment, ecosystems, and evolution.

Unit 2: Earth and Space Science Earth and space science is the study of Earth and the universe. This unit covers skills such as drawing conclusions and reading tables and weather maps. You will read articles about weather, the greenhouse effect, water resources, the solar system, and the International Space Station.

Unit 3: Chemistry Chemistry is the study of matter and how it changes. This unit includes skills such as understanding chemical formulas, comparing and contrasting, and reading line graphs. You will gain an understanding of chemistry by reading articles about the chemistry of household cleaners, chemical reactions in cooking, mixtures and solutions, and combustion.

Unit 4: Physics Physics is the study of energy and forces and how they affect matter. In this unit, you will practice reading diagrams, summarizing information, and applying ideas. You will read articles about how machines work, force and motion, computers and electronics, and laser surgery.

Pretest and Posttest

The Pretest is a self-check of what you already know and what you need to study. After you complete all of the items on the Pretest, check your work in the Answers and Explanations section at the back of the book. Then fill out the Pretest Evaluation Chart. This chart tells you where each skill is taught in this book. When you have completed the book, you will take a Posttest. Compare your Posttest score to your Pretest score to see your progress.

Lessons

Each unit is divided into lessons. Each lesson is based on the Active Reading Process. *Active reading* means doing something before reading, during reading, and after reading. By reading actively, you will improve your reading comprehension skills.

The first page of each lesson has three sections to help prepare you for what you are about to read. First, you will read some background information about the passage presented in the lesson. This is followed by the Relate to the Topic section, which includes a brief exercise designed to help you relate the topic of the reading to your life. Finally, Reading Strategies will provide you with a pre-reading strategy that will help you to understand what you read and a brief exercise that will allow you to practice using that strategy. These are activities you do before reading. Vocabulary words important to the lesson are listed down the left-hand side of the page.

The articles you will read are about interesting topics in science. As you read each article, you will see Skills Mini-Lessons. Here you learn a reading, science, or graphic skill, and you do a short activity. After completing the activity, continue reading the article. Two Skills Mini-Lessons appear in every article. These are the activities you do during reading.

After reading the article, you answer fill-in-the-blank, short-answer, and multiple-choice questions in the section called Thinking About the Article. Answering these questions will help you decide how well you understood what you just read. The final question in this section relates information from the article to your own real-life experiences.

Science at Work

Science at Work is a two-page feature at the end of each unit. Each Science at Work feature introduces a specific job, describes the science skills the job requires, and includes a related activity. It also gives information about other jobs in the same career area.

Unit Reviews and Mini-Tests

Unit Reviews tell you how well you have learned the skills in each unit. Mini-Tests follow each Unit Review. These timed practice tests allow you to practice your skills with the kinds of questions that you will see on the actual GED Tests.

Answers and Explanations

Answers and explanations to every exercise question are at the back of this book, beginning on page 228. The explanation for multiple-choice questions tells why one answer choice is correct.

Setting Goals

A goal is something you aim for, something you want to achieve. What is your long-term goal for using this book? You may want to get your GED or you may just want to learn more about science. These are large goals that may each take you some time to accomplish.

Write your long-term goal for science.

____

____

This section of the book will help you to think about how you already use science and then to set some goals for what you would like to learn in this book. These short-term goals will be stepping stones to the long-term goal you wrote.

Check each activity that you do. Add more activities.

I use science in my everyday life when I

_____ cook

_____ watch the weather report

_____ recycle

_____ take antibiotics when I am sick

_____ other ______________________________

____

____

List your experiences with learning and using science.

What I've Liked	What I Haven't Liked
________________	________________
________________	________________
________________	________________
________________	________________
________________	________________

Think about your science goals.

1. I decided to improve my science skills when I ______________________

____

____

2. My science goals include (check as many as you like)

- ☐ reading science charts and graphs
- ☐ understanding science diagrams
- ☐ understanding the benefits of recycling
- ☐ knowing how issues in genetic research affect me
- ☐ learning about ecosystems and my role in them
- ☐ understanding about daily weather
- ☐ knowing Earth's place in the universe
- ☐ learning how to use chemical reactions in everyday tasks
- ☐ understanding how to conserve our natural resources
- ☐ knowing how computers work
- ☐ other ______________________

____

____

3. I will have met my long-term goal for science when I am able to

____

____

____

Keep track of your goals.

As you work through this book, turn back often to this page. Add more goals at any time you wish. Check each goal that you complete.

Learn about the skills you have.

Complete the Pretest that begins on the next page. It will help you learn more about your strengths and weaknesses in science. You may wish to change some items in your list of goals after you have taken the Pretest and completed the Pretest Evaluation Chart on page 13.

PRETEST

Use this Pretest before you begin Unit 1. Don't worry if you can't answer all the questions. The Pretest will help you find out in which science areas you are strong in and which you need to practice. Read each article, study any graphics, and answer the questions that follow. Check your answers on pages 228–229. Then enter your scores in the chart on page 13.

The Plant Cell

All living things are made of cells, the working units of the body. Plant cells differ from animal cells. Plant cells have a cell wall for strength. They also have a chemical called chlorophyll for making food. The food gives the plant cell energy and substances needed for growth. The diagram shows the structures of a plant cell and describes the function of each structure.

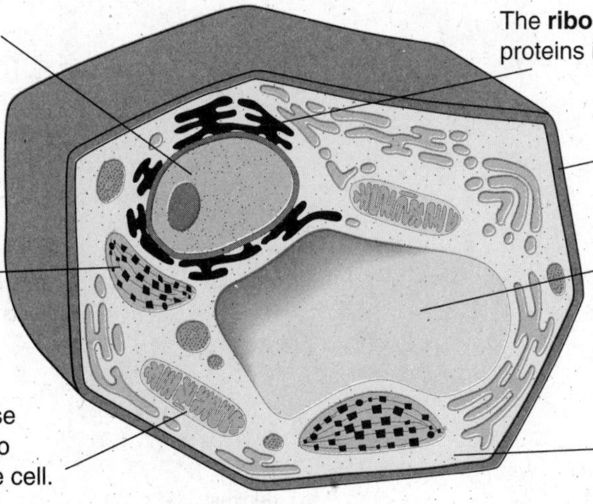

The **nucleus** is the control center of the cell. It contains the genetic material.
The **ribosomes** make proteins in the cell.
The **cell wall** is the stiff outer layer around the cell. It provides support for the whole plant.
The **chloroplasts** use chlorophyll and sunlight to make food in the cell.
The **vacuole** is a storage space for water and minerals.
The **cell membrane** is a layer around the cell. It controls what may enter or leave the cell.
The **mitochondria** use the plant's own food to release energy for the cell.

Fill in the blank with the word or words that best complete each statement.

1. The control center of a cell is its ____________________.

2. The ____________________ makes the plant cell stiff.

Circle the number of the best answer.

3. A plant cell needs water when its
   (1) mitochondria are empty.
   (2) chloroplasts are empty.
   (3) vacuole is empty.
   (4) ribosomes are empty.
   (5) cell membrane is empty.

Go on to the next page.

The Muscles of the Arm

Pick up a cup of coffee. You bend your elbow and raise your lower arm. This action is caused by a muscle in the upper arm. Now put down the cup of coffee. You straighten your elbow and move your lower arm down. This action is caused by another muscle in the upper arm.

Muscles work in pairs. The biceps muscle bends the elbow joint. The triceps muscle straightens the elbow joint. Why does it take two muscles to operate one joint? Muscles pull, but they cannot push. A muscle works by contracting, or shortening. When the biceps contracts, it pulls on the bones of the lower arm. The elbow joint bends. When the triceps contracts, it pulls on the same bones but in the opposite direction. When one muscle is contracting, its partner is relaxing.

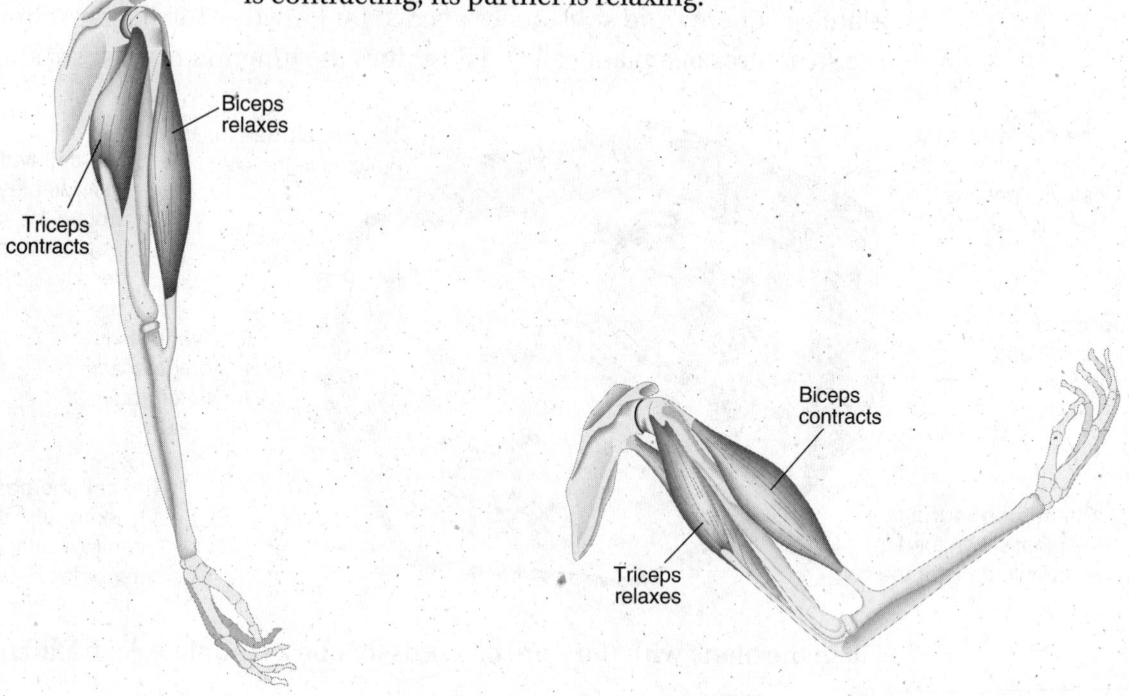

Fill in the blank with the word or words that best complete each statement.

4. When a muscle ____________________, it gets shorter.

5. When one muscle in a pair is contracting, the other muscle is

____________________.

Circle the number of the best answer.

6. The large muscles at the back of the thigh bend the knee joint. Where are the muscles that straighten the knee joint?
   (1) at the back of the thigh
   (2) at the front of the thigh
   (3) at the front of the lower leg
   (4) at the back of the lower leg
   (5) at the hip

Bacteria

Bacteria are simple one-celled organisms. They can be found just about anywhere. The action of bacteria can be good for people, or it can be harmful. The bacteria that turn milk into cheese or yogurt are useful. These same bacteria also turn the milk in your refrigerator sour. Then they are not so useful.

If sour milk and yogurt are made by the same bacteria, why does sour milk taste so bad? The difference is in how the bacteria are controlled. When yogurt is made, the bacteria are killed before they make the product too sour. In your refrigerator, the bacteria keep on going. The result is that the milk gets much too sour. The bacteria that make milk sour use the sugar in the milk for energy. Their waste product, lactic acid, is the sour substance you taste in the spoiled milk.

The activity of bacteria depends on the temperature. People are often surprised when they find that food has gone bad in the refrigerator. Keeping food cool does slow down the bacteria. However, it does not stop their action. Freezing food does stop the action of bacteria. But it does not necessarily kill the bacteria. So food that has been in the freezer can spoil after it has been defrosted.

Bacteria can be killed by high temperatures. Milk and other dairy products are pasteurized. In this process, the milk is heated to a high temperature, then quickly cooled. The heat kills the bacteria. But once you take the milk home and open it, new bacteria may get in. Then the spoiling process begins.

Fill in the blank with the word or words that best complete each statement.

7. ____________________, which is a waste product of bacteria, makes spoiled milk taste sour.

8. Milk is turned into yogurt by the action of ____________________.

Circle the number of the best answer.

9. How does the pasteurizing process affect bacteria?
   (1) Pasteurizing kills bacteria with high temperatures.
   (2) Pasteurizing kills bacteria with low temperatures.
   (3) Pasteurizing slows bacteria with low temperatures.
   (4) Pasteurizing slows bacteria with high temperatures.
   (5) Pasteurizing poisons bacteria with chemical preservatives.

The Flower

The reproductive organ of a plant is the **flower.** Flowers come in many shapes and sizes. Some are large and bright. Others are so small, you might not notice them.

Flowers make pollen. The pollen contains sperm, which is made in the anthers of the flower. The pollen is carried from one flower to another by insects, birds, or the wind. When pollen from one flower reaches another flower of the same kind, the sperm in the pollen joins with the egg, which is made in the ovary of the flower. The fertilized egg becomes a seed. The seed begins the next generation.

Flowers that are pollinated by insects such as bees often are bright in color. They have large petals, which give the bees a place to land. Many of these flowers also make nectar. This sweet juice attracts bees to the flower. When the bees drink the nectar, some of the sticky pollen gets on their bodies. This pollen rubs off when the bees get to the next flower.

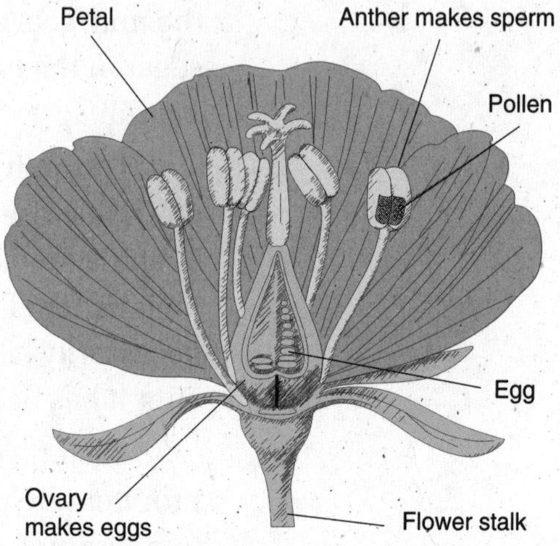

The flowers of many trees and grasses are pollinated by the wind. These flowers usually have tiny petals. Some have no petals at all. The pollen is dry and dusty. These features make it easy for the pollen to blow from one plant to another.

Identify each of the following as a characteristic of a plant that is pollinated by insects or by the wind. Write *insects* or *wind* in the space provided.

10. Sticky pollen ____________________

11. Sweet nectar ____________________

12. Very small petals ____________________

13. The flower shown on this page ____________________

Circle the number of the best answer.

14. Which part or parts of the flower are necessary for reproduction?
    (1) petals
    (2) anthers only
    (3) ovary only
    (4) petals and anthers
    (5) anthers and ovary

Biomes

You probably know that Earth's climate is coldest near the poles and warmest near the equator (an imaginary circle drawn around the Earth halfway between the poles). The climate determines the living things that are found in any area. Large regions with the same climate throughout have the same kinds of living things. A large region with a certain climate and certain living things is called a **biome.**

There are many kinds of biomes on Earth. Most of the eastern and northeastern United States is a forest biome. This biome is home to many kinds of trees and birds. There are also many **mammals,** such as deer, foxes, squirrels, and chipmunks.

Most of the central United States is a grassland biome. Because this biome is drier than the forest biome, there are few trees. The animals of the grassland feed on the many kinds of grasses there. Once there were huge herds of bison grazing the grasslands. Now there are herds of sheep and cattle. The most common wild animals are small. These are rabbits, prairie dogs, and badgers.

Much of the southwestern United States is a desert biome. It is so dry that few plants can grow there. Rain is sometimes heavy in the desert, but it does not rain often or for long. Then it dries up quickly. The cactus plant survives here because it is able to store water. Most of the animals of the desert live underground to escape the heat. They come out at night or early morning when it is cool. Small animals feed on the plants and their seeds. In turn, these animals are food for coyotes, hawks, and rattlesnakes.

Fill in the blank with the word or words that best complete each statement.

15. The ______________________ biome is home to many trees and deer.

16. The ______________________ biome is home to rabbits and prairie dogs.

17. A desert plant that can store water is the ______________________.

Circle the number of the best answer.

18. In general, the biomes of the United States change as you move from east to west because the climate becomes
    (1) cooler
    (2) drier
    (3) windier
    (4) less sunny
    (5) wetter

The Water Cycle

When you are caught in a sudden rainstorm, you probably don't think about where all that water came from. But you are experiencing one step in the water cycle. The **water cycle** is the circulation of water on Earth and in its atmosphere.

Water covers more than half of the planet. This surface water is found in oceans, lakes, and rivers. Surface water constantly evaporates. Water in the atmosphere condenses and forms clouds. When the clouds become too full of water, it falls as **precipitation.** Rain, snow, and sleet are forms of precipitation. When it rains, some water soaks into the ground and some moves along the land to rivers and lakes.

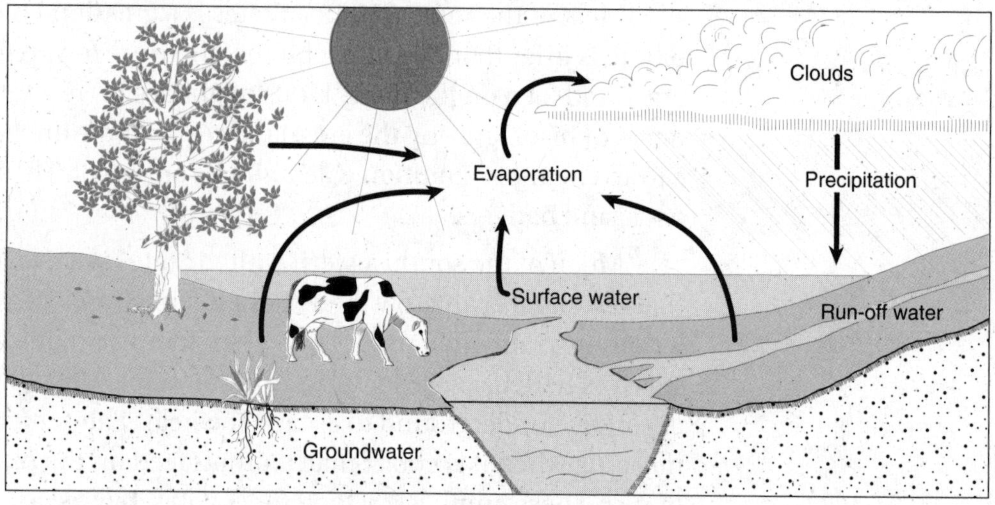

Match the part of the water cycle with its description. Write the letter of the part of the cycle in the blank at the left.

	Description	Part of the Water Cycle
______	19. rain and snow	a. clouds
______	20. lakes and oceans	b. groundwater
______	21. water that soaks into the soil	c. precipitation
		d. run-off water
______	22. water that condenses in the atmosphere	e. surface water
______	23. water flowing over the top of the soil	

Rocks

Have you ever washed your hands with gritty soap? The soap probably had ground pumice in it. Pumice is a kind of rock. This rock forms when lava from a volcano cools and hardens. **Igneous rocks,** such as pumice and granite, form when melted rock hardens. Some buildings are made of granite.

Over a long period of time, wind and water can wear down rocks. Small pieces of the rocks are blown or washed away. These pieces may settle slowly and form layers. Such particles are called sediment. Slowly the layers harden, forming **sedimentary rocks**. Sandstone, limestone, and shale are sedimentary rocks. Sedimentary rocks are not as hard as igneous rocks. Sandstone and limestone wear away much faster than granite.

Igneous and sedimentary rocks can be changed into new forms. This is caused by high temperatures or great pressure. Rocks formed in this way are called **metamorphic rocks.** Marble is a metamorphic rock. You may have seen statues made of marble.

Fill in the blank with the word or words that best complete each statement.

24. Rocks that form as layers of hardened particles are called

_______________________.

25. Rocks that form under high temperatures or great pressure are called

_______________________.

Circle the number of the best answer.

26. Which of these is an example of an igneous rock?
   (1) granite
   (2) limestone
   (3) marble
   (4) sandstone
   (5) shale

27. An area where many igneous rocks are found may once have had
   (1) many rivers
   (2) large amounts of sediment
   (3) high pressure
   (4) volcanoes
   (5) earthquakes

The Atom

All matter is made up of atoms. An **atom** is made up of three types of particles. **Protons** are particles with a positive electrical charge. **Neutrons** have no charge. Protons and neutrons are found in the **nucleus,** or center, of an atom. All atoms of a particular element have the same number of protons. The number of neutrons can vary.

Orbiting around the nucleus are **electrons,** particles with a negative electrical charge. Electrons are much lighter than protons or neutrons. The number of electrons in an atom is equal to the number of protons. That means the amount of positive and negative electric charge is the same, so overall an atom has no charge. If an atom gains or loses an electron, it is called an **ion.** An ion has a charge.

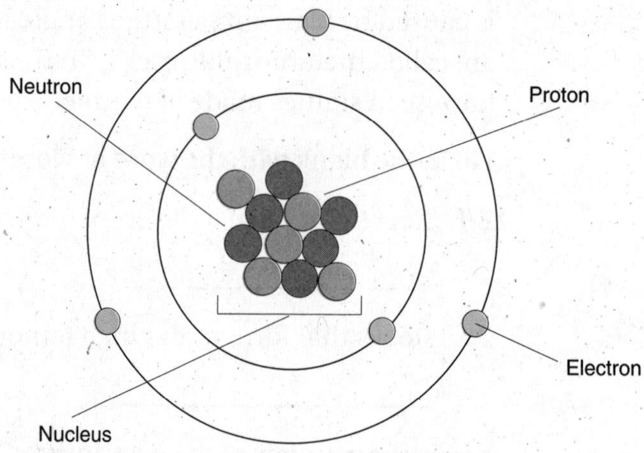

Match the name of the particle with its description. Write the letter of the particle in the blank at the left. Letters may be used more than once.

	Description	Particle
______	28. has no electric charge	a. proton
______	29. not found in the nucleus	b. neutron
______	30. has a positive electric charge	c. electron
______	31. a negatively charged ion has an extra one	
______	32. an ion with a positive charge has an extra one	

States of Matter

On Earth, all matter is found in three states: **solid, liquid,** and **gas.** The table below shows the properties of these states. The state of matter of a substance depends on its temperature. Each substance changes state at different temperatures. At low temperatures, substances are solids. Sugar, salt, and plastic are solids at room temperature. If a solid is heated, it changes to a liquid. Water and alcohol are liquids at room temperature. If a liquid is heated, it changes to a gas. Air is a mixture of substances that are gases at room temperature.

State	Temperature Range	Shape	Volume
solid	lowest	definite (does not change)	definite (does not change)
liquid	middle	not definite; takes the shape of its container	definite (does not change)
gas	highest	not definite; takes the shape of its container	not definite; expands to fill the volume of its container

Circle the number of the best answer.

33. In which state or states of matter does the volume stay the same?
   (1) solid only
   (2) liquid only
   (3) gas only
   (4) solid and liquid only
   (5) solid, liquid, and gas

34. What happens if you cool a liquid enough to make it into a solid?
   (1) Its shape changes from not definite to definite.
   (2) Its shape changes from definite to not definite.
   (3) Its volume changes from not definite to definite.
   (4) It will be in its highest temperature range.
   (5) None of its properties changes.

Forces

A **force** is a push or pull. In a tug of war, two teams pull on a rope. Each team exerts a force on the rope. The forces act in opposite directions. If the two forces are equal, there is no movement. The forces are said to be balanced.

Suppose an extra player joins one team. The extra player increases that team's force. Now the forces are not balanced, and there is movement. A change in movement is called acceleration. The rope accelerates, moving in the direction of the greater force. The team with the extra player wins.

If you hold a ball in your hand, the forces on the ball are balanced. **Gravity** pulls down on the ball. Your hand exerts an upward force that balances the force of gravity. If you let go of the ball, your force changes, but gravity does not. Gravity "wins," and the ball accelerates in the direction of the pull of gravity.

If you throw a ball, the forces involved get more complicated. When you throw the ball, you exert a force on it. The forward force of your hand is opposed by the force of **friction** between the ball and the air. These forces are not balanced. Because your force is greater, the ball moves in the direction you throw it. Once the ball leaves your hand, you exert no force on it. Friction continues to act on the ball. This force is not balanced, so it changes the motion of the ball. The ball slows down. At the same time, gravity pulls on the ball. This downward force is not balanced by another force. So the ball falls down as it moves forward.

Fill in the blank with the word or words that best complete each statement.

35. A ____________________ is a push or a pull.

36. A change in movement is called ____________________.

Circle the number of the best answer.

37. Which of the following is an effect of an unbalanced force?
    (1) acceleration
    (2) gravity
    (3) friction
    (4) a push
    (5) a pull

Pretest Evaluation Chart

The chart below will help you determine your strengths and weaknesses in the four content areas of science.

Directions

Check your answers on pages 228–229. Circle the number of each question that you answered correctly on the Pretest. Count the number of questions in each row that you answered correctly. Write the number in the Total Correct space in each row. (For example, in the Life Science row, write the number correct in the blank before *out of 18*). Complete this process for the remaining rows. Then add the four totals to get your total correct for the whole Pretest.

Content Area	Questions	Total Correct	Pages
Life Science (Pages 14–101)	1, 2, 3 4, 5, 6 7, 8, 9 10, 11, 12, 13, 14 15, 16, 17, 18	______ out of 18	Pages 22–27 Pages 34–39 Pages 52–57 Pages 58–63 Pages 82–87
Earth and Space Science (Pages 102–141)	19, 20, 21, 22, 23 24, 25, 26, 27	______ out of 9	Pages 116–121 Page 123
Chemistry (Pages 142–175)	28, 29, 30, 31, 32 33, 34	______ out of 7	Pages 144–149 Pages 150–155
Physics (Pages 176–215)	35, 36, 37	______ out of 3	Pages 184–189

Total Correct for Pretest ______ out of 37

If you answered fewer than 34 questions correctly, look more closely at the four content areas of science listed above. In which areas do you need more practice? Page numbers to refer to for practice are given in the right-hand column above.

Unit 1

Life Science

Life science is the study of living things and biological processes. Living things include plants, animals, and other organisms. You use knowledge of life science when you make choices that affect your personal health and environment. Understanding life science can help you better understand yourself and your world.

List three living things you saw today. ________________________________

____

List two things you did today to keep yourself healthy. ________________

____

Life Science

Thinking About Life Science

You may not realize how often you use life science as you go about your daily life. Think about your recent activities.

Check the box for each activity you have done recently.

- ☐ Did you exercise?
- ☐ Did you choose to eat one food over another?
- ☐ Did you take care of a pet?
- ☐ Did you water a plant?
- ☐ Did you go to a doctor?
- ☐ Did you recycle an item?

Write some other activities where you used life science.

____

____

____

Previewing the Unit

In this unit, you will learn:

- how scientists study living things
- what living things have in common
- how different parts of your body work
- how organisms pass traits to their offspring
- how germs cause disease
- how living things relate to one another and to their environment
- how plants and animals grow, develop, and change over time

Lesson 1	**Scientific Methods**	**Lesson 7**	**Bacteria and Viruses**
Lesson 2	**The Cell**	**Lesson 8**	**Plants**
Lesson 3	**Blood Vessels**	**Lesson 9**	**Animal Behavior**
Lesson 4	**Bones and Muscles**	**Lesson 10**	**Life Cycles**
Lesson 5	**Reproduction and Development**	**Lesson 11**	**Environmental Issues**
		Lesson 12	**Ecosystems**
Lesson 6	**Genetics**	**Lesson 13**	**Evolution**

Lesson 1

Scientific Methods

When astronauts go into space, they feel weightless. If you have ever hit a big dip in the road or ridden down in a fast elevator, then you have a small idea of what weightlessness feels like. In space, however, weightlessness is continuous.

Scientists are interested in how weightlessness affects humans. Being in space for a long time can cause changes in the body. What are these changes? To answer this question, scientists gather information and test ideas.

Vocabulary

scientific methods

observation

hypothesis

embryo

prediction

experiment

experimental group

control group

conclusion

Relate to the Topic

This lesson is about the methods used in science. It describes an actual experiment done aboard the space shuttle to show how scientific discoveries are made. Think about an important scientific discovery.

What was the discovery? ________________________

Has it affected your life or the life of someone you know? How?

____

____

Reading Strategy

SKIMMING **Skimming** means to quickly look over something to get the main idea. A good way to do this is to start with the **title,** or name, of an article. Also look at the **headings,** which are the names of sections within the article. The title tells you the main topic, and headings summarize what supporting topics are discussed in smaller sections. Before you read the article, first skim the title and headings on pages 17 through 19. Then answer the questions.

1. What is the article about? ________________________
   Hint: Look at the title on page 17.

2. List the main scientific methods that are discussed in the article.

   ____

   Hint: Look at the headings on pages 17 through 19.

Check your answers on page 229.

An Experiment in Space

When people fly in space, they are not affected by the pull of Earth's gravity. Being weightless may be fun, but it can also cause problems. Some astronauts get space-motion sickness. Others come back from long flights with weak bones and muscles. Some scientists worry that such conditions may limit the future of space travel.

It is important to understand how weightlessness affects the body. Flights to distant planets may take years. People may live and work for long periods in space stations. How will their bodies react? Will they be able to raise families?

Weightless astronauts aboard the space shuttle

Scientific Methods

Questions like these are not easy to answer. To find answers, scientists have ways to get information and test ideas. These processes are **scientific methods.** The basic scientific method includes four main steps. These steps are observation, hypothesis, experiment, and conclusion.

Observation

A high school student named John Vellinger became curious about weightlessness. Through **observation,** he learned about what was already known. He watched astronauts on TV. He read as much as he could. He wondered how weightlessness would affect people in space for long periods. Would they be able to raise animals for food? Would they be able to have children? The answers to these questions may be important if people are to go on long voyages in space.

Hypothesis

Once scientists observe things, they try to explain them. A **hypothesis** is a possible explanation of how something works. It is based on many observations. Would weightlessness affect the development of an **embryo,** an unborn living thing in an early stage of life? One hypothesis is that an embryo would not be affected by weightlessness.

Making Predictions A hypothesis is useful because it is the basis for predicting—or foretelling—what will happen. For example, Vellinger might predict that a chicken embryo would hatch normally in space. A **prediction** is a good guess about a future event.

Reread the first paragraph on this page.

Which of the following statements is a better prediction of what will happen next? Circle the letter of the correct answer.

a. Vellinger will try to develop chicken embryos in the weightlessness of space to see whether they hatch normally.
b. Vellinger will try to develop young chicks in the weightlessness of space to see if they grow to adulthood.

Experiment

Scientists must test whether a hypothesis is supported by facts. They do this with an **experiment.** With help from scientists, Vellinger designed an experiment to test whether weightlessness would affect chicken embryos. NASA chose his experiment for a space shuttle mission.

Vellinger decided to use 64 fertilized chicken eggs. He divided the eggs into two groups. One group of eggs would spend five days in space on the shuttle *Discovery.* This group was the **experimental group.** The other group of eggs would stay on Earth. The second group was the **control group.** The two groups differed in only one way. The group of experimental eggs would be weightless for five days. The eggs in the control group would remain in Earth's gravity.

Vellinger then divided both the experimental and control groups. 16 eggs from each group were fertilized nine days before the shuttle launch. The other 16 eggs in each group were fertilized just two days before the launch. This meant that some embryos in the experimental group would be "young" and some would be older when they were launched into space.

What happened in the experiment? Did the evidence support the hypothesis? If so, all 64 eggs should have hatched after the normal 21-day development period. Instead, something surprising happened. None of the 16 younger embryos that had been aboard the shuttle survived. Yet the older group that had also spent time in space hatched normally.

 Check your answer on page 229.

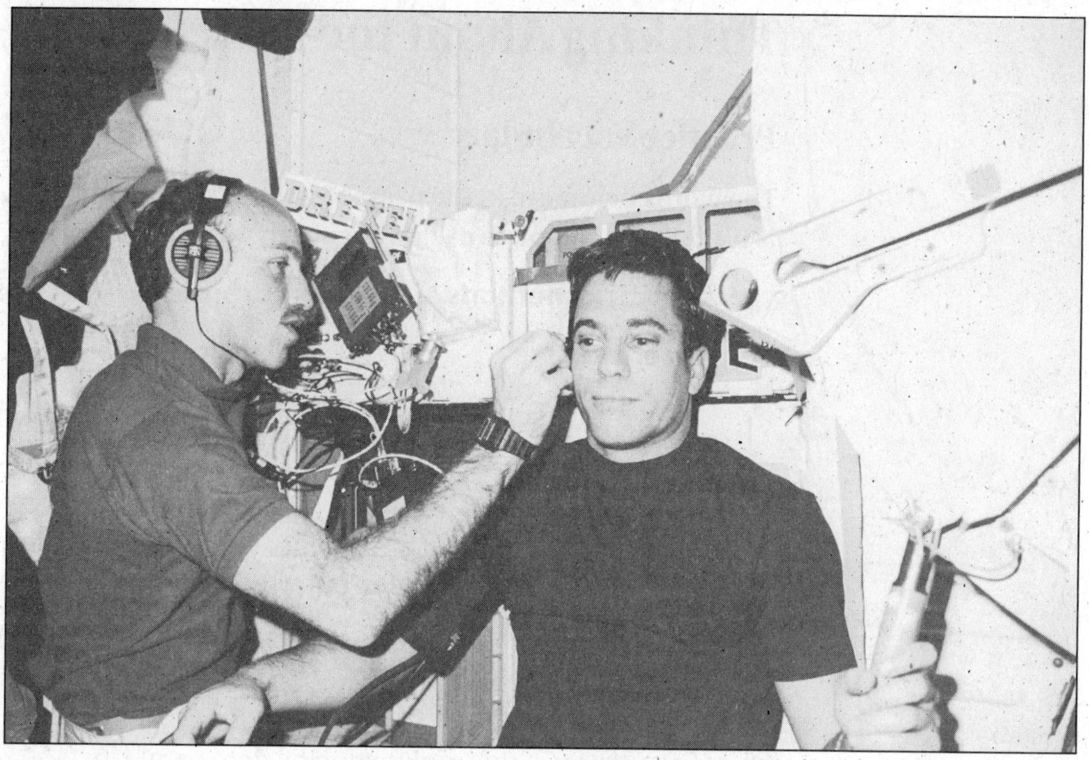

Astronaut John E. Blaha participates in an experiment on the space shuttle *Discovery.*

Using the Glossary or Dictionary When you read, you may see words you do not understand. Circle any words you do not know. You can look up the meaning of words in **bold print** in the glossary at the back of this book. Other unfamiliar words can be found in a dictionary.

Match each term with its correct definition. Use the glossary or a dictionary.

______	1. experiment	a.	an unborn living thing in an early stage of life
______	2. embryo	b.	the act of noting a fact or event in nature
______	3. observation	c.	a procedure that tests a hypothesis

Conclusion

The results of an experiment are stated in a **conclusion.** This experiment shows that our hypothesis was not supported by what happened. Our conclusion is that weightlessness does seem to affect embryos. But it does not seem to affect embryos at different stages of growth in the same way. The embryos that died were all weightless during the first third of the 21-day development period. The embryos that hatched were in the second third of the development period when they were weightless.

Astronaut John E. Blaha, the pilot of *Discovery,* said, "What looked like a simple experiment may have . . . generated thousands of questions." With the results of this experiment, scientists will make new hypotheses and do more experiments. Someday they may be able to answer the question: *Can people have children in outer space?*

Check your answers on page 229.

Thinking About the Article

Practice Vocabulary

The words below are in the passage in bold type. Study the way each word is used. Then complete each sentence by writing the correct word.

scientific methods **hypothesis** **observation**

experiment **conclusion**

1. In science, ways of getting information and testing ideas are called ____________________.
2. Through ____________________, scientists note things that happen in nature. They try to figure out why or how these things happen.
3. The scientists then come up with an explanation, called a(n) ____________________, that will explain the observations.
4. Scientists test this explanation by doing a(n) ____________________ that is designed to see if the explanation is correct.
5. The results of this work are stated in a(n) ____________________.

Understand the Article

Circle the letter of the correct answer.

6. How did the control and experimental groups of chicken embryos differ?
   a. The control group developed under normal gravity, and the experimental group developed in weightlessness.
   b. The control group consisted only of older embryos, and the experimental group consisted only of younger embryos.
7. What were the results of the chicken embryo experiment?
   a. All the embryos in the experiment hatched.
   b. All the embryos that stayed on Earth hatched, but only the older embryos that were weightless in space hatched.
8. What conclusion can you draw from this experiment?
   a. Weightlessness does not seem to affect embryo development.
   b. Weightlessness does seem to affect embryo development.
9. What hypothesis do these results suggest about space travel?
   a. Women may be unable to bear children on long space voyages.
   b. Young children may not grow and mature in space.

Apply Your Skills

Circle the number of the best answer for each question.

10. Look in the glossary. Which of the following is the best definition for the word *hypothesis?*
    (1) a question
    (2) the answer to a question
    (3) an observation
    (4) a procedure for testing an observation
    (5) a possible explanation for something observed

11. Which of the following is an example of making a hypothesis?
    (1) proposing how weightlessness would affect embryos
    (2) watching embryos develop on the space shuttle
    (3) watching embryos develop on Earth
    (4) measuring the length of time it takes embryos to hatch
    (5) calculating the percentage of embryos that fail to hatch

12. Which of the following is the best prediction of what would happen if duck eggs fertilized at different times were taken aboard a shuttle flight?
    (1) None of the eggs would hatch.
    (2) Eggs that were fertilized nine days before the launch would hatch.
    (3) Eggs that were fertilized two days before the launch would hatch.
    (4) All of the eggs would hatch.
    (5) The baby ducks would be abnormal.

Connect with the Article

Write your answer to each question.

13. Why do you think it is important to test a hypothesis by experimenting?

____

____

____

14. Suppose you were in charge of shuttle experiments. A pregnant woman has volunteered to go into space to test the effects of weightlessness on a human embryo. Would you let her go? Why or why not?

____

____

____

Check your answers on page 229.

LESSON 2

The Cell

The Cell
The Cell

Sitting in the sun feels good. It feels so good that many people find it hard to believe that the sun can be harmful. In the past, a tan was even considered a sign of good health.

Tanning is no longer considered safe. And getting a sunburn is even more dangerous. Both tanning and burning can cause skin cancer. Harmful rays in sunlight can cause skin cells to grow in abnormal ways.

Vocabulary

ultraviolet light

basal cell skin cancer

squamous cell skin cancer

melanoma

cell

cytoplasm

ribosome

mitochondria

nucleus

cell membrane

Relate to the Topic

This lesson is about skin cancer, the abnormal growth of skin cells. It explains the types of skin cancer, how sunlight can cause it, and how you can prevent it. Have you or someone you know ever had any problems from staying out in the sun?

Describe what happened. ______________________________

____

What do you usually do to help yourself stay safe when you go out in the sun?

____

Reading Strategy

SCANNING BOLDFACED WORDS **Scanning** means to quickly look over something to find specific information. Scanning and skimming are two ways to preview something. Technical terms in science materials are often highlighted in **bold type**—type that is darker than the type around it. Look at the boldfaced terms on page 23. Then answer the questions.

1. What is ultraviolet light? ______________________________

   ____

   Hint: Look at the first paragraph.

2. Write the technical terms for two kinds of skin cancer.

   ____

   ____

   Hint: Look under the heading Types of Skin Cancer.

Check your answers on page 229.

Sunlight and Skin Cancer

Each year, millions of Americans relax at beaches or swimming pools and in the mountains. Many people work outdoors in the sun. Some people go to tanning parlors to get a bronzed look. However, exposure to **ultraviolet light,** a type of light given off by the sun and by tanning lamps, can cause skin cancer. In fact, there are more than one million new cases of skin cancer in the United States each year. That makes skin cancer the most common cancer in this country. Skin cancer is also the easiest form of cancer to treat and cure.

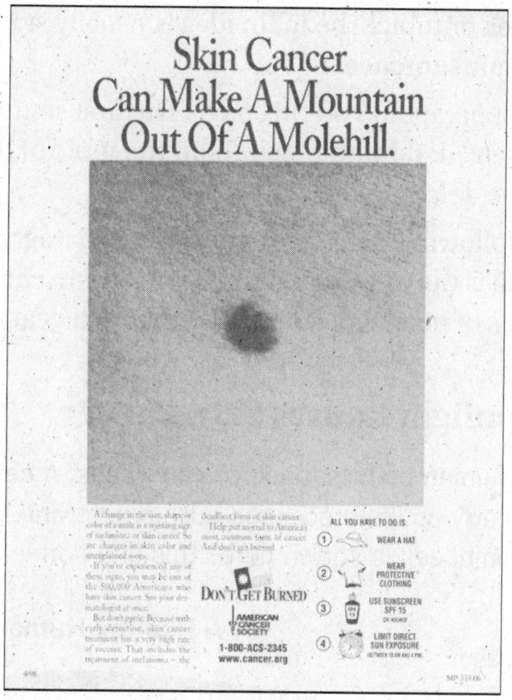

Types of Skin Cancer

There are three types of skin cancer. They are called basal cell, squamous cell, and melanoma.

The most common and least dangerous skin cancer is **basal cell skin cancer.** About 975,000 people develop this type of skin cancer each year. Basal cell skin cancer often appears on the hands or face. It may look like an open sore, reddish patch, mole, shiny bump, or scar. Basal ce!! skin cancer grows slowly and rarely spreads to other parts of the body. When found early and removed, basal cell skin cancer can almost always be cured.

Squamous cell skin cancer is more dangerous than basal cell skin cancer. It affects about 325,000 people each year. Squamous cell skin cancer looks like raised pink spots or growths that may be open in the center. This cancer grows faster than basal cell skin cancer. Squamous cell skin cancer can spread to other parts of the body. If it is not treated, this type of skin cancer may lead to death.

The most dangerous of the three types of skin cancer is **melanoma.** There are about 53,600 new cases each year. This type of skin cancer may grow in a mole or on clear skin. Melanomas are oddly shaped blotches that turn red, white, or blue in spots. They become crusty and bleed, and they grow fast. When melanomas reach the size of a dime, it's likely that they have spread and become deadly. About 7,400 people die of melanoma each year in the United States.

Finding the Main Idea One way to make sure you understand what you read is to find the main idea of each paragraph. A paragraph is a group of sentences about one **main idea** or topic. The main idea is usually stated in one sentence which is called a **topic sentence.**

Reread the first paragraph on this page. The first sentence is the topic sentence. It makes a general statement about the topic of the paragraph. All the other sentences give details about the topic.

Which of the following is the main idea of this paragraph?

a. Melanoma is the most dangerous type of skin cancer.
b. Thousands of people die of melanoma each year.

How Sunlight Causes Skin Cancer

The human body is made of many cells. A **cell** is the smallest unit of a living thing that can carry on life processes such as growing, responding, and reproducing itself. A typical animal cell is shown here. This is a normal cell, not a cancer cell.

A Healthy Human Cell

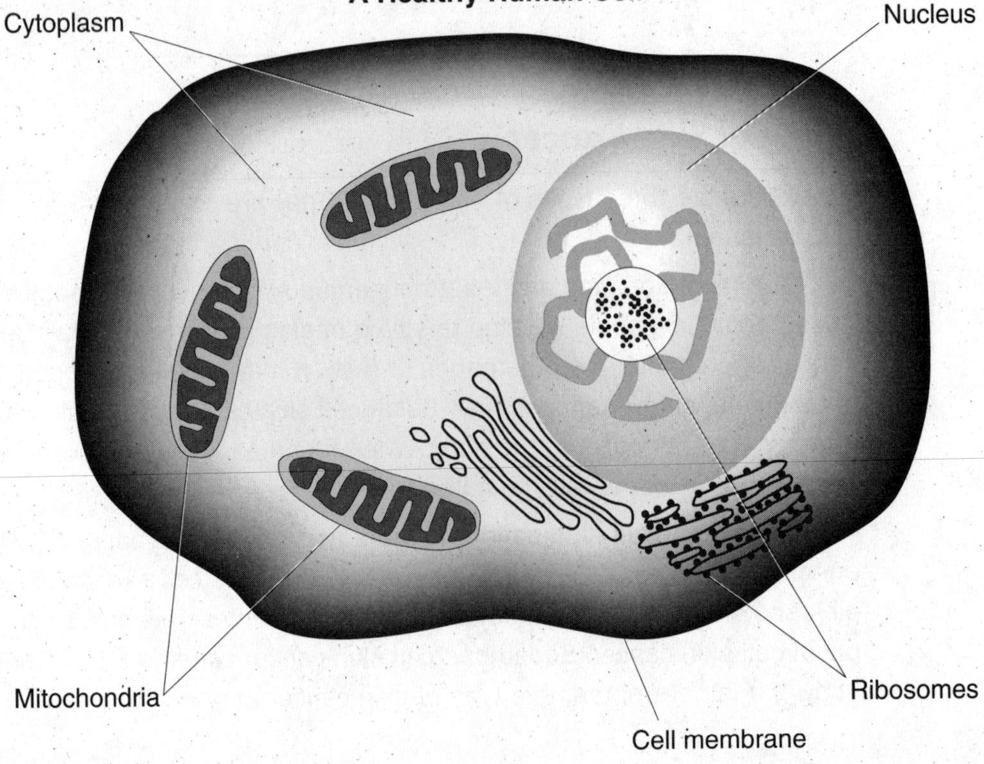

A cell has many parts. A jellylike material, called **cytoplasm,** makes up most of the cell. **Ribosomes** are cell parts that make the proteins the cell needs to grow. **Mitochondria** give the cell the energy it needs to grow and reproduce.

The part of the cell that controls all cell activities is the **nucleus.** When a normal cell reproduces, it divides into two cells. Each new cell gets its own complete copy of the nucleus. The ultraviolet rays in sunlight can cause changes in the nucleus of a skin cell. When this happens, the cells divide abnormally. Cancer is cell division that is out of control.

The **cell membrane** covers the cell. Most cells stop dividing when they touch another cell. However, cancer cells keep dividing, even if they crowd the cells near them.

Interpreting Diagrams A **diagram** is a picture that explains what something looks like or how it works. A diagram usually has a title and labels. The title tells the main idea of the diagram. The labels point out different parts of the diagram. Lines usually connect each label to the part of the diagram it names.

Look at the diagram on page 24. Read the diagram's title and labels. Which of the following types of information are you likely to learn from this diagram? Circle the letter of the correct answer.

a. the growth stages of a cancer cell
b. the main parts of a healthy cell

Preventing Skin Cancer

The color of your skin has a lot to do with how likely you are to get skin cancer. In general, people with light skin are the most likely to get skin cancer. People with darker skin, including most Asians and Hispanics, are less likely to get skin cancer. African Americans are least likely to get skin cancer.

Here are some things you can do to protect yourself from skin cancer.

- Spend less time in the sun, especially between 10 A.M. and 4 P.M.
- Wear long sleeves and a hat to protect your skin.
- Always wear a sunscreen with an SPF (Sun Protection Factor) of at least 15. Apply it to all of the exposed areas of your body, including the tops of your ears and your lips. Use a sunscreen even on cloudy days. Sunscreens may not protect against melanomas, but they do give important protection against sunburn and less harmful skin cancers.
- Do not use tanning parlors.
- Check your skin for new growths or sores that do not heal. If you find any of these, see a doctor right away. Early treatment for skin cancer is very important.

Check your answer on page 229.

Thinking About the Article

Practice Vocabulary

The words below are in the passage in bold type. Study the way each word is used. Then match each word with its meaning. Write the letter.

_____ 1. cell membrane

_____ 2. cytoplasm

_____ 3. cell

_____ 4. nucleus

_____ 5. mitochondria

_____ 6. ribosome

a. the outer covering of a cell

b. the control center of a cell

c. smallest unit of a living thing that carries on life processes

d. the jellylike material that makes up most of the cell

e. the cell part that makes proteins

f. the parts of the cell that provide energy

Understand the Article

Write or circle the answer to each question.

7. Describe the three types of skin cancer.

____

____

____

8. How can sunlight cause skin cancer?
   a. The ultraviolet rays in sunlight cause bacteria and viruses to grow on skin.
   b. The ultraviolet rays can cause skin cells to grow and reproduce abnormally.

9. What is the relationship between skin color and the likelihood of getting skin cancer?
   a. The lighter the skin, the more likely a person is to get skin cancer.
   b. The darker the skin, the more likely a person is to get skin cancer.

10. List three ways to protect yourself from skin cancer.

____

____

____

Apply Your Skills

Circle the number of the best answer for each question.

11. What is the main idea of the first paragraph on page 23?
    (1) Millions of Americans enjoy the sun.
    (2) Many people work outdoors in the sun.
    (3) Sunlight can cause skin cancer.
    (4) More than one million Americans get skin cancer each year.
    (5) Skin cancer can usually be treated and cured.

12. Look at the diagram on page 24. Where in the cell are the mitochondria located?
    (1) outside the cell membrane
    (2) in the nucleus
    (3) in the cytoplasm
    (4) under the ribosomes
    (5) in a cancer cell

13. Under which heading in the article would you find information about protecting yourself from skin cancer?
    (1) The Cell
    (2) Sunlight and Skin Cancer
    (3) Types of Skin Cancer
    (4) How Sunlight Causes Skin Cancer
    (5) Preventing Skin Cancer

Connect with the Article

Write your answers in the space provided.

14. Why would it be a good idea to have any moles checked periodically by a doctor?

15. How will you protect your skin the next time you go outdoors?

Lesson 3

Blood Vessels

We've been hearing the message for years: Americans eat too many fatty foods, and fat is bad for the heart. Some people have listened to the message and changed their diet to include more fruits, whole grains, and vegetables and less meat and dairy products.

But it's also true that fat gives food a satisfying flavor, so many people find it hard to cut down. For those who can't resist potato chips, there are new versions of snack products to try. However, these products have pros and cons that you should consider.

Vocabulary

fat

cholesterol

saturated fat

monounsaturated fat

polyunsaturated fat

plaque

artery

Relate to the Topic

This article is about fats and cholesterol and how they affect the heart. It explains that cutting down on fats in the diet can help prevent heart disease.

List three of your favorite snack foods. ______________________

____

Do you think these foods are good for your heart? Why or why not?

____

____

____

Reading Strategy

SKIMMING CIRCLE GRAPHS A **circle graph** shows how parts of an amount are related to a whole amount. The circle represents the whole amount. The title tells you what kind of information is presented. Labels also tell you the name and amount of the parts, or wedges, that make up a circle graph. When you skim something, you read it quickly to get the main ideas. Skim the two circle graphs on page 31. Then answer the questions.

1. What is the topic of the two graphs? ______________________
   Hint: Look at the title.

2. What is each graph about? ______________________
   Hint: Look at the labels below each circle graph.

Check your answers on page 230.

Eating Right for a Healthier Heart

Food labels can be confusing. They are full of words like *cholesterol, saturated fat, polyunsaturated fat,* and *monounsaturated fat.* Since eating too much fat and cholesterol can cause heart disease, it's important to know what's in your food.

Help with Reading the Labels

Many people confuse cholesterol and fat, although these substances are not the same. **Fats** are substances that provide energy and building materials for the body. Fats are found in oils, butter, milk, cheese, eggs, meat, and nuts. When the body takes in more food of any kind than it needs, it stores the extra food as fat. **Cholesterol** is a fatlike substance found in all animals, including humans. Some foods, such as egg yolks and shellfish, contain cholesterol. But most of the cholesterol in our bodies is made from the saturated fats in the foods we eat.

Saturated fat is a type of fat that is solid at room temperature. Most saturated fats come from animal products such as butter, cheese, meat, and egg yolks. Some vegetable oils, such as palm oil, also have saturated fat. Saturated fat increases cholesterol in the blood.

Monounsaturated fat is a type of fat found in some vegetable products, including olive oil, peanut oil, and peanut butter. Some scientists think monounsaturated fat lowers the body's cholesterol. Others believe it has no effect on cholesterol.

Polyunsaturated fat is a type of fat found in some vegetable foods and fish. Corn oil, almonds, mayonnaise, soybean oil, and fish are common sources of this fat. Polyunsaturated fat lowers the amount of cholesterol in the blood.

Fried foods, potato chips, and lunchmeats are usually high in fat and cholesterol.

The Effect of Fat and Cholesterol

Your body needs fat. Fat insulates the body from hot and cold. Fat stores energy. The body uses fats to build cells. Fats are needed to absorb certain vitamins. Women need fat to help regulate menstruation.

Your body also needs cholesterol. Cholesterol is an important part of all animal cells. It also helps protect nerve fibers. The body needs cholesterol to make vitamin D and other substances.

Using the Index Is the word *cells* familiar? Cells were mentioned in the article on skin cancer. You can find other discussions of cells in this book by using the index on pages 261–266. An index lists words alphabetically, with the page numbers on which the words appear.

Turn to the index and find the word *cells.* It is on page 261, in alphabetical order under the letter C. Cells are discussed on pages 24 through 25, as well as other pages. Now look up *fat* in the index. The index tells you that fat is mentioned on pages 28 through 33, and ______.

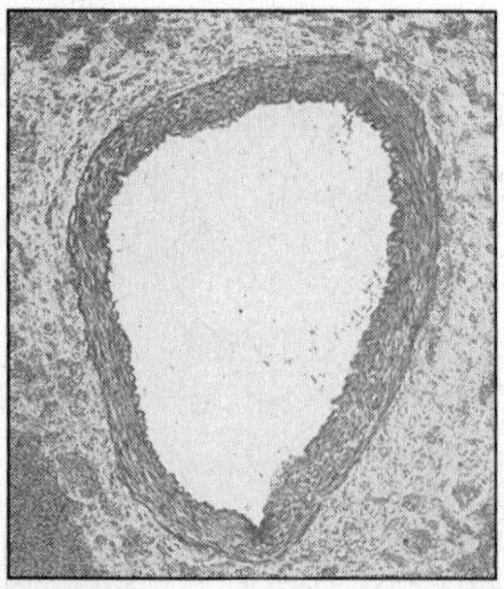

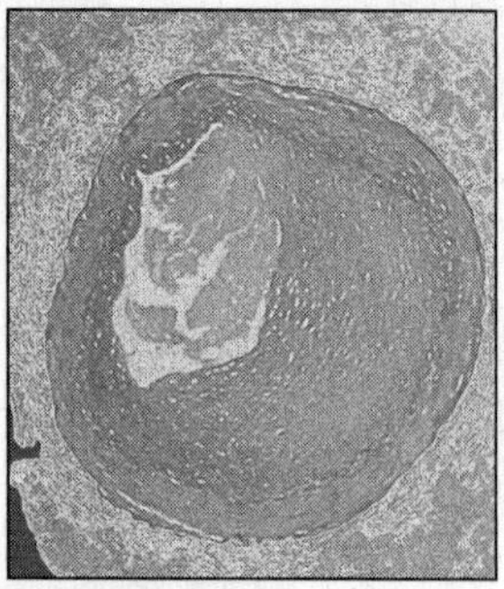

Cross sections of a healthy artery (top) and an artery clogged with plaque (bottom)

If fat and cholesterol have so many benefits, what is the problem? The problem is that too much fat and too much cholesterol can be harmful. Fat should provide less than 30 percent of the total daily calories in an average person's diet. Many people have trouble keeping their fat intake within these guidelines. Also, the body can make cholesterol.

What happens when there is too much fat and cholesterol in the diet? Extra cholesterol circulates in the blood. There it forms deposits called **plaque** on the inside walls of arteries. Too much fat can add to this problem. **Arteries** are large blood vessels that carry blood to all parts of the body. When they are clogged with plaque, arteries cannot carry as much blood. The heart must work harder to pump the same amount of blood through them. When the flow of blood to the heart muscle is blocked, a heart attack occurs. As a result, the person may die.

Studies have shown that people with a lot of cholesterol in their blood are most likely to have heart attacks. Reducing blood cholesterol can lower the risk of having a heart attack. The best way to do this is to eat less food that is high in cholesterol and saturated fats.

Food Companies Respond

Since so many people are looking for foods low in cholesterol and saturated fat, food companies have responded. One chain of fast-food restaurants changed its frying oil to one with less saturated fat and less trans fats (artificially produced solid fats). The new oil is high in polyunsaturated fats. They also added a salad bar and put more chicken and fish, which have less fat than beef, on the menu.

 Check your answer on page 230.

Blood Vessels

Some snack food companies have switched from saturated to polyunsaturated fats. Many have cut the fat content of their products. Some are using a controversial fat substitute called Olestra. Still, you have to read the labels carefully. "No cholesterol" does not mean "no saturated fat." Also, even low-fat versions of some products may still have a lot of fat.

Percent of Total Calories from Various Nutrients

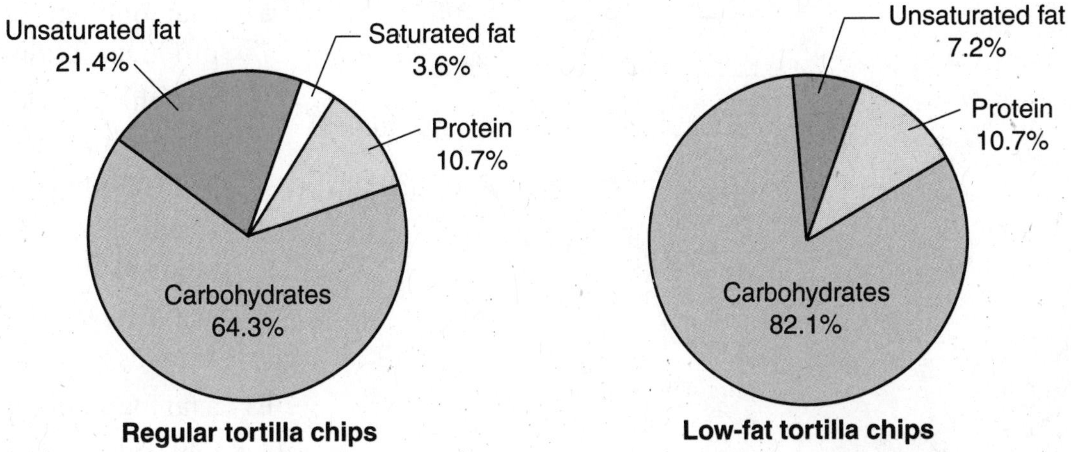

Reading a Circle Graph Think of a circle graph as a pie. The circle is the whole pie. Each wedge is a piece of the pie. In the circle graphs above, the whole pie is the total percent of calories in one serving of tortilla chips (100%). Each wedge shows the percent of calories for one nutrient. Big wedges show big percents, and small wedges show small percents. For example, most of the calories in tortilla chips come from carbohydrates: 64.3 percent for the regular chips and 82.1 percent for the low-fat chips.

Look at the circle graphs to answer these questions.

1. What percent of the calories in the regular chips comes from unsaturated fat?
   a. 21.4%   b. 3.6%

2. The regular tortilla chips have about ______ times the amount of unsaturated fat as the low-fat chips.

What You Can Do

There are some simple things you can do to reduce your chances of heart disease. Start with your diet. Eat less meat, eggs, butter, ice cream, cheese, whole milk, and snack foods. Eat more whole grains, fruits, vegetables, lean meats, and low-fat dairy products. You also should get more exercise. Walking, running, swimming, and other aerobic exercises all help lower the body's cholesterol level. Stop smoking—that's also bad for your heart. Last, have your cholesterol level checked by your doctor. If it is too high, your doctor will probably suggest a diet and exercise.

 Check your answers on page 230.

Thinking About the Article

Practice Vocabulary

The words below are in the passage in bold type. Study the way each word is used. Then match each word with its meaning. Write the letter.

_____ 1. cholesterol

_____ 2. saturated fat

_____ 3. monounsaturated fat

_____ 4. polyunsaturated fat

_____ 5. artery

a. a fat found in some vegetable products like olive oil

b. a fat that is solid at room temperature and usually comes from animals

c. a large blood vessel that carries blood to all parts of the body

d. a fatlike substance found in all animals

e. a fat found in some vegetables and fish

Understand the Article

Write or circle the answer to each question.

6. What are fats?
   a. substances that provide energy and building materials for the body
   b. substances found only in animals, including humans

7. What happens to the extra cholesterol that the body cannot use?

____

____

8. Why does the heart have to work harder in a person with clogged arteries?
   a. The arteries become narrower, so the heart has to work harder to pump the same amount of blood through them.
   b. The heart becomes weaker because the person is not getting exercise.

9. What can you do to reduce your chance of getting heart disease? Circle the letter next to each action that will help.
   a. Eat more meat, butter, and eggs.
   b. Eat more whole grains, fruits, and vegetables.
   c. Get more exercise.
   d. Stop smoking.
   e. Have your cholesterol level checked.

Apply Your Skills

Circle the number of the best answer for each question.

10. This article discusses the effect of fat on the heart. Look in the index. Which page(s) have information about exercise and the heart?
    (1) 26–28
    (2) 34–35
    (3) 95–96
    (4) 148–151
    (5) 201–203

11. Look at the circle graphs on page 31. Which category contributes no calories to low-fat tortilla chips?
    (1) unsaturated fat
    (2) saturated fat
    (3) any kind of fat
    (4) carbohydrates
    (5) protein

12. If you were on a low-salt diet, which tortilla chips would be better for you?
    (1) The regular chips would be better because they have less salt.
    (2) The low-fat chips would be better because they have less salt.
    (3) The low-fat chips would be better because they have less fat.
    (4) Both types of chips would be okay.
    (5) You cannot tell because the graphs do not show the salt content.

Connect with the Article

Write your answer to each question.

13. Avocados, which are fruit, contain a large amount of saturated fat. Does this surprise you? Why or why not?

____

____

____

14. Suppose you want to reduce the amount of fat in your diet. Which foods would be easiest for you to give up? Which would be hardest for you to give up? What would you eat instead?

____

____

____

Check your answers on page 230.

LESSON 4

Bones and Muscles
Bones and Muscles

Bones and Muscles

Vocabulary

aerobic

osteoporosis

joint

sprain

ligaments

Walking is a simple activity with excellent health benefits. It strengthens the heart, muscles, and bones. Because walking is a low-impact exercise, there is little chance of damaging your bones, muscles, or joints.

Best of all, walking doesn't require expensive gear, special clothing, or lessons. In this lesson, you will learn about the benefits of walking and other exercise to your bones and muscles.

Relate to the Topic

This lesson is about walking as a form of exercise. It explains the benefits of walking and shows its effects on muscles and joints. Suppose you wanted to convince a friend to start an exercise program.

Why might you recommend walking as a way to get started?

____

____

What are some of the points you would make to convince your friend of the importance of exercising regularly?

____

____

____

Reading Strategy

SKIMMING DIAGRAMS A diagram usually has a title and labels. The title tells you the topic of the diagram. You can skim a diagram to find its topic by looking at its title. Skim the diagrams on pages 36 and 37. Then answer the questions.

1. What is the topic of the diagram on page 36? ____________________
   Hint: Look at the title.

2. What is the topic of the diagram on page 37? ____________________
   Hint: Look at the title.

Check your answers on page 230.

Walking for Fitness

Strolling through the mall or around town is a pleasant way to spend time. But did you know that by walking faster, you can improve your fitness and health? Walking at a fast pace gives the heart, lungs, muscles, and bones a good workout.

The Benefits of Walking

Walking is easy and it's convenient. You don't need expensive equipment, special clothing, or lessons to walk. All you need is a good pair of shoes and a little time. You can walk anywhere—around the block, on a track, or even indoors. Some malls open early so walkers can exercise before the shoppers arrive.

Walking is easy on the body. It doesn't jar the joints as jogging or tennis does. That makes walking safe for many people. In fact, doctors often recommend walking to patients recovering from heart attacks, operations, or some injuries.

Walking is a safe and inexpensive way to exercise.

Walking can be an aerobic exercise like jogging, swimming, or cycling. An **aerobic** exercise requires the body to take in extra oxygen. It strengthens the heart, because the heart is required to beat faster. It also increases the amount of oxygen taken in by the lungs. As you exercise, your heart delivers the oxygen-rich blood to your muscles, which helps them grow stronger.

Studies have shown that brisk walking may reduce the risk of heart disease, stroke, and high blood pressure. Other studies have shown that a brisk walk three times a week may lower cholesterol, lower stress, and even provide protection against certain types of cancer.

Walking uses up stored fat. Walking burns about the same number of calories per mile as jogging. It just takes longer to walk a mile than to jog. People who walk regularly and do not increase the amount they eat can lose weight slowly.

Improving Bones and Muscles

Walking uses major muscle groups in the legs, abdomen, and lower back. Walkers who exercise their arms as they walk can make the muscles of the upper body stronger, too.

Muscles work in pairs to move bones. The diagram below shows that when you push off the ground with your foot, you straighten your ankle. To do this, the calf muscles of the leg contract, or shorten. At the same time, the shin muscles relax, or lengthen. Then as you swing your leg forward, your foot lifts up. To bend the ankle this way, the shin muscles contract. At the same time, the calf muscles relax. This repeated movement improves the tone of the leg muscles.

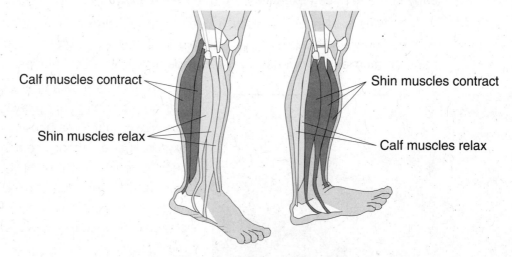

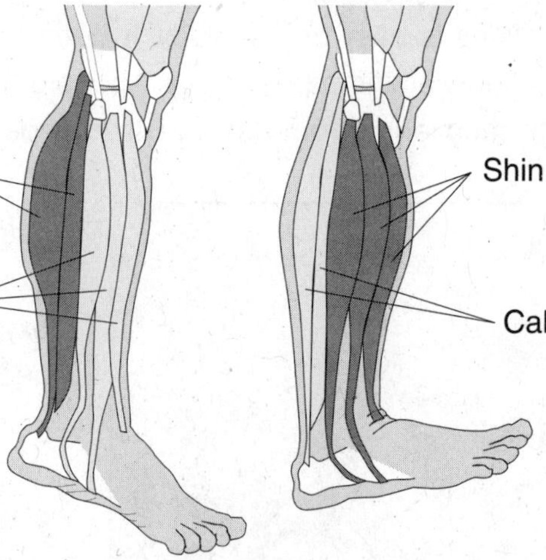

Muscles Work in Pairs

Exercise that increases muscle strength also benefits the bones. Exercise causes muscles to pull on the bones. As a result, the bones become stronger and more solid. This can help prevent **osteoporosis,** a condition of brittle bones. This problem affects many older people, especially women.

Finding the Implied Main Idea Sometimes the main idea of a paragraph is not stated. Instead, it is hinted at, or **implied.** To find the implied main idea, you have to think about how the details in the paragraph are related to each other and to the topic of the article.

Reread the paragraph on this page that begins, "Exercise that increases. . . . " It discusses the effect of exercise on bones. The implied main idea is that **walking can benefit bones,** even though the word *walking* is never used.

Read the first paragraph on this page. What idea is implied?

a. Walking reduces pain in your lower back.
b. Walking strengthens muscles throughout your body.

 Check your answer on page 231.

Easy on the Joints

Walking is considered one of the safest forms of exercise because it doesn't jar the joints of the body. A **joint** is the place where two or more bones come together. There are several types of joints. Most allow some kind of movement. For example, a hinge joint works like the hinge on a door. The hinge allows the door to open and close. A hinge joint allows your knee to bend and straighten.

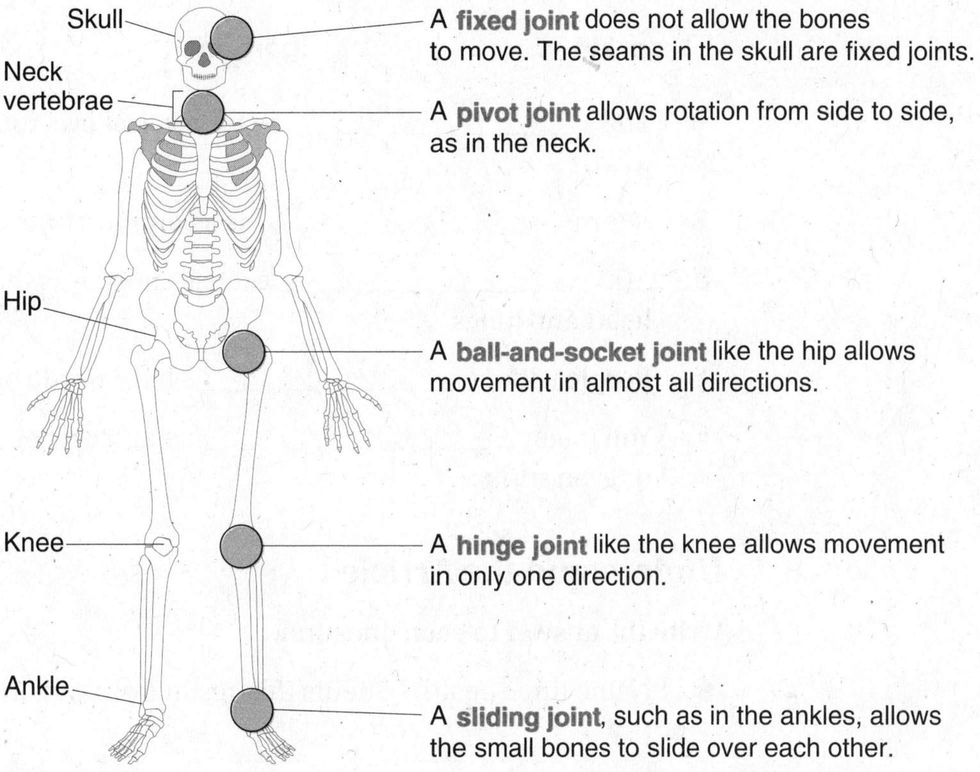

Skull
Neck vertebrae
Hip
Knee
Ankle
A **fixed joint** does not allow the bones to move. The seams in the skull are fixed joints.
A **pivot joint** allows rotation from side to side, as in the neck.
A **ball-and-socket joint** like the hip allows movement in almost all directions.
A **hinge joint** like the knee allows movement in only one direction.
A **sliding joint**, such as in the ankles, allows the small bones to slide over each other.

The Joints of the Body

Some physical activities, such as jogging, can put a lot of stress on joints. In some cases, runners sprain a leg or ankle. A **sprain** is a joint injury in which the ligaments are stretched too far or torn. **Ligaments** are strong bands that connect bones at joints. A ligament stretches much like a rubber band. Unlike joggers, walkers rarely hurt their ligaments.

Comparing and Contrasting with Diagrams When you tell how things are alike, you are **comparing**. When you tell how things are different from one another, you are **contrasting**.

Look at the diagram above. How do neck joints and knee joints differ? Circle the letter of the correct answer.

a. Neck joints are fixed, while knee joints have a ball and socket.
b. Neck joints are pivot joints, while knee joints are hinge joints.

 Check your answer on page 231.

Thinking About the Article

Practice Vocabulary

The words below are in the passage in bold type. Study the way each word is used. Then complete each sentence by writing the correct word.

aerobic	**osteoporosis**	**joint**
sprain	**ligament**	

1. The ______________________ in the neck allows rotation from side to side.
2. A torn ______________________ is a common injury for runners.
3. A(n) ______________________ exercise improves the condition of your heart and lungs.
4. People with ______________________ have brittle bones.
5. You might ______________________ an ankle if you run on a hard, uneven surface.

Understand the Article

Write the answer to each question.

6. Name three health benefits that result from walking.

____

____

____

7. Why is it necessary for muscles to work in pairs?

____

____

____

____

8. You decide to go for a fast walk to get some exercise. How can you tell whether you are walking fast enough for your exercise to be aerobic?

____

____

Apply Your Skills

Circle the number of the best answer for each question.

9. How can walking and jogging burn about the same number of calories per mile?
   (1) Both walking and jogging reduce the risk of heart disease.
   (2) It takes longer to walk a mile than to jog one.
   (3) Any kind of exercise can help you lose weight.
   (4) Both kinds of exercise help to increase muscle strength.
   (5) Runners are more likely to sprain their ankles.

10. Reread the paragraph below the diagram on page 37. What main idea is implied?
   (1) Sprains heal slowly.
   (2) Ligaments stretch or tear easily.
   (3) Walking does not put a lot of stress on joints.
   (4) Joint injuries are painful.
   (5) Jogging is an unsafe form of exercise.

11. Look at the diagram on page 36. How is the leg on the left different from the leg on the right?
   (1) The calf muscles are relaxed.
   (2) The calf muscles are contracted.
   (3) The shin muscles are contracted.
   (4) Both the shin and the calf muscles are relaxed.
   (5) Both the shin and the calf muscles are contracted.

Connect with the Article

Write your answer to each question.

12. Choose one of the types of joints from the diagram on page 37. Explain how the joint works by comparing it to a common object.

____

____

____

13. Suppose you want to start an exercise program to lose weight and improve your overall health. Would you choose walking or jogging? Why?

____

____

____

Check your answers on page 231.

5 LESSON

Reproduction and Development

Reproduction and Development

Vocabulary

hereditary

zygote

uterus

embryo

placenta

fetus

fetal alcohol synrome

The maternity ward of a hospital is a joyful place. Beaming relatives hold healthy babies. In contrast, the neonatal intensive care unit is stressful. Tiny babies are hooked up to tubes and monitors. Nurses and worried parents hover over them.

Some babies in a neonatal intensive care unit have conditions that could have been prevented. Not all birth defects and problems can be prevented, but pregnant women can help their babies by being careful about what they take into their bodies.

Relate to the Topic

This lesson explains how drugs like alcohol can pass from mother to baby. It describes birth defects and problems caused by certain drugs.

List three substances that might affect the development of an unborn baby.

____

How would you persuade a friend not to drink alcohol during pregnancy?

____

____

Reading Strategy

ASKING QUESTIONS Ask yourself questions as you read. This will help you understand what you read, by making you more aware of important details as well as main ideas. Read the first paragraph on page 41. Then answer the questions.

1. What is one question you could ask after reading the first paragraph?

____

Hint: Follow your own interests.

2. What is one question that is likely to be answered later in the article?

____

Hint: Look at the last sentence in the first paragraph.

Check your answers on page 231.

Having a Healthy Baby

Scientists once thought that almost all birth defects were **hereditary.** This means that a problem is passed from parent to child through the father's sperm or the mother's egg. People did not realize that what a mother did could affect the health of her unborn child.

Then in the 1950s and 1960s, many pregnant women in Europe took a drug called *Thalidomide.* Thousands of these women had babies born with misshapen arms and legs. Over a 30-year period in the United States, millions of women took a drug called *DES.* This drug prevented miscarriages. But by 1970, daughters of many of these women had cancer. Studying the effects of these two drugs helped scientists focus their research. Since then, scientists have learned that unborn babies are affected by what their mothers eat, drink, and smoke.

A mother and her healthy baby

The Development of an Unborn Baby

In nine months, a new human being develops from one cell into an organism with billions of cells. A developing baby goes through three stages before it is born. First it is a zygote, then an embryo, and finally a fetus.

Zygote. A sperm from the father joins with the egg produced by the mother. This fertilized egg is called a **zygote.** The zygote divides and forms a hollow ball of cells, which makes its way toward the **uterus,** or womb. It floats freely in the uterus for a few days. Around the tenth day, the zygote attaches to the woman's uterus.

Embryo. From the third to the eighth week, the developing baby is called an **embryo.** The embryo is attached to the uterus by the placenta. The **placenta** is a structure that allows substances to pass between the embryo and the mother.

The placenta is like a filter. The mother's blood passes along one side of the placenta. The embryo's blood passes along the other side. The two bloodstreams are separated by thin blood vessels, through which food substances and oxygen pass from the mother's blood to the embryo's. Waste and carbon dioxide pass from the embryo's blood to the mother's. Other substances in the mother's blood, such as drugs or chemicals, can pass through, too.

During this stage, the baby's main body organs and systems form. Birth defects are most likely to occur at this time. A harmful substance in the mother's blood can cause serious damage to the embryo.

Fetus. From the ninth week until the end of the ninth month, the developing baby is called a **fetus.** During these months, the fetus grows. Harmful substances are less likely to cause birth defects during this stage because the main systems and body have been formed. If damage occurred in the embryo stage, the damaged organ or system in the fetus may not work properly.

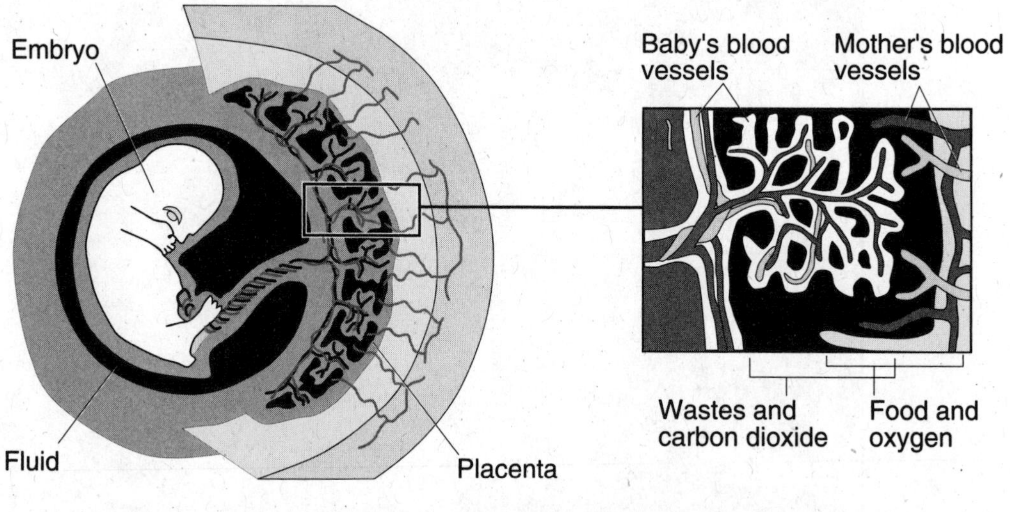

The Exchange of Substances Between Mother and Embryo

Finding the Main Idea of a Diagram A diagram is a picture that helps you see how something looks or works. Like a paragraph or an article, a diagram has a main idea. You can figure out the main idea by looking at the diagram or by studying its title. Look back at the diagram on page 24. The title tells you the main idea: *This is what a healthy human cell looks like.*

Which of the following tells the main idea of the diagram above?

a. Substances pass between mother and embryo.

b. The embryo is attached to the mother by the placenta.

 Check your answer on page 231.

The Effects of Drugs

What happens when a pregnant woman smokes a cigarette, drinks a beer, or takes an aspirin? It's hard to prove what is harmful and what is not. But over the years, scientists have started to link some substances with certain problems.

Cocaine. The mother's use of cocaine can cause a miscarriage, early labor, or stillbirth (death of the fetus). Cocaine babies are often underweight. They may have damage to the brain, lungs, urinary system, or sex organs.

Cigarettes. The nicotine in cigarettes makes the blood vessels in the placenta shrink. Less oxygen and fewer nutrients reach the developing baby. Smoking has been linked to miscarriages and stillbirths. Babies born to smokers are often underweight at birth.

Finding Details **Details** are specific facts that describe or explain the main idea of a paragraph, article, or diagram. For example, the main idea of the previous paragraph is that smoking cigarettes during pregnancy can affect the baby. A detail that supports this main idea is that the babies of smokers often are underweight at birth.

Place a check mark beside any details that you can find in the paragraph about smoking cigarettes during pregnancy.

_____ a. Nicotine shrinks placenta blood vessels.

_____ b. Nicotine can damage the baby's brain.

_____ c. Smoking is linked to stillbirths.

_____ d. Fewer nutrients reach the baby's blood.

Alcohol. A condition called **fetal alcohol syndrome (FAS)** can occur when the mother drinks alcohol while pregnant. Children with FAS may have abnormal heads, faces, arms, or legs. They often have low birth weights. Some are mentally retarded.

Common Medications. Few medications are known to cause serious harm to a developing baby. This doesn't mean, however, that most medications are safe. A pregnant woman should not take any medication without consulting her doctor. Even over-the-counter medications should be avoided. For example, some headache medications can cause problems when taken during the last three months of pregnancy.

Preventing Birth Defects

There is no way to guarantee a healthy baby. However, women can help lower the risks to their babies. A pregnant woman should eat a well-balanced diet. She should get regular medical care. A woman who is pregnant should not smoke or drink alcohol. She should not take cocaine or other illegal drugs. Also, she should check with her doctor before taking any medicines.

Check your answers on page 231.

Thinking About the Article

Practice Vocabulary

The words below are in the passage in bold type. Study the way each word is used. Then complete each sentence by writing the correct word.

zygote	**uterus**	**embryo**
placenta	**fetus**	

1. The fertilized egg, called a(n) ____________________, attaches to the wall of the ____________________, or womb, by the tenth day.
2. From the third to the eighth week, the developing baby is called a(n) ____________________.
3. The ____________________ is a structure through which substances pass between mother and baby.
4. From the ninth week until the end of the ninth month, the developing baby is called a(n) ____________________.

Understand the Article

Write or circle the answers to each question.

5. What two drugs helped focus research on what happens when a woman takes drugs during pregnancy?

    ____

6. List the three stages of a baby's prebirth development in the proper order.

    ____

7. During which stage of development is the most serious damage to the unborn baby likely to occur?

    ____

8. List three drugs that have been linked with problems for babies.

    ____

9. What can a pregnant woman do to help ensure she has a healthy baby? Circle the letter next to each correct answer.
    a. eat a well-balanced diet
    b. not smoke at all
    c. drink alcohol in moderation
    d. check with her doctor before taking medicine

Apply Your Skills

Circle the number of the best answer for each question.

10. The diagram on page 42 has two parts. What is the main idea of the part on the left?
    (1) The embryo stage is from three to eight weeks.
    (2) The placenta is part of the mother, not the baby.
    (3) The embryo is connected to the placenta, which is connected to the mother.
    (4) The baby and mother exchange substances via the placenta.
    (5) Food and oxygen pass from the mother to the baby.

11. Why are harmful substances least likely to cause birth defects in the last few months of pregnancy?
    By the last few months of pregnancy,
    (1) all of the body organs have formed
    (2) the placenta blocks harmful substances
    (3) the fetus has stopped growing
    (4) the fetus can control what it takes in
    (5) the fetus is not connected to the placenta

12. What should a pregnant woman who wants to have a healthy baby do?
    (1) eat a well-balanced diet
    (2) stop smoking if she smokes
    (3) stop drinking alcohol if she drinks
    (4) take medication only with the advice of a doctor
    (5) do all of the above

Connect with the Article

Write your answer to each question.

13. Many states have laws that require alcoholic beverages to have a warning label stating the dangers of drinking while pregnant. Do you think this is a good law? Give a reason for your answer.

____

____

____

14. If you had a friend who was pregnant and you saw her lighting a cigarette, what would you do? Why?

____

____

Check your answers on page 231.

LESSON 6

Genetics

Vocabulary

inherit

traits

heredity

genetics

dominant trait

recessive trait

Punnett square

genetic screening

amniocentesis

Down synrdome

chromosome

Do you and your mother have the same eye color or the same hair color? Do you have a nose shaped like your father's? Parents pass on features like these to their children. In fact, parents pass on more than appearance to their children.

For example, parents can pass on certain disorders or diseases to their children. Tests can detect if people are likely to get a disorder passed on by their parents. These tests cannot tell for sure whether a person will get a disorder—only if they are likely to get it.

Relate to the Topic

This lesson is about genetics. It explains how some features, including disorders, are passed from parents to children. Think about your family.

List a disorder that runs in your family. ______________________

If you could take a test to determine whether you are likely to develop the disorder, would you? Why or why not?

____

____

Reading Strategy

RELATING TO PERSONAL EXPERIENCE Link your personal experiences to the topic you are reading about. Look at the photograph on page 47. Then answer the questions.

1. In what ways do you look like your parents?

____

____

Hint: Has anyone told you that you look like your parents?

2. What features do you share with your other relatives?

____

____

Hint: Think about ways that you resemble different relatives.

Check your answers on page 232.

Genetic Screening

When Kristi Betts was 15, her mother came down with Huntington's disease. This disorder, which starts in middle age, slowly attacks the brain. People with Huntington's lose control over their physical and mental functions. This takes place over a period of about 20 years. There is no cure.

At first, Kristi was concerned only for her mother. Then she realized that she and her sisters and brothers were at risk for Huntington's disease, too. You cannot catch Huntington's disease like a cold or the flu. You **inherit** the disease. This means that you receive genetic material from one or both of your parents that causes you to develop the disease. Huntington's disease is passed on in the same way as brown eyes or curly hair. Each child of a parent with Huntington's disease has a chance of inheriting it.

How Traits Are Passed from Parent to Child

All organisms inherit features, or **traits,** from their parents. Some traits, such as hair color, are easily seen. Others, such as blood type, cannot be seen. **Heredity** is the passing of traits from parents to their young, or offspring. Traits are passed on when organisms reproduce. The study of how traits are inherited is called **genetics.**

Each parent gives its offspring genetic material for a form of the trait. In some cases, one form of a trait shows and the other does not. The form of a trait that shows whenever it is present is called a **dominant trait.** The form of a trait that doesn't always show is called a **recessive trait.** In humans, for example, dark hair and dark eyes are dominant traits. Light hair and light eyes are recessive traits. A person must inherit a recessive trait from both parents in order for it to show.

A four-generation birthday party

Scientists show how traits combine by using a diagram called a **Punnett square,** which shows all the possible combinations of traits among the offspring of two parents. Look at the Punnett square on the left. It shows the combinations that may result when one parent has the trait for Huntington's disease and the other parent does not. The trait for Huntington's disease is a dominant trait. It is labeled with a capital *H*. The healthy form of the trait is recessive. It is labeled with a lowercase *h*.

Father \ Mother	H	h
h	Hh	hh
h	Hh	hh

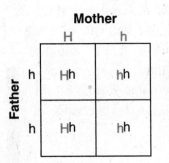

In this Punnett square, the mother with the trait for Huntington's disease is shown on top. She has a dominant and a recessive form of the trait. The healthy father is shown on the left. He has two recessive forms of the trait. When these two people have a child, each gives one form of the trait to the child. Their traits can combine as shown in the four boxes. A child who inherits a dominant and a recessive form (Hh) or two dominant forms (HH) will develop Huntington's disease as an adult. A child who inherits two recessive forms (hh) will not develop the disease.

Using Details Details are very important in science. When you come to a passage with a lot of details, slow down. The previous paragraph explains how to read the Punnett square. Reread the paragraph one sentence at a time. If you read slowly and carefully, you will understand the details. For example, you will find out that the father is healthy because he has two recessive forms of the trait for Huntington's. The mother has Huntington's because she has one dominant and one recessive form of the trait.

Look back at the paragraph to find the details to help you answer these questions.

1. Will a child who inherits hh develop Huntington's disease? ______
2. Will a child who inherits Hh develop Huntington's disease? ______

Testing for Inherited Disorders

You can see from the Punnett square above that Kristi Betts had a two out of four chance of inheriting Huntington's disease. At one time, people had to live with this uncertainty. Since Huntington's disease doesn't appear until middle age, young people with an ill parent didn't know their own fate. But now people at risk can be tested. **Genetic screening** is the name for tests that can tell people if they have inherited certain disorders.

It is hard to decide whether to be tested for Huntington's disease. Is it better to know or not know if you are going to get the disease? Kristi decided it was better to know. She was lucky. She found out that she had not inherited Huntington's disease.

Unlike Huntington's, many genetic diseases are recessive. In such cases, when two recessive forms combine, the child inherits the disorder even though both parents may be healthy. There are tests to see if adults carry the recessive traits for certain disorders, such as sickle-cell anemia.

 Check your answers on page 232.

Genetic Screening of the Unborn

Genetic screening of fetuses is becoming more common, even among people with no history of genetic disorder in their families. For example, **amniocentesis** is a test that can be performed after the sixteenth week of pregnancy. This test can detect several disorders caused by genetic abnormalities, including Down syndrome. **Down syndrome** is a disorder caused by the presence of an extra **chromosome.** Children who have Down syndrome are mildly to severely mentally retarded. They may also have other health problems.

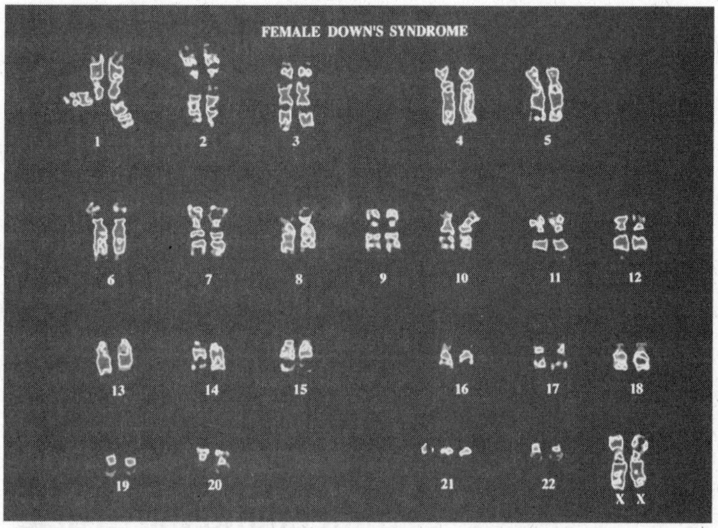

The developing baby receives genetic material from each parent in the form of chromosomes. Each baby should have 23 pairs of chromosomes, with one in each pair coming from the mother, and the other coming from the father. In amniocentesis, the baby's chromosomes are photographed and examined. The extra chromosome 21 in this photograph indicates that this baby has Down syndrome.

When genetic screening shows a disorder, prospective parents must make a decision. Genetic counselors help them explore their choices. People may decide not to have children. They may also accept the risk and the possible outcome of having a disabled child. Some people believe that genetic screening is wrong. Others feel that the knowledge, even if it is bad news, is worth having.

Distinguishing Fact from Opinion **Facts** are things that can be proved true. **Opinions,** on the other hand, are beliefs. They may or may not be true. When reading science, it's important to distinguish fact from opinion. One way to do this is to look for words that signal an opinion: *believe, feel, think,* and *opinion.* For example, in the previous paragraph the phrase "Some people believe" signals that an opinion is coming.

Write the word *fact* or *opinion* next to each statement. If the statement includes an opinion, circle the word that signals an opinion.

1. Genetic counselors help parents explore their choices. ______
2. Some people feel that even bad news is knowledge worth having. ______

 Check your answers on page 232.

Thinking About the Article

Practice Vocabulary

The words below are in the passage in bold type. Study the way each word is used. Then complete each sentence by writing the correct word.

traits	**heredity**	**genetics**
dominant trait	**recessive trait**	

1. In humans, dark hair is a ____________________ that always shows when it is present.
2. ____________________, or characteristics, are features inherited from parents.
3. ____________________ is the study of how traits are inherited.
4. The passing on of traits from parents to their children is called ____________________.
5. Light hair is a ____________________.

Understand the Article

Write or circle the answer to each question.

6. Unlike a cold or pneumonia, Huntington's disease is not spread by contact with other people's germs. How is Huntington's disease transmitted?
   a. You inherit it from a parent.
   b. You get it from contact with poisonous chemicals.
7. Name a human trait that is dominant.

   ____
8. Name a disorder or disease that results when a child inherits two recessive forms of the trait.

   ____
9. Name a disorder that can be identified by performing amniocentesis.

   ____
10. What is the job of a genetic counselor?

    ____

    ____

Apply Your Skills

Circle the number of the best answer for each question.

11. Which of the following is a genetic screening test for a fetus?
    (1) Huntington's disease
    (2) amniocentesis
    (3) Punnett square
    (4) heredity
    (5) Down syndrome

12. According to the Punnett square on page 48, what is the chance that a child of a parent with Huntington's disease will inherit the disease?
    (1) zero out of four
    (2) one out of four
    (3) two out of four
    (4) three out of four
    (5) four out of four

13. Which of the following statements includes an opinion rather than a fact?
    (1) To test whether a person has inherited a disease, he or she undergoes genetic screening.
    (2) A person with one parent who has Huntington's has a chance of inheriting the disease.
    (3) Some young people think it is better to be tested and know whether they will develop Huntington's in middle age.
    (4) Some parents undergo amniocentesis to find out whether their unborn babies have Down syndrome or other disorders.
    (5) Children born with Down syndrome are mildly to severely retarded and may have other health problems.

Connect with the Article

Write your answer to each question.

14. If both of your parents had Hh traits for Huntington's, what would be your chances of inheriting this disease?

____

15. If you were about to become a mother or father, would you want genetic screening done during pregnancy? Why or why not?

____

____

____

Check your answers on page 232.

Lesson 7

Bacteria and Viruses

Vocabulary

rhinovirus

virus

influenza (flu)

vaccination

antibody

pneumonia

bacteria

antibiotic

Colds can make you feel miserable. That's why many people try to avoid them. You may have heard of different ways to avoid getting a cold or to treat a cold so it doesn't get worse.

If you've ever had a cold, then you probably know that colds can be passed from person to person. Colds and certain other diseases are caused by germs. Sharing germs is one way to get sick. Scientists are trying to find out exactly how cold germs are passed from person to person and how to treat diseases effectively.

Relate to the Topic

This lesson is about the viruses and bacteria that cause some common diseases. Think back to a time when you had a cold or the flu.

How do you think you caught it? ______________________________

____

What were your symptoms? ______________________________

____

What did you do to make yourself feel better? ______________________________

____

____

Reading Strategy

RELATING TO WHAT YOU KNOW The topic of this lesson is bacteria and viruses. When you read, think about what you already know about the topic. Then answer the questions.

1. What are bacteria and viruses? ______________________________
   Hint: Think about what you have heard about them.

2. What kinds of illnesses can bacteria and viruses cause?

   ____

   ____

   Hint: Think about some illnesses you have had.

Check your answers on page 232.

Colds, Flu, and Pneumonia

First you feel a small ache or a tickle in your throat. Soon your nose is running, your head is congested, and your eyes are watering. Your throat is now sore, too. Yes, it's another cold.

Catching a Cold

In spite of what your mother may have told you, simply getting wet and chilled won't give you a cold. Instead, you catch a cold from a sick person near you.

For many years, scientists have researched ways that colds are passed from person to person. Jack Gwaltney, a scientist at the University of Virginia, thinks that colds are passed by touch. Gwaltney says that people with colds have many cold-causing viruses on their hands. When these people touch something, such as a telephone, they leave viruses on the surface. You come along and touch the telephone. Then you touch your nose or eyes, and the virus settles in.

Another scientist, Elliot Dick, focused on a different theory. While at the University of Wisconsin, he performed an experiment in which he gathered 60 card players for a 12-hour poker game. 20 players had colds. Of the 40 healthy players, half wore braces or collars that kept them from touching their faces. The other half were free to touch their faces. Players in both healthy groups caught colds. Since players who could not touch their faces also got sick, Dick concluded that cold viruses spread through the air. Someone who is sick sneezes or coughs, and you breathe in the virus. Soon you are sick, too.

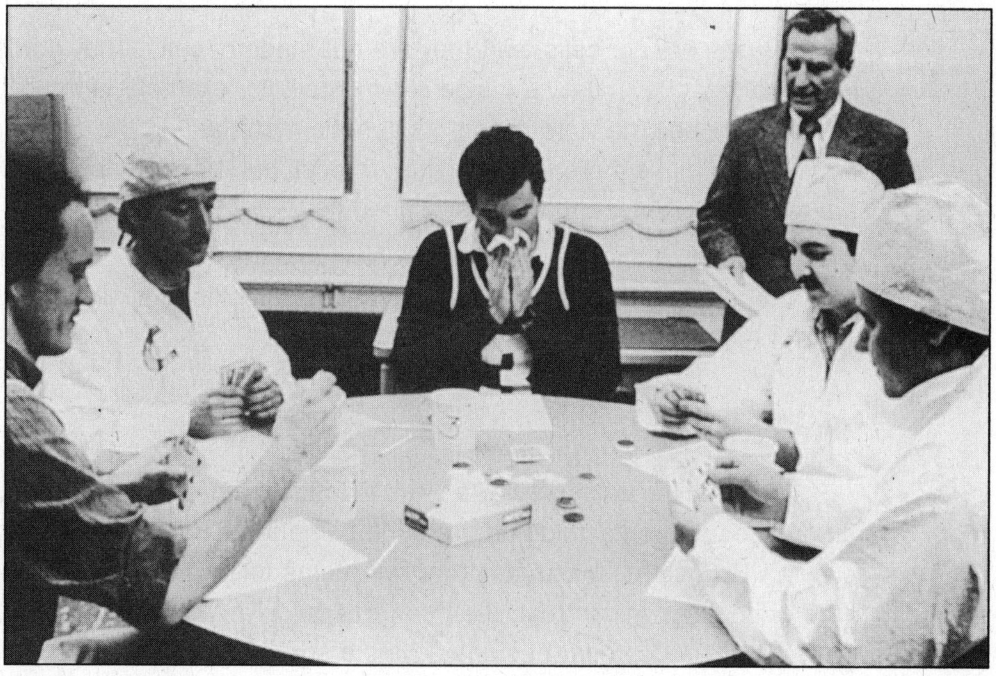

Elliot Dick's cold virus experiment

Treating a Cold

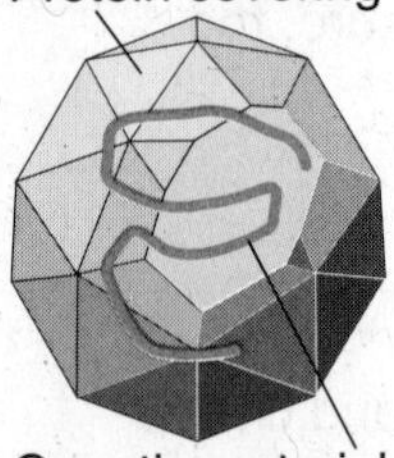

A Rhinovirus

Stroll through any drugstore and you'll see hundreds of sprays, pills, capsules, and syrups to make the cold sufferer feel better. Many of these products do help. But none can cure a cold. For years, scientists have been trying to find a cure for the common cold. The problem is that colds are caused by about 200 different viruses. About half of all colds are caused by a group of viruses called **rhinoviruses.**

Just what is a virus? A **virus** is a tiny particle made up of genetic material with a protein covering. The genetic material holds directions for making more viruses. The protein covering protects the virus.

Finding Details in a Diagram Besides providing a general picture of something, a diagram has many specific things, or details, in it. You have to look carefully to find the details. Often there's help: The most important details are labeled. The words with lines pointing to parts of the diagram are called *labels.* Labels direct your attention to important details. In the diagram of a rhinovirus above, labels point out two details: the protein covering and the genetic material.

Now look at the diagram of a bacterial cell on the next page. List the details you can find in this diagram.

____________________ ____________________

____________________ ____________________

Viruses are not cells, and they are not made of cells. They don't grow. To make more viruses, they must be inside a living cell. For example, a rhinovirus latches onto a cell in the nose. The virus injects its genetic material into the cell and uses the cell's materials to make more viruses. Then the cell bursts open and dies. The new viruses are released to infect other cells.

Infections caused by viruses are hard to cure. The best way to fight viruses is to stop them before they invade. Researchers are looking for ways to block the rhinoviruses from attaching to cells in the nose.

The Flu

Another illness caused by a virus is **influenza,** usually called the **flu.** The difference between a cold and the flu is sometimes hard to know. A cold usually starts slowly, with a scratchy throat. Other symptoms follow in a day or two. Usually there is little or no fever. In contrast, the flu starts quickly. Within twelve hours you may have a fever over 101 degrees. Besides having a sore throat, stuffy nose, and a cough, you ache and feel very tired. Recovering from the flu can take up to three weeks. Although there are some drugs to help people feel better, there is no cure.

 Check your answers on page 232.

One defense against the flu is to get a flu vaccination each year. A **vaccination** is an injected dose of a dead or weakened disease-causing agent. This causes the body to form antibodies. An **antibody** is a substance the body makes to fight a disease. Once antibodies form, you are protected against that specific agent. This protection lowers your chance of getting the disease.

Pneumonia

People weakened by a bad cold or the flu are more likely to develop pneumonia. Symptoms include a high fever, chest pain, breathing problems, and a bad cough. **Pneumonia** is an infection of the lungs caused by a virus or bacterium. **Bacteria** are one-celled organisms and are many times larger than viruses. A bacterial cell is shown in the following diagram.

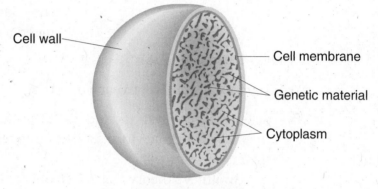

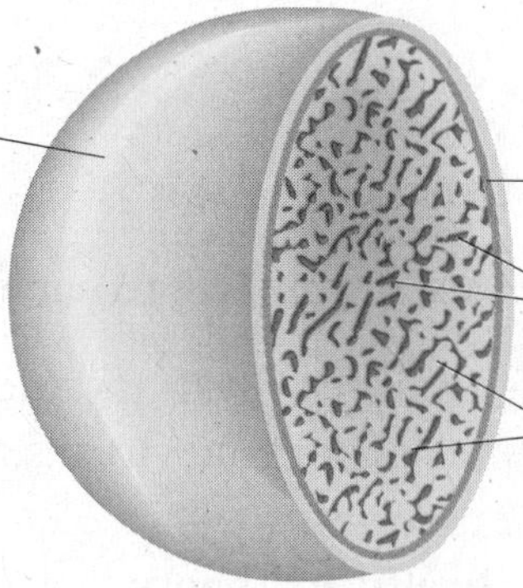

A Bacterial Cell

About 90 percent of flu-related pneumonia is caused by bacteria. As the infection takes hold, the lungs produce fluid and mucus to fight the bacteria. The fluid blocks the air passages in the lungs. The person has trouble breathing and may have to go to a hospital. He or she is given **antibiotics,** drugs that fight bacteria. The antibiotics kill the disease-causing bacteria, and the person gets better.

Making Inferences When you read, you can sometimes figure out things that the author hints at but doesn't actually tell you. A fact or idea that is not stated in the text but that you figure out is an **inference.** Reread the first paragraph about pneumonia. The author says that people who have the flu sometimes develop an infection called pneumonia. One thing you can infer is that a good way to avoid getting pneumonia is to avoid getting the flu.

Which of the following ideas can be inferred from the information in the paragraph that begins "About 90 percent"? Circle the letter of the correct inference.

a. About 10 percent of flu-related pneumonia is caused by a virus.
b. Antibiotics can help cure pneumonia caused by a virus.

 Check your answer on page 232.

Thinking About the Article

Practice Vocabulary

The words below are in the passage in bold type. Study the way each word is used. Then match each word with its meaning. Write the letter.

______	1. virus	a. one-celled organisms
______	2. influenza	b. an infection of the lungs caused by bacteria or a virus
______	3. pneumonia	c. an illness caused by a virus; also called the flu
______	4. bacteria	d. a drug that fights bacteria
______	5. antibiotic	e. a tiny particle made of genetic material and a covering

Understand the Article

Write or circle the answer to each question.

6. Scientists Jack Gwaltney and Elliot Dick have focused on different theories about cold viruses. What is the main difference between their theories?
   a. Gwaltney's theory focuses on only one type of cold virus, while Dick's theory focuses on many types of cold viruses.
   b. Gwaltney's theory focuses on the transmission of cold viruses through touch, while Dick's theory focuses on the transmission of cold viruses through the air.

7. What can cause each of the following diseases? Write *bacteria* and/or *virus* in the space provided.
   a. a cold ______________________
   b. the flu ______________________
   c. pneumonia ______________________

8. How does a virus make more copies of itself?
   a. It splits in half, as in cell division.
   b. It takes over a cell and uses cell materials to copy itself.

9. What is a vaccination?

____

____

10. What is an antibody?

____

Apply Your Skills

Circle the number of the best answer for each question.

11. Which of the following is found in both a bacterial cell and in a virus?
    (1) cell wall
    (2) cell membrane
    (3) antibody
    (4) genetic material
    (5) cytoplasm

12. Based on the information in this article, what can you infer is the best way to prevent getting a cold?
    (1) Avoid touching anything that people with colds touch.
    (2) Avoid breathing air in spaces where people with colds are.
    (3) Avoid people with colds.
    (4) Stay dry and warm in the winter.
    (5) Get a vaccination against colds.

13. Antibiotics are not used to treat colds and the flu. What can you infer from this?
    (1) Antibiotics do not fight viruses.
    (2) Antibiotics do not fight bacteria.
    (3) People with colds or the flu do not go to the hospital.
    (4) Antibiotics cost too much to use them on colds and the flu.
    (5) Antibiotics are used to prevent colds and the flu.

Connect with the Article

Write your answer to each question.

14. Winter is the season when most cases of colds, flu, and pneumonia occur. Why do you think that is so?

____

____

____

15. What can you do to keep yourself and your family healthy next winter?

____

____

____

____

Check your answers on pages 232–233.

Lesson 8

Plants

Vocabulary

species

root

stem

bark

leaf

bud

flower

When you reach into the medicine cabinet for an aspirin, do you realize that you are using a drug that comes from a plant? Aspirin comes from the bark of the willow tree. It has been used for thousands of years to relieve fever and pain by many peoples, including Native Americans and the ancient Greeks.

Many medicines we use today come from plants. Rain forests are home to many different plants. Some of these could provide cures for cancer or other diseases. Scientists are working to find these useful plants before rain forests disappear.

Relate to the Topic

This lesson is about plants that are used as medicines. People use plants for many purposes, not just as medicines. Think about how you use plants.

List two kinds of plants that you eat.

____

List two kinds of plants that are used to build things.

____

What other ways do you use plants everyday?

____

Reading Strategy

SKIMMING CHARTS Information is often summarized in **charts**. A chart usually has a title and labels. The title tells you what kind of information the chart contains. The labels help you locate specific information in the chart. Skim the chart on page 61. Then answer the questions.

1. What is the topic of the chart?

   ____

   Hint: Look at the title.

2. What kinds of information can you find in the chart?

   ____

   Hint: Look at the labels above each column.

Check your answers on page 233.

Medicines from Plants

In the Amazon rain forest, a type of tropical daisy is used as an antibiotic medicine. In Indonesia, certain plants are used to cure tetanus (lockjaw). In India and Nepal, coleus is used to get rid of body worms. These are just a few of the plants that are used as medicines. People have been using plants to treat and cure diseases for thousands of years. Plant medicines work in two ways. Some affect the body's chemistry. Others affect the bacteria and viruses that cause diseases.

Searching for Medicinal Plants

There is an urgent need to search for plants that can be used as medicines. The tropical rain forests contain two-thirds of the world's plant **species,** or kinds of plants. Many of these species have not yet even been identified. But the rain forests are disappearing at a rapid rate. Useful plants may become extinct before they can be identified and studied.

This vine can be brewed into a tea that is used to treat stomachaches. It grows in rain forests.

One scientist is using a shortcut to find useful plants. Dr. Mark Plotkin has been working with native shamans, or traditional healers, in the Amazon rain forest. These healers have a knowledge of plants that dates back thousands of years. They use about 300 different plants as medicines. Dr. Plotkin has to work quickly, though. Most young people in the Amazon rain forest are more interested in modern ways. As a result, the shamans' knowledge is dying out. The plants they use may soon be gone, too.

Scientists must test a plant if they think it may be a source for a medicine. An extract, or strong solution, is made from the plant. The extract is placed in test tubes that contain cancer cells, bacteria, or viruses. Extracts that seem to work as a medicine are tested on mice. Then the extract is broken down into its chemical parts. The parts are tested until the active chemical is found. Then scientists must figure out how much of the extract is safe to use. Many plant products are poisonous in large doses.

Parts of a Plant

Medicines have been made from all parts of plants. Often only one part of a plant can be used to make a medicine. The diagram shows the parts of a typical seed plant.

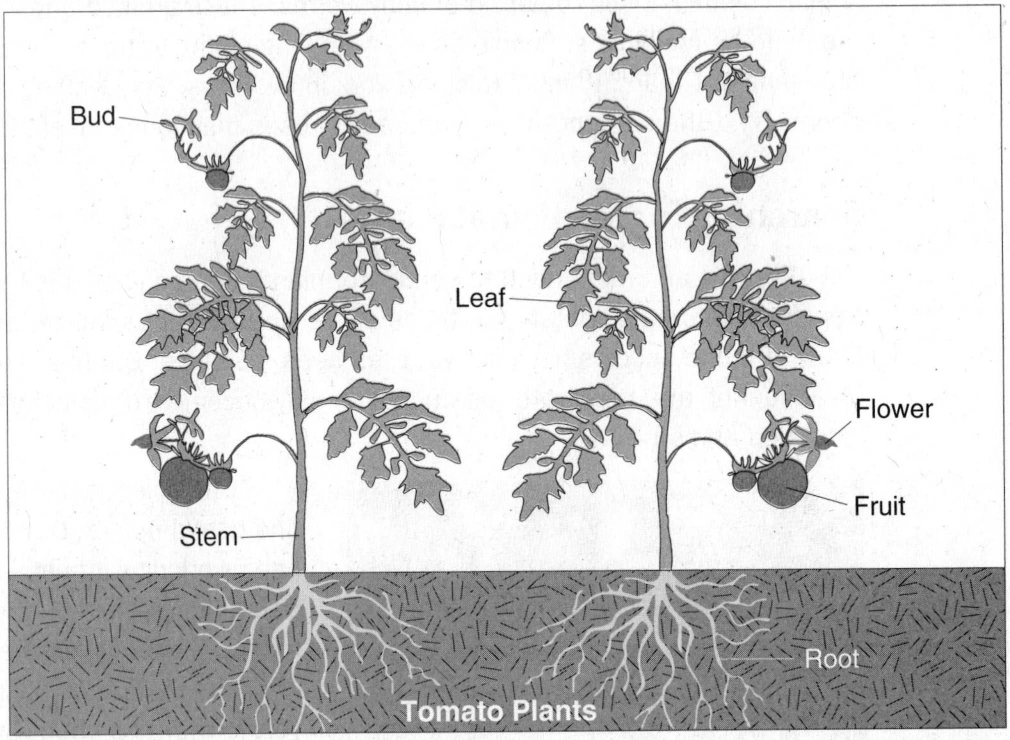

The **roots** of a plant hold the plant in the ground. They also absorb minerals and water from the soil. The **stem** supports the plant. It also transports water and minerals from the roots to the top of the plant. **Bark** is the outer part of the stem of a woody plant. **Leaves** use sunlight to change water and carbon dioxide into food for the plant. **Buds** are areas of growth. New leaves or flowers grow from buds. **Flowers** are the reproductive organs of plants. Fruits develop from flowers. The fruits contain the seeds, which will grow into new plants.

Getting Meaning from Context You may not understand every word you read in science. But sometimes you can figure out the meaning of words you don't know from clues nearby. Reread the description of the stem in the paragraph above. Can you guess what the word *transport* means? Look at the **context**—the rest of the words in the sentence. There are clues. Water and minerals are moving up from the roots to the rest of the plant. The stem is carrying water and minerals. The word *transport* means "to carry or move."

In the paragraph that describes the parts of a plant, what does *reproductive organs* mean? Circle the letter of the correct meaning.

a. the parts of the plant that produce offspring
b. the parts of the plant that produce many copies of the leaves

 Check your answer on page 233.

Using Medicines Made from Plants

Even in modern cultures, plants are the source of many drugs. There are more than 265,000 different plant species known in the world. Less than two percent of them have been tested as medicines. Yet about 40 percent of all medicines have come from that tiny number of plants. Many medicines are made directly from natural plant products. Others are synthetic, or artificial, copies of the plants' helpful substances. These synthetic substances make more medicine available than people could gather from the plants alone. The chart shows some of these medicines and their plant sources.

Medicines and Their Plant Sources

Medicine	Plant Source	Use
quinine	cinchona bark	treating malaria
curare	several tropical plants	muscle relaxant during surgery
digitalis	purple foxglove	treating heart disorders
vinca alkaloids	rosy periwinkle	treating Hodgkin's disease and leukemia
expectorant	horehound	in cough syrup to discharge mucus
menthol	peppermint leaves	in pain relievers and decongestants
valepotriates	root of valerian	sedative
reserpine	roots of several shrubs	sedative; treating high blood pressure
salicylate	wintergreen	in liniments to soothe muscle aches
taxol	bark of Pacific yew	treating ovarian and other cancers

The chart shows that many common medicines come from plants. For example, Valium, a well-known sedative, is a synthetic form of substances found in the roots of the valerian plant. (Sedatives are medicines that help people relax.) Horehound is used to make cough syrups and throat lozenges.

Some plants are used in the treatment of serious diseases, such as cancer. Many forms of chemotherapy use natural products from plants. One recent discovery is taxol. It is used to treat ovarian cancer. The Pacific yew must be harvested to produce natural taxol. Synthetic taxol has been produced, but is still in the experimental stage.

Interpreting Charts Charts can provide a large amount of information in a small space. To find the information you are looking for in a chart, you must read the labels at the top of each column. These labels tell you what types of information are listed in each column. Once you find the information you are looking for in one column, trace your finger across the row to find related information.

What types of medicines include menthol from peppermint leaves? Circle the letter of the best answer.

a. pain relievers and decongestants
b. cough syrup and sedatives

Check your answer on page 233.

Thinking About the Article

Practice Vocabulary

The words below are in the passage in bold type. Study the way each word is used. Then match each word with its meaning. Write the letter.

_____ 1. leaf
_____ 2. stem
_____ 3. bark
_____ 4. flower
_____ 5. bud
_____ 6. root

a. transports water to leaves
b. reproductive organ of the plant
c. absorbs water and minerals from soil
d. outer part of the stem of a woody plant
e. area of growth
f. makes food for the plant

Understand the Article

Write or circle the answer to each question.

7. List two ways that plants work as medicines.

____

____

8. Why do scientists test plants in laboratories before trying them on people? Circle the letter of each correct reason.
   a. They have to find out which chemical in the plant is active.
   b. They cannot find volunteers to take the plant extracts.
   c. They have to figure out how much of the plant extract to use.
   d. They have to see whether the plant destroys cancer, bacteria, or viruses.

9. Why has Dr. Mark Plotkin been working with shamans in the Amazon rain forest?

____

____

____

10. According to the chart on page 61, how are reserpine and valepotriates alike? Circle the letter of each correct similarity.
   a. Both are made from roots.
   b. Both are sedatives.
   c. Both are used in cough syrups.

Apply Your Skills

Circle the number of the best answer for each question.

11. Reread the first paragraph under the heading "Searching for Medicinal Plants" on page 59. What does the word *species* mean?
    (1) type of culture
    (2) type of organism
    (3) medicines that come from plants
    (4) treatment for a disease
    (5) type of disease

12. Reread the last paragraph on page 59. What does the phrase *active chemical* mean?
    (1) the extract of the plant
    (2) the strong solution that contains cancer cells, bacteria, or viruses
    (3) the chemical that works as a medicine
    (4) the most poisonous chemical in the plant
    (5) the amount of chemical that is safe to use

13. Look at the chart on page 61. According to the chart, which plant is used to soothe muscle aches?
    (1) quinine
    (2) purple foxglove
    (3) salicylate
    (4) wintergreen
    (5) Pacific yew

Understand the Article

Write your answer to each question.

14. What are two ways modern culture has helped limit the use of rain forest plants as medicines?

____

____

____

15. Have you or someone you know ever used any of the medicines listed on page 61? If so, write why the medicine was used. If not, describe some other medicine you have taken.

____

____

____

Check your answers on page 233.

LESSON 9

Animal Behavior

Vocabulary

mammal

sound waves

echolocation

density

language

Dolphins intrigue people. Many people visit marine parks and aquariums to see dolphin shows. Some people even pay to watch dolphins along the coast or to swim beside them in the water.

Like humans, dolphins are mammals and they are very intelligent. Perhaps this is why people are so interested in dolphins. Scientists have been trying to find out how dolphins communicate in the wild and in captivity. Some scientists have even tried to teach dolphins different kinds of languages.

Relate to the Topic

This lesson is about dolphin communication. It describes some of the sounds that dolphins make. Think about a time you saw dolphins at a marine park, at an aquarium, or on TV.

What did the dolphins do? ______________________________

____

Did they make any sounds? What did you hear?

____

Reading Strategy

USING HEADINGS TO ASK QUESTIONS When you come to a heading, think about it for a moment before reading the information that follows it. Think of a question that might be answered in that section. As you continue reading, look for answer to your question. Read the headings on pages 65 through 67. Then answer the questions.

1. What is one question that is likely to be answered on page 65?

   ____

   Hint: Read the heading.

2. What is one question that is likely to be answered on page 66?

   ____

   Hint: Read the heading.

Check your answers on page 233.

How Do Dolphins Communicate?

At a signal from their trainer, the dolphins leap out of the pool, curve high over the water, and then dive back in. They perform beautifully, and the audience at the marine park loves them. While they resemble fish, they are actually **mammals.** Dolphins are not just charming entertainers. They are the subject of many research studies, including several on how dolphins communicate. In the wild, dolphins communicate using a variety of sounds. They use whistles, grunts, and repetitive clicks, many of which humans cannot hear. In captivity, they have been taught to communicate using simple sign language or computer-generated sounds.

Signature Whistles

One type of sound that dolphins use is the whistle. To most people, all dolphin whistles sound alike. But research indicates that each dolphin has its own unique signature whistle.

Studying signature whistles is difficult. Although people can hear the whistles underwater, we cannot locate a whistle's source. Even when underwater microphones are used to pick up the whistles, their source cannot be pinpointed. One solution to this problem is to isolate a single dolphin for a short time and record its whistle. Another solution, invented by Peter Tyack of Stanford University, is a device called a vocalight. The vocalight is attached to a dolphin's head by a suction cup. A microphone inside the vocalight picks up sounds, which are displayed as lights. The louder the sound, the more lights go on.

Tyack used vocalights to study two dolphins, Spray and Scotty, at the Sealand aquarium in Brewster, Massachusetts. One dolphin had green lights and the other red. Tyack and his colleagues observed the dolphins and recorded the number and color of the lights. Tyack found that each dolphin made two types of whistles. One type was Spray's signature, and the other type was Scotty's. Each dolphin used the other's signature whistle some of the time, perhaps as a label or a name. And each signature whistle had many variations in duration, pitch, and shape of the sounds. Tyack concluded that the dolphins could detect these variations.

Most dolphins at marine parks and aquariums are bottlenose dolphins.

Spray died soon after these experiments, leaving Scotty alone. Two years later, Tyack returned to test Scotty's whistles. He found that Scotty no longer used Spray's favorite whistle. His whistles had become shorter and quieter. Tyack thinks this is evidence that the whistles are a form of social communication among dolphins.

Echolocation

In addition to whistles, dolphins use high-pitched clicks to identify objects. The dolphin produces a burst of sound from its head. The **sound waves** strike objects and bounce back. The waves are then received in the dolphin's lower jaw and interpreted. This process, called **echolocation,** is similar to a submarine's use of sonar.

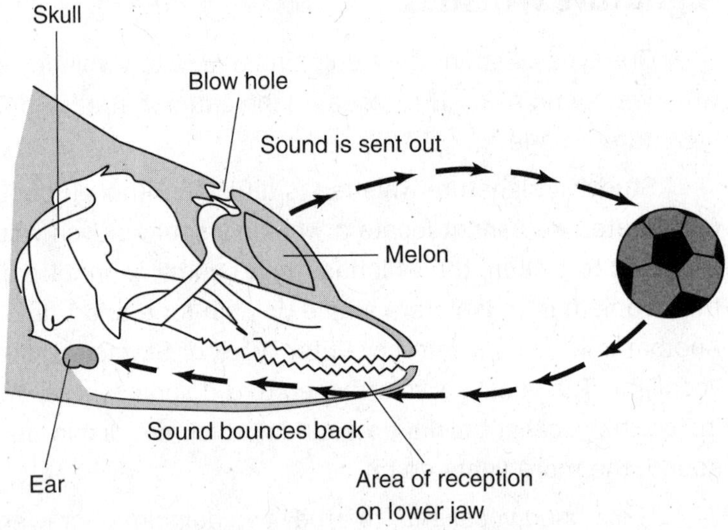

Echolocation in Dolphins

Through echolocation, a dolphin can "see" the shape of objects. In addition to providing information about an object's surface, echolocation provides information on **density.** A dolphin can sense the amount of matter in a particular amount of space. For example, a dolphin can detect a swimmer's lungs, which are less dense than the rest of his or her body because they are filled with air. In this way, echolocation is similar to ultrasound, which provides images of the inside of the human body.

Interpreting Process Diagrams Science articles often use **process diagrams** to explain how something works. Arrows are usually used to show the progression of steps in a process. Study the process diagram of echolocation in dolphins. Then answer the question.

What is the path of the sound waves in the diagram above? Circle the letter of the best answer.

a. They start and end at the dolphin's head.
b. They start and end at the soccer ball.

 Check your answer on page 233.

Teaching Dolphins Artificial Language

Dolphins do communicate in the wild, but so far there is no proof that their communication is a form of language. A **language** is a system of sounds, symbols, signs, or gestures that refer to objects or ideas and that can be combined in many different ways to produce different meanings. Human language uses sounds to represent meaning and grammar to combine sounds into an infinite number of messages.

Can dolphins be taught a simple language? Louis M. Herman and his colleagues at the University of Hawaii thought so. They taught four captive dolphins two artificial languages. One language uses computer-generated high-pitched "words." The other language uses hand and arm movements (sign language) to signify words. Each language has about forty words, including nouns such as *channel, gate, person,* and *ball;* verbs such as *fetch;* and modifiers such as *right, left, surface,* and *bottom.* Herman wanted to know if the dolphins could learn these words and understand the difference between them.

The dolphins were able to learn both what each word referred to and how to interpret the order of words. For example, the dolphins could distinguish between two sign language sentences such as "right hoop left Frisbee fetch" and "left hoop right Frisbee fetch." The first sentence means "take the Frisbee on the left to the hoop on the right," and the second means "take the Frisbee on the right to the hoop on the left." Herman's experiments seem to provide further evidence of dolphins' ability to understand and communicate.

One dolphin, Ake, went beyond responding as trained. She was able to invent responses to unusual situations. For example, there were two large paddle-shaped switches labeled "yes" and "no." If Ake was asked to move an object and it was not in the pool, she pressed the "no" paddle. If she was given a command that was impossible to carry out, such as "fetch the water to the person," she ignored it. If she was given a command with too many nouns, such as "fetch the water and the hoop to the person" she ignored the word "water" and simply fetched the hoop. Herman sees these untaught responses as evidence that dolphins have learned the grammar rules of the artificial language and can use them to interpret new messages.

Drawing Conclusions A **conclusion** is an idea that follows logically from facts or evidence. Scientists are careful not to draw a conclusion unless they have evidence to support it. For example, Ake's ability to make up her own responses to unusual messages and situations supports Herman's conclusion that dolphins can learn grammar rules and use them to interpret new messages.

Which of the following is a conclusion that can be drawn from the evidence provided by the artificial language experiments? Circle the letter of the correct answer.

a. Dolphins can learn "words" that refer to specific objects or ideas.
b. Dolphins use language to communicate in the wild.

 Check your answer on page 233.

Thinking About the Article

Practice Vocabulary

The words below are in the passage in bold type. Study the way each word is used. Then complete each sentence by writing the correct word.

mammals	**sound waves**	**echolocation**
density	**language**	

1. Scientists taught dolphins, which are marine __________________, an artificial __________________ that involved gestures.
2. Dolphins send out __________________ from their heads and receive them in their lower jaws.
3. Through __________________, dolphins can identify objects in the environment.
4. In addition to sensing the shape of an object, a dolphin can sense its __________________.

Understand the Article

Write or circle the answer to each question.

5. How did Peter Tyack solve the problem of identifying the source of underwater sounds?

____

____

____

6. What is a dolphin's signature whistle?

____

____

7. How does echolocation work?
   a. by bouncing sound waves off objects in the environment
   b. by creating light signals that represent sounds in the environment
8. What led Louis Herman to conclude that dolphins could learn the grammar rules of the artificial language and use them to interpret new messages?
   a. Ake was able to create new responses to unusual situations.
   b. Ake was able to fetch the Frisbee and hoop when commanded.

Apply Your Skills

Circle the number of the best answer for each question.

9. According to the article, how are dolphins classified?
   (1) as fish
   (2) as rodents
   (3) as mammals
   (4) as primates
   (5) as amphibians

10. Scotty's whistles changed after Spray died. Tyack cited this fact as evidence supporting which conclusion about dolphin signature whistles?
    (1) They are unique to each animal.
    (2) They are stable over many years.
    (3) They are inaudible to the human ear.
    (4) They are a form of social communication.
    (5) They are a language with "words" and "grammar."

11. According to the diagram on page 66, dolphins receive sound waves that have bounced off of objects. Where do dolphins receive these sound waves?
    (1) in their blow hole
    (2) in their lower jaw
    (3) in their tail
    (4) in their melon
    (5) in their nose

Connect with the Article

Write your answer to each question.

12. Some scientists say that research on dolphins living in tanks is not valid because dolphins behave differently in tanks than they do in the wild. If you were a researcher working with captive dolphins, what would you say in response?

    ____

    ____

    ____

13. Have you or someone you know ever trained a dog or cat? What did this experience teach you about animal communication?

    ____

    ____

    ____

Check your answers on pages 233–234.

LESSON 10

Life Cycles

Vocabulary

life cycle

egg

egg mass

caterpillar

pupa

adult

Roaches, silverfish, carpenter ants, termites, aphids—the list of insect pests is long. One destructive pest is the gypsy moth. Gypsy moths are leaf-eating insects that have damaged millions of acres of trees. They can strip all the leaves off a tree in just a few weeks.

One way to fight insect pests is to try to attack them at different stages of their life cycle. People have tried many methods of wiping out gypsy moths at each stage of their life cycle. Still, gypsy moths continue to spread in the United States.

Relate to the Topic

This lesson is about an insect pest, the gypsy moth. It describes the life cycle of the moth. Think about the stages of the human life cycle.

Which stages have you experienced so far? ______________________

____

How would you describe each stage? ______________________

____

____

____

Reading Strategy

SCANNING DIAGRAMS Science materials often use diagrams to display important concepts. A diagram usually has a title and labels. The title tells you what the diagram is about. The labels name the different parts of the diagram. Scan the diagram on page 72. Then answer the questions.

1. What is the diagram about? ______________________
   Hint: Look at the title.

2. What are the four forms of the gypsy moth?

   ____
   Hint: Look at the labels.

Check your answers on page 234.

Fighting the Gypsy Moth

You may take the trees in your neighborhood for granted. Yet in the Northeast, gypsy moth caterpillars have stripped the leaves off millions of oak, birch, aspen, gum, and other trees. People in the northeastern United States have been fighting the gypsy moth for a hundred years.

The Spread of the Gypsy Moth

A Frenchman brought gypsy moth eggs from Europe to Massachusetts in the 1860s. He hoped to breed the moths with American silk-producing moths. Unfortunately, several moths escaped from his house. 50 years later, the gypsy moth had spread throughout the Northeast. Today many scientists, government agencies, and private citizens are fighting the gypsy moth as far south as North Carolina and as far west as Wisconsin. The moths have been seen even in California and Oregon.

Gypsy moth caterpillars do a great deal of damage. They will eat every leaf on trees they like, such as oak trees. However, they skip other types of trees, such as spruce. Healthy trees can survive a gypsy moth attack. The leaves usually grow back the next year. But trees weakened by disease or inadequate rainfall may die after a year or two.

In addition to damaging trees, gypsy moth caterpillars make a mess. They leave half-eaten leaves everywhere. Their droppings ruin the finish on cars. The caterpillars make their way onto porches, screens, and windows. When they die, the smell of decay is terrible.

Tree leaves damaged by gypsy moth caterpillars

The Life Cycle of the Gypsy Moth

To find ways to get rid of gypsy moths, scientists study the insect's life cycle. A **life cycle** is the series of changes an animal goes through in its life. There are four stages in the life cycle of a gypsy moth.

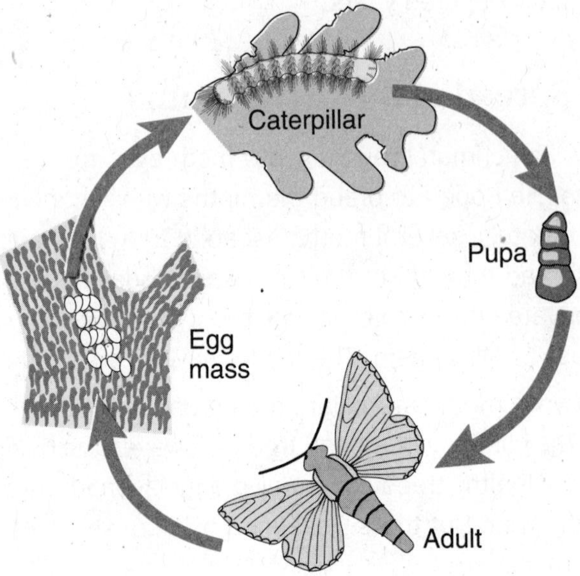

The Gypsy Moth's Life Cycle

1. **Egg.** Gypsy moth eggs are laid during the summer. Each female lays from 75 to 1,000 eggs in a clump called an **egg mass.** Egg masses are tan and slightly fuzzy.
2. **Caterpillar.** Gypsy moth eggs hatch into caterpillars. The caterpillars climb up trees to find leaves to eat. They grow to more than two inches long.
3. **Pupa.** During the pupa stage, the caterpillar encloses itself in a case for about two weeks. Its body changes into an adult moth.
4. **Adult.** When the pupa case breaks open, the adult moth comes out. Adult gypsy moths do not eat, so they do not live long. The female gives off a smell that attracts males. After mating, the male dies. The female lives long enough to lay eggs, and then she dies.

Understanding Sequence in a Diagram A **sequence** is the order in which things happen. Often, arrows are used to indicate a sequence, as they are in the diagram of the gypsy moth life cycle above.

1. In the life cycle of the gypsy moth, what stage comes after the caterpillar?

____

2. What three stages come before the adult stage?

____

Life Cycles

A life cycle is often shown in the circular style used on page 72. However, it can also be shown in a timeline, such as the one below.

Life Cycle of a Gypsy Moth

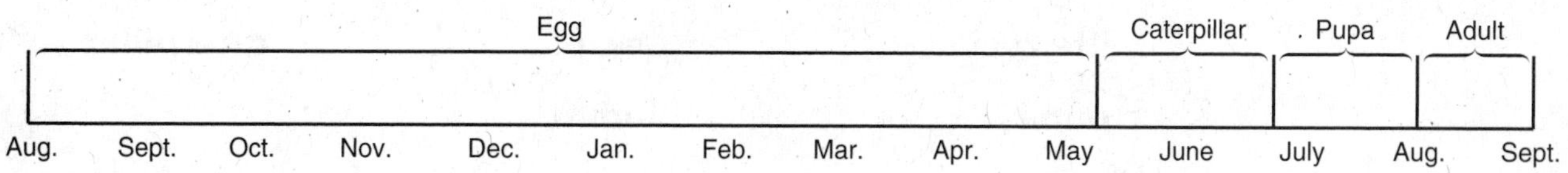

Reading a Timeline A **timeline** is a way to show a sequence. In addition to showing the sequence of events, a timeline shows when an event happens. When you see a timeline, look at its title first. It will tell you what the timeline is about. This one is about the life cycle of the gypsy moth. Next, look at the labels. The labels along the bottom of this timeline are months. The labels at the top show the stages of a gypsy moth's life. For example, you can see that most adult gypsy moths emerge in August and die in September. This stage only lasts a month.

1. How long does the caterpillar stage of the life cycle last? ____________________

2. When do caterpillars go into the pupa stage?

____

Controlling the Gypsy Moth

The gypsy moth damages trees during the caterpillar stage. The caterpillars can be killed by spraying the trees. Some sprays are chemicals that can harm other animals and the environment. Other sprays contain bacteria that kill only the moths. Caterpillars can be caught by wrapping sticky tape around trees. When the caterpillars climb, they get stuck on the tape and die. Gypsy moths can also be killed by destroying their eggs. Egg masses can be found on trees, buildings, fences, and outdoor furniture. They can be scraped into a bucket of kerosene, bleach, or ammonia. These chemicals kill the eggs.

Pupa cases can be removed from trees and crushed. Adult males can be caught in scented traps, which contain a bait that smells like a female moth. The male flies into the trap and dies there.

Some birds prey on gypsy moths. Birds that eat the moths can be attracted into an infested area. People can put out food, water, and nesting materials to encourage the birds to stay. Another natural control method uses parasites. A **parasite** is an organism that lives on or in another organism and harms it. Many parasites have been released in areas with gypsy moths.

Diseases can lower the number of moths. One year there was a very rainy spring, and many moths died of a fungus disease. Perhaps one day scientists will be able to use the fungus to kill gypsy moths.

Check your answers on page 234.

Thinking About the Article

Practice Vocabulary

The words below are in the passage in bold type. Study the way each word is used. Then complete each sentence by writing the correct word.

life cycle	**egg**	**caterpillar**
pupa	**adult**	

1. The ____________________ is the first stage of the gypsy moth's life.
2. The caterpillar is enclosed in a case during the ____________________ stage.
3. During the ____________________ stage, the gypsy moth crawls around and damages trees.
4. A mature gypsy moth, capable of laying eggs, is in the ____________________ stage.
5. An animal goes through stages during the course of its life, which are called its ____________________.

Understand the Article

Write the answer to each question.

6. How were gypsy moths introduced into the United States?

____

____

____

7. What damage does the gypsy moth caterpillar do?

____

____

Match the stage of the gypsy moth's life cycle with the control method used during that stage.

_____ 8. egg

_____ 9. caterpillar

_____ 10. pupa

_____ 11. adult

a. spraying insecticide

b. soaking in ammonia, kerosene, or bleach

c. putting out scent traps

d. crushing

Apply Your Skills

Circle the number of the best answer for each question.

12. Look at the diagram on page 72. Which of the following is the correct sequence of stages in the gypsy moth life cycle?
    (1) egg, pupa, caterpillar, adult
    (2) egg, adult, pupa, caterpillar
    (3) egg, pupa, adult, caterpillar
    (4) egg, caterpillar, adult, pupa
    (5) egg, caterpillar, pupa, adult

13. According to the timeline on page 73, which is the longest stage of the gypsy moth's life cycle?
    (1) egg
    (2) egg mass
    (3) caterpillar
    (4) pupa
    (5) adult

14. During the month of March, which control method can people use to destroy gypsy moths?
    (1) Crush the pupa cases.
    (2) Spray the caterpillars with insecticide.
    (3) Kill the caterpillars by catching them on sticky tape.
    (4) Put out scented bait traps for adult male moths.
    (5) Soak the egg masses in kerosene, bleach, or ammonia.

Connect with the Article

Write your answer to each question.

15. What other animals do you know about that look different at different stages of the life cycle? Pick one of these animals and describe how it looks and acts during different parts of its life cycle.

____

____

____

16. Describe an experience you or someone you know has had with gypsy moths or other insect pests. What did you do to control them?

____

____

____

Check your answers on page 234.

11 LESSON

Environmental Issues

Environmental Issues
Environmental Issues
Environmental

Vocabulary

recycling

internal recycling

external recycling

asphalt

landfill

pollute

raw material

ore

natural resources

When you take out your garbage, notice how much your family throws away each day. Paper and plastic packaging, food leftovers, even old junk—where does it all go?

Most of it goes to landfills. However, since the 1960s, the amount of garbage that is recycled has increased steadily as recycling programs have become more and more popular. The number of communities offering curbside recycling programs increased from 15 percent to 61 percent between 1990 and 1999.

Relate to the Topic

This lesson is about recycling. It describes both the benefits and the costs of recycling.

Does your community offer a recycling program? If so, describe how it works.

____

____

Do you recycle? Why or why not? ______________________

____

Reading Strategy

RELATING TO WHAT YOU KNOW When you read, think about what you already know about the topic. The topic of this lesson is recycling. Then answer the questions.

1. What is recycling? ______________________________

   ____

   Hint: Think about how you have heard this word used.

2. What types of materials can be recycled?

   ____

   ____

   Hint: Think about the recycling instructions you've seen.

Check your answers on pages 234–235.

Is Recycling Working?

About 226 million Americans have access to a curbside recycling program or a local drop-off center where they can recycle used paper and other materials. **Recycling** is the process of collecting and reprocessing waste materials so they can be used again. There are two main types of recycling. **Internal recycling** takes place when manufacturing businesses recycle their waste materials. **External recycling** is what you do when you return your waste materials so they can be made into new things.

How Does Recycling Work?

Metals, glass, wood, paper, and plastic are commonly recycled. You may have seen glass jars, plastic containers, and aluminum cans in a recycling bin. Newspaper, cardboard, office paper, and other kinds of paper are also recyclable.

First, the materials are collected and processed. You might toss them in your recycling bin or drop them off at a recycling center. When you return aluminum cans for a deposit, you are also recycling. The cans are reprocessed into sheet metal.

Next, the recycled materials are made into new things. Newspapers, paper towels, soft-drink containers, and plastic laundry detergent bottles are often made from recycled materials. There are also new ways to use recycled materials. For example, recycled glass is used to make **asphalt** roads. Recycled plastic is used to make carpet and park benches. Buying things that are made from recycled materials is another way that you can help with recycling.

Three Steps of Recycling

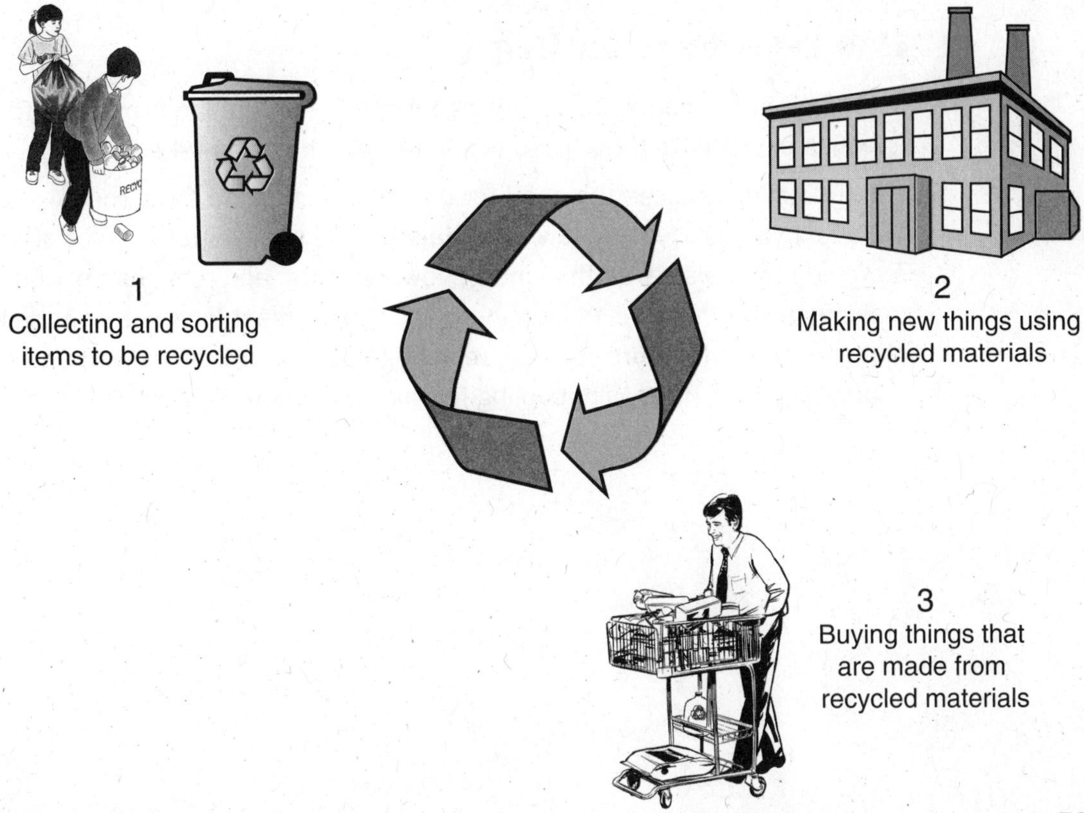
1
Collecting and sorting items to be recycled
2
Making new things using recycled materials
3
Buying things that are made from recycled materials

This bar graph shows the recycling rate for commonly recycled items.

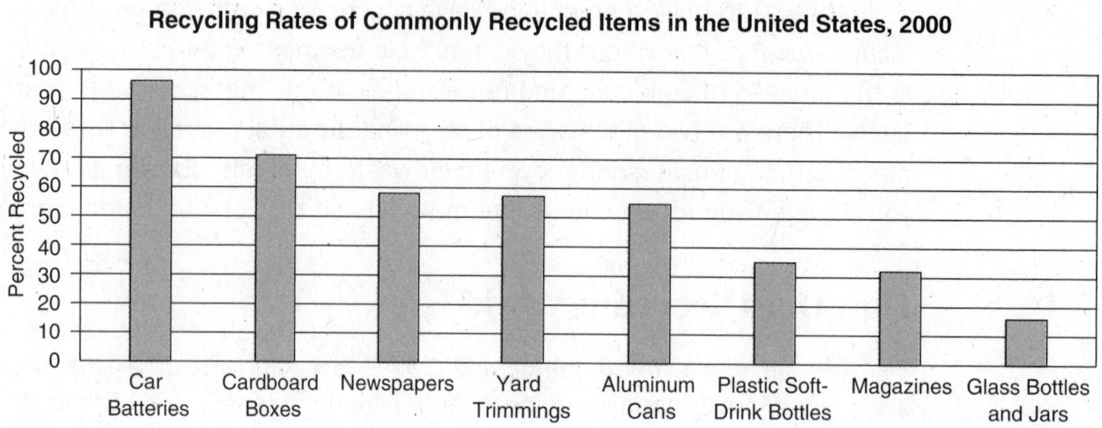

Reading a Bar Graph **Bar graphs** are used to compare sets of information. The height of each bar shows you the amounts of each item. To read a bar graph, first look at the title to find the main idea. This graph compares the percentages of different items that get recycled. The words along the bottom edge of the graph identify the items represented by the bars. To find the recycling rate for a particular item, locate its label and line up the top of the bar with the vertical scale. For example, 58 percent of all newspapers in 2000 were recycled.

1. Which item had the highest recycling rate in 2000? ______________________
2. Which item had the lowest recycling rate in 2000? ______________________

How Does Recycling Help?

Most of our garbage goes into a **landfill**—a plot of land reserved for garbage. Landfills can **pollute** the air and water nearby. They also take up space.

Recycling reduces the need for landfills. It can also save energy and money. Extracting and processing **raw materials** into new things takes a lot of energy. Using recycled materials saves this energy, lowers costs, and reduces pollution. For example, making cans from recycled aluminum uses 95 percent less energy than does making aluminum cans from **ore**. Overall, recycling in the year 2000 saved enough energy to supply electricity, heat, and cooling for six million households.

 Check your answers on page 235.

Recycling is good for the American economy, too. It protects and expands manufacturing jobs and creates jobs in the recycling industry. More than one million Americans work in the recycling industry.

Most importantly, recycling saves **natural resources**. Natural resources are materials found in nature that are needed for human activity and life. Many of our natural resources, such as aluminum and other metals, are available in limited quantities. Once these resources are used up, they will be gone forever. Recycling allows us to use resources over and over again and keeps them available for future generations.

Is Recycling Worth It?

In some cities, recycling is more expensive than using landfills or burning garbage. Recycling glass, metal, and plastic was costing the city of New York about twice what it would have cost the city to throw these materials away. Thus, in 2002, New York City temporarily stopped recycling plastic, glass, and some metal containers. The city hoped to save 57 million dollars by cutting recycling. Both Baltimore, Maryland, and Charleston, West Virginia, have proposed similar plans to cut recycling programs due to costs. The cost of recycling depends on how close a city is to landfills and the cost of labor in the city. The method of recycling and how much material is actually recycled also affect the cost of recycling programs.

If you recycle containers from your home, you know that recycling not only costs money, it also takes time. You have to rinse and sort items before recycling them.

Applying Knowledge to Other Contexts General knowledge can be put to use in new situations. Scientists and others apply their knowledge to solve problems. The previous two paragraphs describe how some cities are debating whether to temporarily stop recycling by weighing the benefits and costs of recycling.

Which of the following is another example of weighing the benefits and costs before making a decision?

a. Deciding to buy a snack from a vending machine after weighing the extra cost of the item versus the benefit of convenience
b. Deciding to buy bananas at the grocery store after weighing the cost of bananas versus the cost of apples

What Can You Do?

Supporters of recycling say that it is not about saving money, time, or energy. They say that recycling is about conserving natural resources. For recycling to work, we all have to do our part. That means buying items in containers that can be reused or recycled, participating in local recycling programs, and buying new things made from recycled materials.

 Check your answer on page 235.

Thinking About the Article

Practice Vocabulary

The words below are in the passage in bold type. Study the way each word is used. Then complete each sentence by writing the correct word.

internal recycling **external recycling** **raw material**

natural resources **pollute** **landfill**

1. Garbage can ______________ the environment.
2. A plot of land set aside for the disposal of garbage is called a ______________.
3. Mineral ores, petroleum, natural gas, and water are examples of ______________.
4. Manufacturing businesses practice ______________ when they reuse their waste materials.
5. Curbside recycling programs are examples of ______________.
6. Wood chips are an example of a ______________ used to make paper products.

Understand the Article

Write the answer to each question.

7. What happens to most of the garbage in the United States?

____

8. What kinds of things can be recycled?

____

____

9. List two benefits of recycling.

____

____

____

Apply Your Skills

Circle the number of the best answer for each question.

10. Why are some cities temporarily stopping their recycling programs?
    (1) The cities don't have the time to recycle materials.
    (2) There aren't enough workers in these cities to collect the materials.
    (3) Recycling costs more in these cities than landfill disposal does.
    (4) Residents of these cities are not recycling.
    (5) There are no landfills near these cities for the garbage.

11. According to the bar graph on page 78, which items have a recycling rate of 35 percent?
    (1) aluminum cans
    (2) glass containers
    (3) newspapers
    (4) plastic soft-drink bottles
    (5) plastic water bottles

12. Recycling is the process of collecting materials so they can be used again. Which of the following applies the same principle?
    (1) buying a newly released video
    (2) returning a purchase for a refund
    (3) using a coupon to buy something
    (4) baking a loaf of bread from scratch
    (5) donating used clothing to a charity

Connect With the Article

Write your answer to each question.

13. What are two reasons that people do not recycle?

____

____

14. Based on the article, do you think cities should continue recycling even if recycling costs as much or more than landfill disposal? Why or why not?

____

____

____

Check your answers on page 235.

LESSON 12

Ecosystems

What do Brazil nuts, mahogany, and natural rubber have in common? They are all products of tropical rain forests. Tropical rain forests are warm, wet regions near the equator.

Although tropical rain forests cover only a small part of Earth, they contain a large proportion of the world's plants and animals. Tropical rain forests benefit the whole world, but they are disappearing because of farming, logging, and ranching.

Vocabulary

tropical rain forest

ecosystem

equator

photosynthesis

respiration

carbon dioxide–oxygen cycle

greenhouse effect

global warming

Relate to the Topic

This lesson is about tropical rain forests. Think about what you already know about tropical rain forests.

Describe something you know or have heard about tropical rain forests.

____

____

Imagine that you are in a tropical rain forest. What do you see, hear, and feel?

____

____

Reading Strategy

SCANNING MAPS Maps are a simple way to present a lot of information. You can preview a map to find out what kind of information it includes. Scan the title, labels, and key for the map. The key tells what the colors or symbols on the map represent. Scan the map on page 85. Then answer the questions.

1. What is the topic of the map? ______________________
   Hint: Look at the title.

2. What do the colors on the map represent?

   ____

   Hint: Look at the map key.

Check your answers on page 235.

Tropical Rain Forests

Do you like rice cereal with bananas? Coffee with sugar? Did you know that the foods in this breakfast first came from a **tropical rain forest?** Tropical rain forests are the source of many foods that are now grown commercially.

Take a look around you. Offices, libraries, and department stores may have furniture made of mahogany or teak. These woods grow in tropical rain forests. Check out your medicine cabinet. About 40 percent of all drugs have ingredients that first came from tropical rain forest plants.

What Is a Tropical Rain Forest?

A tropical rain forest is a large ecosystem. An **ecosystem** is an area in which living and nonliving things interact. Tropical rain forests are found near the **equator** (the imaginary line that goes around the middle of Earth, halfway between the poles). In these areas, there is a great deal of rainfall, and it is warm throughout the year. The temperature may vary more from day to night than from season to season.

The conditions in tropical rain forests support a wealth of plant and animal life. More than half of all types of plants and animals live in tropical rain forests. The variety of life is tremendous. For example, just one square mile of rain forest in Peru has 1,450 types of butterflies. Together, the United States and Canada have only 730!

A tropical rain forest

The Global Effects of the Rain Forests

The Carbon Dioxide-Oxygen Cycle

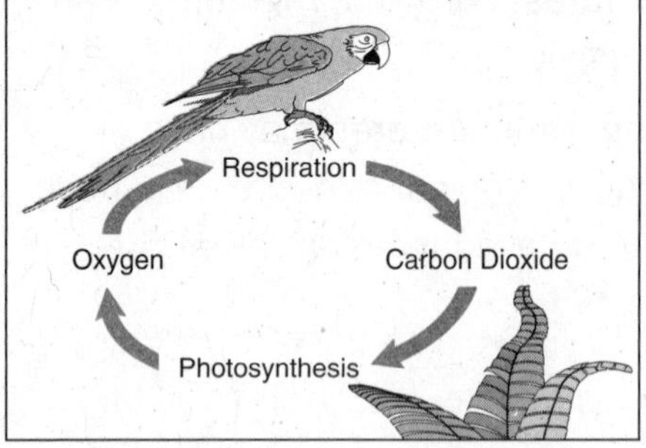

The plants of the rain forests absorb carbon dioxide from the atmosphere. Through the process of **photosynthesis,** plants use energy from sunlight to combine carbon dioxide and water to make food. This process gives off oxygen. Oxygen is used by animals for respiration. **Respiration** is the process by which living things use oxygen to get energy from food. This process gives off carbon dioxide. Carbon dioxide is also given off when fuels are burned and when organic material, such as plants and animals, decompose. The carbon dioxide is then used by plants, completing the **carbon dioxide–oxygen cycle.**

Recognizing Cause and Effect There are many situations in which one thing (a cause) makes another thing (an effect) happen. For example, plants make their own food during photosynthesis (cause). The process of photosynthesis results in plants' giving off oxygen (effect). Science is full of cause-and-effect relationships. Watch for words such as *cause, effect, because, result, leads to, due to, therefore, thus,* and *so*. These words often signal cause-and-effect relationships.

In the previous diagram and paragraph, you learned about the carbon dioxide–oxygen cycle. If more forests were planted, what would be the effect on the amount of carbon dioxide in the air?

a. There would be less because more plants would use carbon dioxide for photosynthesis.
b. There would be more because plants give off carbon dioxide during photosynthesis.

The amount of carbon dioxide in the air affects Earth's temperature. Carbon dioxide absorbs heat and helps keep Earth warm. The role of carbon dioxide and other gases in warming Earth is known as the **greenhouse effect.** By taking carbon dioxide from the air, the plants of the rain forests help control Earth's temperature.

Destruction of the Rain Forests

Over 50,000 square miles of tropical rain forests are destroyed each year by farmers, ranchers, and loggers. Many tropical countries don't have enough farmland, so farmers clear forests and burn the trees. When the soil is no longer able to nourish crops, they move on and clear new places. Ranchers cut down trees to make room for their cattle. Loggers also destroy the forests by cutting down trees for the wood.

This destruction affects the carbon dioxide–oxygen cycle in two ways. First, many trees are burned to clear the land. This burning adds tons of carbon dioxide to the air. Second, destroying trees leaves fewer plants to take carbon dioxide from the air. Scientists think that more carbon dioxide in the air is causing **global warming,** a worldwide increase in temperature.

 Check your answer on page 235.

Tropical rain forests cover about one-twentieth of Earth's land area. They are found along the equator, as shown in the map below. Large areas of the rain forests have already been destroyed.

The World's Tropical Rain Forests

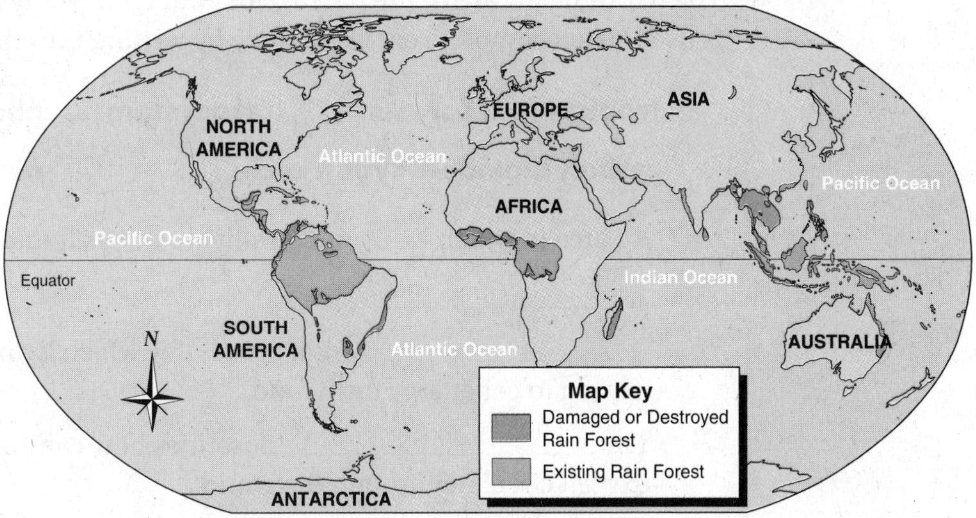

Reading a Map To study a map, first look at the title. It tells you what the map shows. This map shows the world's tropical rain forests. Then look for the map key. The map key tells you how information is shown on the map. In this map, existing rain forests are in dark gray, and damaged or destroyed forests are in dark orange. Look at the compass rose in the lower left. It shows the directions north, south, east, and west.

Study the map above. Which of the following continents has the smallest area of tropical rain forest? Circle the letter of the correct answer.

a. North America   c. Africa
b. South America   d. Asia

Stopping the Destruction

People in tropical countries do not destroy the forests with bad intentions. In these countries, the forests are a source of land, fuel, food, and cash. It's not possible to keep farmers, ranchers, and loggers out of the rain forests. Many countries are now trying to save some areas in the forests by making them off-limits. Some areas are set aside for tourism. In addition, new methods of farming and logging can help people use the forests without destroying them.

Other countries can help, too. They can buy products, such as Brazil nuts, that are grown without damaging the forests. They can refuse to buy products that damage the forests. This includes tropical woods, such as teak. It also includes beef ranched on lands that were once tropical rain forests.

Check your answer on page 235.

Thinking About the Article

Practice Vocabulary

The words below are in the passage in bold type. Study the way each word is used. Then complete each sentence by writing the correct word.

tropical rain forests **ecosystem** **photosynthesis**

carbon dioxide–oxygen cycle **respiration**

1. An area in which living and nonliving things interact is called a(n) ____________________.
2. ____________________ is a process by which living things use oxygen to get energy from food.
3. The ____________________ describes how carbon dioxide and oxygen circulate through the world.
4. ____________________ is a process by which plants use carbon dioxide, water, and energy from sunlight to make food.
5. Some scientists think that the destruction of the ____________________ is contributing to global warming.

Understand the Article

Write or circle the answer to each question.

6. What are some foods we eat that originally came from tropical rain forests?

____

____

7. What role do animals play in the carbon dioxide–oxygen cycle?
   a. Animals take in oxygen and give off carbon dioxide during the process of respiration.
   b. Animals take in carbon dioxide and give off oxygen during the process of photosynthesis.

8. Which three industries are most destructive to the tropical rain forest? Explain why.

____

____

____

Apply Your Skills

Circle the number of the best answer for each question.

9. People burn more fuel now than ever before. What effect does this have on the amount of carbon dioxide in the air?
Carbon dioxide has
   (1) increased
   (2) decreased
   (3) first increased, then decreased
   (4) first decreased, then increased
   (5) remained the same

10. Which of the following causes global warming?
   (1) a decrease in the amount of oxygen in the atmosphere
   (2) an increase in the amount of oxygen in the atmosphere
   (3) a decrease in Earth's animal species
   (4) a decrease in the amount of carbon dioxide in the atmosphere
   (5) an increase in the amount of carbon dioxide in the atmosphere

11. Refer to the map on page 85. Which of the following statements is true?
   (1) All tropical rain forests are located north of the equator.
   (2) All tropical rain forests are located south of the equator.
   (3) Most tropical rain forests are located near the equator.
   (4) There are no tropical rain forests in Asia.
   (5) There are no tropical rain forests in Australia.

Connect with the Article

Write your answer to each question.

12. List three ways that tropical rain forests are important to human health and to the health of Earth's ecosystems.

____

____

____

13. What can you do to help prevent the destruction of tropical rain forests?

____

____

____

____

Check your answers on pages 235–236.

LESSON 13

Evolution

In one scene of the movie *Jurassic Park,* dinosaurs hunt children who are hiding in a kitchen. The dinosaurs turn the knob to open the kitchen door. These dinosaurs can open doors because they have flexible wrists that allow them to swivel their hands.

Flexible wrists are also characteristic of birds. A flexible wrist allows powered flight. This—and other shared characteristics—have led many scientists to hypothesize that birds and dinosaurs are related.

Vocabulary

fossil

paleontologist

adaptation

mutation

natural selection

evolution

convergence

Relate to the Topic

This lesson is about the theory of evolution. It explains how birds probably evolved from small, feathered dinosaurs. Think about birds you have seen.

What do birds look like? ______________________________

____

What are some characteristics of birds that help you recognize them as birds?

____

____

Reading Strategy

SKIMMING PICTURES Science articles often use photographs and illustrations to help the reader understand the text. Skimming a picture and its caption can also help you preview an article. Skim the photograph on page 89 and the illustration on page 91. Then answer the questions.

1. What does the picture on page 89 show?

   ____

   Hint: Read the caption.

2. What does the picture on page 91 show?

   ____

   Hint: Read the caption.

Check your answers on page 236.

Dinosaurs with Feathers

Mammals have fur or hair, fish have scales, and dinosaurs have—feathers? New fossils indicate that some dinosaurs did indeed have feathers. A **fossil** is a trace or the remains of an organism that lived in the distant past. By comparing fossils over time, scientists can trace the development of species over time. Some scientists think that these feathered fossils settle the longstanding debate over the dinosaur-bird link. According to this view, feathered dinosaurs provide evidence that modern birds evolved from dinosaurs.

Dinosaur-Bird Links

The first scientist to suggest that birds and dinosaurs are related was Thomas Henry Huxley. His theory was based on the 1861 discovery of a primitive bird fossil, *Archaeopteryx* (ar-kee-AHP-tuhr-iks). This creature had many similarities to dinosaurs, including clawed fingers and a long bony tail. It also had feathers. While many scientists believed Huxley's theory, there was little evidence to support it. However, **paleontologists**—scientists who study prehistoric life—predicted that fossils of birdlike dinosaurs would eventually be discovered. In recent decades, this prediction was proved correct. During the 1990s, a number of fossils of birdlike dinosaurs were found. All of the different species of birdlike dinosaurs had feathers.

A model of the feathered dinosaur *Caudipteryx*

One species of bird-like dinosaurs is *Protoarchaeopteryx* (proh-toh-ar-kee-AHP-tuhr-iks). It is similar in many ways to the fast, meat-eating dinosaur *Velociraptor* (vuh-LAH-suh-rap-tuhr), made famous by the movie *Jurassic Park. Protoarcheopteryx* had a cluster of long feathers at the end of its tail.

Another species, *Caudipteryx* (caw-DIP-tuhr-iks), may have been even more feathery. Feathers covered the arms, much of the body, and the tail. Some feathers were tiny and soft like down, and others were large and stiff like quills.

A third species, *Confuciusornis* (con-few-shus-OR-nis), may have actually been able to fly. *Confuciusornis* may provide evidence for how a dinosaur's grasping hand evolved into a flying hand. *Confuciusornis* had unique wing feathers that were longer than its body, and the male had very long, narrow tail feathers.

The Usefulness of Feathers

Despite their feathers, neither *Protoarchaeopteryx* nor *Caudipteryx* could fly. Instead, scientists think that the short feathers may have provided insulation. The long feathers may have been used by males to attract females. Many modern birds have down to keep warm and colorful feathers to display during courtship.

Once feathers developed, they may have given some birdlike dinosaurs a competitive edge. They may have enabled these dinosaurs to run faster or balance better than their nonfeathered relatives. In other species, feathers may have aided gliding or flying. A trait, such as feathers, that makes an organism better able to live in its environment is called an **adaptation.** Another example of an adaptation is an arctic fox's white fur. The color helps the arctic fox blend into the background of snow. Its enemies have trouble seeing it, so the fox has a better chance of surviving.

Many adaptations occur through mutation. A **mutation** is a change in genetic material. Mutations happen by chance and most are harmful. But sometimes a mutation produces a trait, such as feathers on a dinosaur or white fur on a fox, that helps an organism survive.

Making Inferences An inference is a fact or idea that follows logically from what has been said. Readers make inferences all the time from the information in what they read. Review the previous paragraph about mutations. The author states in the paragraph that some mutations cause traits which can help an organism to survive. From what the author says, you can infer that harmful mutations can cause an individual to die.

Which of the following can you infer from the paragraph about adaptations? Circle the letter of the correct inference.

a. White fur is a useful adaptation any place that foxes live.
b. White fur is a useful adaptation only in places with lots of snow.

Evolution through Natural Selection

There are always variations in any population due to mutation. When feathers first appeared, a few dinosaurs may have had them. A dinosaur with this adaptation was more likely to survive, reproduce, and pass the trait to offspring. A dinosaur without this adaptation was more likely to die before it reproduced.

Charles Darwin, a nineteenth-century English scientist, called this process natural selection. **Natural selection** means that the organisms best suited to their environments are most likely to survive and reproduce. Natural selection is sometimes called *survival of the fittest.* What is *fit* depends on the situation. In this case, feathers may have helped some dinosaurs in the competition for resources. However, survival of an individual organism is not enough. It must reproduce to pass on the adaptations to its offspring.

 Check your answer on page 236.

The above illustration depicts evolution from dinosaurs to birds.
Source: Portia Rollings/NGS Image Collection

The make-up of a population of organisms changes slowly over time. Those with useful adaptations reproduce more than others. The useful traits will appear in more of the offspring. Over time, the adaptation may be found in most of the population. This gradual change of a species over time is called **evolution.**

Convergence

Not all scientists are convinced that the feathered dinosaurs show that birds evolved from dinosaurs. They argue that birds and dinosaurs could have developed traits such as feathers independently, a process called **convergence.** Convergence results in similarities among groups of animals that are not closely related through evolution. For example, crows, bats, and butterflies all have wings, but they are not closely related. Crows are birds, bats are mammals, and butterflies are insects. Their wings evolved independently as an adaptation to life in the air.

However, most scientists do think that birds and dinosaurs are related. They point to more than a hundred shared traits, including feathers, air-filled skull bones, and wishbones. Says one scientist, "Dinosaurs are not extinct after all. They're alive and well and represented by more than 10,000 species of living birds."

Applying Knowledge to Other Contexts Using the knowledge you gain in one situation and applying it to another can give you new insights about the world around you. For example, you just learned that birds, bats, and butterflies all have wings but are not closely related. Their traits converge because they each have adapted to their environment by taking up flight; and controlled flight requires wings.

Which of the following is another example of convergence?

a. Sharks and dolphins have similarly shaped bodies and fins, but sharks are fish and dolphins are mammals.

b. Humans and chimpanzees have thumbs that allow them to grasp objects, and both are mammals.

Check your answer on page 236.

Thinking About the Article

Practice Vocabulary

The words below are in the passage in bold type. Study the way each word is used. Then complete each sentence by writing the correct word.

adaptation **mutation** **natural selection**

evolution **convergence**

1. A(n) ________________ is a change in a gene.
2. A trait that makes a plant or animal better able to live in its environment is called a(n) ________________.
3. ________________ is the independent evolution of similar characteristics among unrelated organisms.
4. ________________ means that organisms best suited to their environments are most likely to survive and reproduce.
5. The gradual change in a species over time is called ________________.

Understand the Article

Write or circle the answer to each question.

6. What do all species of birdlike dinosaurs discovered so far have in common?

____

____

7. What do scientists think flightless dinosaurs might have used feathers for?

____

____

____

8. How do species evolve?
   a. Individuals with useful adaptations survive, reproduce, and pass the adaptations to their offspring.
   b. Individuals may develop traits during their lifetime and teach them to their offspring.

Apply Your Skills

Circle the number of the best answer for each question.

9. You can infer that birds, bats, and butterflies are not closely related because they
   (1) have changed over time
   (2) are very different types of animals
   (3) have wings instead of arms
   (4) can fly
   (5) have feathers

10. Antibiotics are drugs that fight disease-causing bacteria. After a few decades, the bacteria develop resistance to the antibiotic, and the drug no longer works. The resistance of bacteria to antibiotics is an example of a(n)
   (1) fossil
   (2) convergence
   (3) adaptation
   (4) paleontologist
   (5) extinction

11. Which would most likely happen over time if people had to do more standing, walking, and running to survive?
   (1) Humans would develop bird-like wings.
   (2) Humans would develop stronger legs.
   (3) Humans would gradually die out.
   (4) Humans would look more like dinosaurs.
   (5) Humans would develop flexible ankles.

Connect with the Article

Write your answer to each question.

12. Which do think is more likely: that birds evolved from dinosaurs, or that the similarities between birds and dinosaurs is the result of convergence? Cite evidence to support your answer.

____

____

13. How did reading this article change the way you think about dinosaurs or birds? _______________________________

____

____

Check your answers on page 236.

Science at Work

Health: Fitness Instructor

Some Careers in Health and Fitness

Aerobics Instructor
conducts fitness classes for groups of people

Assistant Aerobics Coordinator
helps choose and schedule classes; selects instructors and conducts training sessions

Water Fitness Instructor
conducts fitness classes in swimming pools for groups of people

Personal Trainer
works individually with clients on fitness needs

Health and fitness has become a huge industry in our country. People enjoy exercising because it helps them mentally and physically. Fitness instructors teach people to exercise safely and effectively. They design workout routines, demonstrate exercises and gym equipment, teach classes, and monitor clients' progress. Fitness instructors must be able to answer clients' questions clearly and correctly. Because they work closely with people most of the day, they should have excellent communication skills.

Fitness instructors need a good understanding of life science, especially the human body. They need to understand how the body and its systems work. They must know about human anatomy, or the parts of the body, and physiology—how the body parts work and how they interact. Fitness instructors must pay great attention to their clients' bones and muscles and cardiovascular and respiratory systems. They are responsible for helping their clients achieve their workout goals without injury.

Look at the chart showing some of the careers in health and fitness.

- Do any of the careers interest you? If so, which ones?
- What information would you need to find out more about those careers? On a separate piece of paper, write some questions that you would like answered. You can find more information about those careers in the *Occupational Outlook Handbook* at your local library or online.

PRACTICE

Use the following memo to answer the questions below.

FROM: Fitness Instructor Diane

TO: Client Tom

Tom, I have designed an exercise program for you. To get your body in good shape, it is important that you complete all three parts. Only use this workout program 3–4 times a week. Give yourself a day of rest between each day of exercise to avoid injury or stress to your body. Be sure to start each workout session by stretching.

Part 1 – Cardiovascular Workout – to get your heart working more efficiently. Choose one of the following machines: step machine; treadmill; rowing machine; or stationary bicycle. These machines will strengthen lower body muscles. Do a 5-minute warm up, 10 minutes at peak working heart rate, and a 5-minute cool down.

Part 2 – Strength Training – to build muscle and bone density. Use either the weight machines, or leg and hand weights. While using the weights, rotate between body parts to give each part time to rest. For example, first work on an arm muscle, then on a leg muscle. Start with light weights. Lift each weight 15 times. Do this twice. Work on at least 3 muscles in the leg and arm areas.

Part 3 – Stretching – to help your body cool down, relax, and resume its normal state. Stretch the same muscles you worked on in Part 2. Stretch and hold the position for 5–8 seconds. Do each muscle one time.

1. Which of the following will help Tom build muscle and bone density?
   (1) stretching
   (2) rowing machine
   (3) step machine
   (4) hand weights
   (5) stationary bicycle

2. Why is it important for Tom to rest between the days he works out?
   (1) He will get too tired at the gym.
   (2) He might get hurt from too much exercising.
   (3) Diane won't be there to help him.
   (4) Stretching is too difficult.
   (5) He must use all the machines.

3. Match the recommended exercise with its benefit.

______	treadmill	a.	build muscle and bone density
______	weight machines	b.	cool down
______	stretching	c.	improve efficiency of the heart

Check your answers on page 236.

UNIT 1

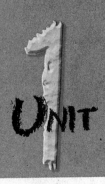

Unit 1 Review Life Science

How Cells Reproduce

The **nucleus** of a cell is the control center. The nucleus contains the chromosomes, which in turn contain the genetic material, or **DNA.** This material has all the instructions the cell needs to live. When the cell reproduces, this information is passed on to the new cells.

A cell reproduces by dividing. This five-step process is called mitosis. In **mitosis,** one cell becomes two cells. Before a cell divides, it makes a copy of its DNA. Each new cell receives one copy of the DNA. These two new cells can then grow and divide.

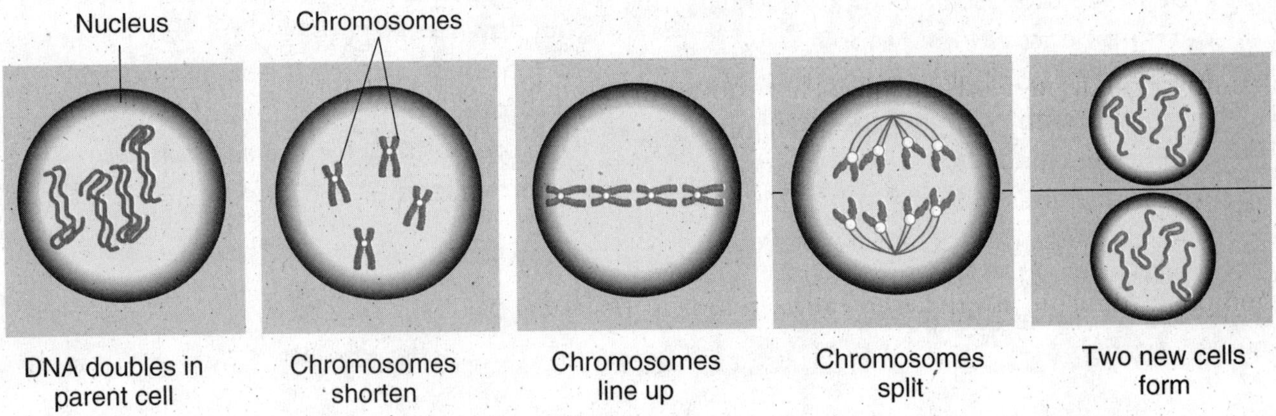
Nucleus
Chromosomes
DNA doubles in parent cell
Chromosomes shorten
Chromosomes line up
Chromosomes split
Two new cells form

Fill in the blank with the word or words that best complete each statement.

1. The genetic material is called ______________________.
2. Cells reproduce by division, or ______________________.

Circle the number of the best answer.

3. Which of the following can you infer from the diagram?
   (1) Chromosomes in new cells are fatter than those in the parent cell.
   (2) New cells have twice as many chromosomes as parent cells do.
   (3) Parent cells pass only half their chromosomes to new cells.
   (4) An X-shaped chromosome consists of two copies of a parent chromosome.
   (5) Parent chromosomes are Y-shaped; new chromosomes are X-shaped.

The Heart

Your heart is a large, muscular pump. As you read this, your heart is pumping blood to your lungs, where the blood absorbs oxygen. Your heart is also pumping blood throughout your body. The blood carries oxygen to the body. The parts of the heart are shown below.

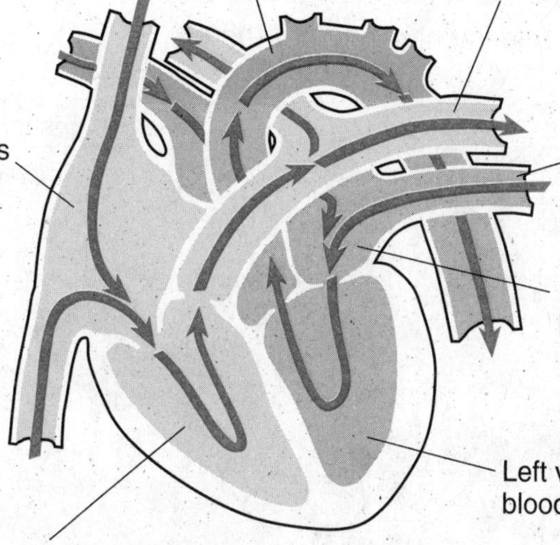

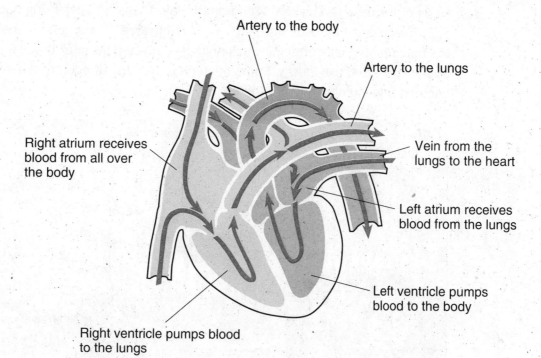

Fill in the blank with the word or words that best complete each statement.

4. If blood is flowing away from the heart, it is in a(n)

_______________________.

5. Blood coming from the lungs flows through a vein to the

_______________________ of the heart.

Circle the number of the best answer.

6. Which is the correct sequence of blood flow in the heart?
   (1) right atrium, right ventricle, lungs, left atrium, left ventricle
   (2) left atrium, left ventricle, lungs, right atrium, right ventricle
   (3) right atrium, lungs, left ventricle, right atrium, left ventricle
   (4) right ventricle, left ventricle, lungs, right atrium, left atrium
   (5) right atrium, right ventricle, left atrium, lungs, left ventricle

Go on to the next page.

The Nitrogen Cycle

All living things need nitrogen in some form. Nitrogen is an important part of proteins. Proteins make up much of the structure of living things. For example, muscles are made mostly of protein.

The air around you is 78 percent nitrogen, which your body cannot use. Only a few kinds of bacteria can use nitrogen from the air. These nitrogen-fixing bacteria live in the soil. They change nitrogen into a form called **nitrates.** Plants take in the nitrates from the soil. Plants make protein, which animals get when they eat the plants. When plants and animals die, they decay. Some bacteria return the nitrogen to the soil. Other bacteria release nitrogen into the air.

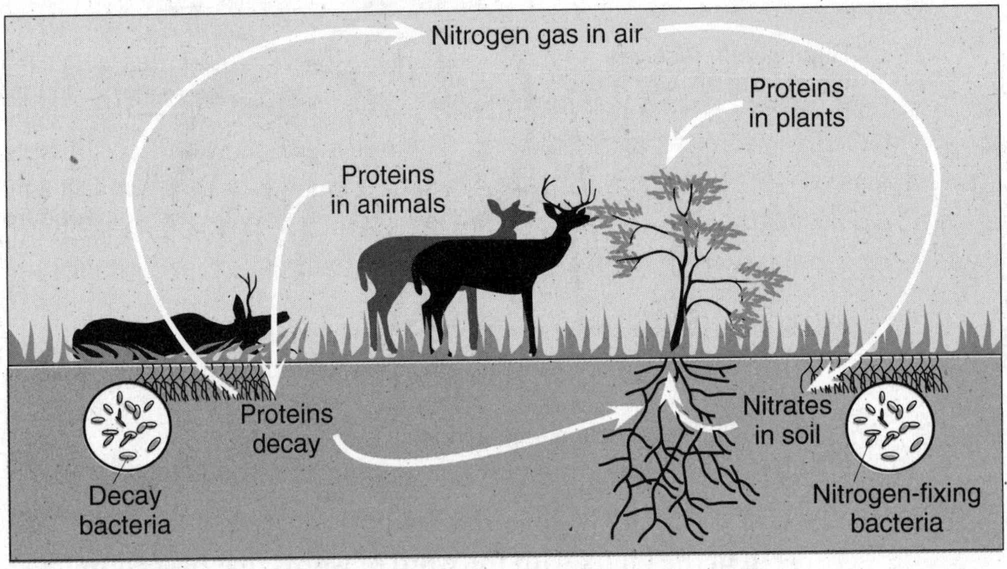

Match each organism with its source of nitrogen.

	Organism	Nitrogen source
______	7. animals	a. air
______	8. plants	b. protein
______	9. nitrogen-fixing bacteria	c. nitrates

Fill in the blank with the word or words that best complete the statement.

10. Lightning can cause a chemical reaction in which nitrogen from the air is changed into nitrates. This result is similar to the action of the

____________________.

The Ant and the Acacia

You have probably seen ants swarming all over a piece of candy dropped on the sidewalk. Cleaning up such bits of food and eating other dead animals is the role that most species of ants fill in nature. These ants are called scavengers.

Not all ant species are scavengers. Some species of ants live in a partnership with acacia plants. Many partnerships in nature involve a give and take. A relationship in which two species help each other is called **mutualism.** Each partner gives the other something it needs. The need may be food, shelter, water, or protection from an enemy. In the case of the ant and the acacia plant, the trade is food and shelter for defense.

The acacia makes a sugary sweet nectar, which the ants eat. The ants also live in the thorns of the acacia plant. The ants protect the plant from insects and other animals that might eat it. If a deer starts nibbling on an acacia leaf, the ants swarm and sting it all over. The deer will probably avoid eating that plant in the future. If any other plants start to grow near the acacia, the ants chew them down.

Fill in the blank with the word or words that best complete each statement.

11. In its relationship with the acacia plant, the ant gets ______________ and ______________.

12. In its relationship with the ant, the acacia plant gets ______________.

13. Animals that eat other dead animals are called ______________.

Circle the number of the best answer.

14. Which of the following is an example of mutualism?
(1) A bird eats ticks that are on the back of an ox.
(2) An ant cleans up a sidewalk by eating spilled food.
(3) Ants carry bits of leaves back to the anthill.
(4) A wild dog eats what is left of an antelope after lions have finished eating.
(5) Two chimpanzees remove fleas from each other's fur.

Science Extension

Visit a drugstore or some other place that has a machine that takes blood pressure. Take your own blood pressure. Find out if it is normal. If it is too high or too low, find out what you can do to improve your blood pressure.

Check your answers on pages 236–237.

Mini-Test • Unit 1

GED PRACTICE

This is a 15-minute practice test. After 15 minutes, mark the last number you finished. Then complete the test and check your answers. If most of your answers were correct but you did not finish, try to work faster next time.

Directions: Choose the one best answer to each question.

Questions 1 and 2 refer to the following diagram.

How West Nile Virus Is Spread

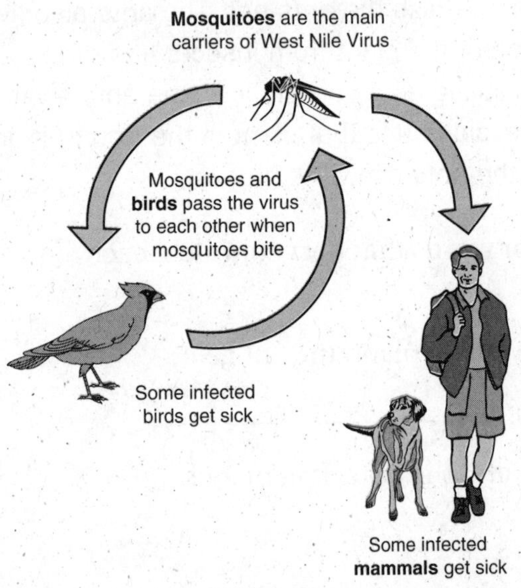
Mosquitoes are the main carriers of West Nile Virus
Mosquitoes and **birds** pass the virus to each other when mosquitoes bite
Some infected birds get sick
Some infected **mammals** get sick

1. A mosquito infected with West Nile virus bites a bird. According to the diagram, which of the following is a possible effect?
   (1) The virus spreads through the air.
   (2) The mosquito gets infected with the virus.
   (3) The bird gets infected with the virus.
   (4) A mammal passes the virus to a bird.
   (5) A mammal passes the virus to a mosquito.

2. Which of the following is an opinion related to the topic of the diagram, rather than a fact?
   (1) Biting mosquitoes can spread germs.
   (2) Mosquitoes spread West Nile virus.
   (3) Birds carry West Nile virus.
   (4) West Nile virus causes human illness.
   (5) West Nile virus is a major health concern.

Questions 3 and 4 refer to the following information.

Germs are all around us, but they rarely make healthy people ill. Any germs that enter the body are seen as foreign substances. A foreign protein is called an **antigen.** When an antigen enters a healthy body, white blood cells begin to make antibodies. An antibody is a protein that the body makes to defend itself. Antibodies attack and kill germs. When your white blood cells produce sufficient antibodies against invading germs, you remain healthy.

3. Based on this information, what can you infer about infections?

   When a person has an infection, his or her white blood cells are
   (1) attacking and killing antibodies
   (2) not producing enough antibodies
   (3) producing too many antibodies
   (4) not producing enough antigens
   (5) producing too many antigens

4. Why do healthy people rarely become ill?
   (1) Germs are foreign substances.
   (2) Our environment is generally germ-free.
   (3) Most germs do not attack humans.
   (4) White blood cells protect the body.
   (5) Antigens attack invading germs.

5. Your physical traits are determined by genetic material that you inherit from your parents. For every trait you inherit, each of your parents has contributed genetic material for that trait. Some traits are dominant or recessive. For example, the ability to roll the tongue is a dominant trait; the inability to roll the tongue is a recessive trait. If you have a recessive trait, you inherited recessive genetic material for that trait from both of your parents. If you have a dominant trait, you inherited dominant genetic material for that trait from one or both parents. Dominant genetic material for a trait can mask the recessive genetic material.

   Right-handedness is a dominant trait. Can two right-handed parents produce a left-handed child?

   (1) Yes, if neither parent has recessive genetic material for the handedness trait.
   (2) No, since one parent has recessive genetic material for the handedness trait.
   (3) Yes, if both parents have recessive genetic material for the handedness trait.
   (4) No, since one parent has dominant genetic material for the handedness trait.
   (5) Yes, since handedness is a trait that does not show dominance.

Questions 6 and 7 refer to the following information.

A biologist wanted to answer the question "How much time do plant cells spend in each phase of cell division?" She used a chemical to stop cell division in an onion root tip. Then she examined a sample of the cells and counted the number of cells in each phase of division. The biologist knew that the percentage of cells in each phase was equal to the amount of time the cells spent in that phase. She then summarized her observations in the circle graph below.

Time Cells Spend in Cell Division

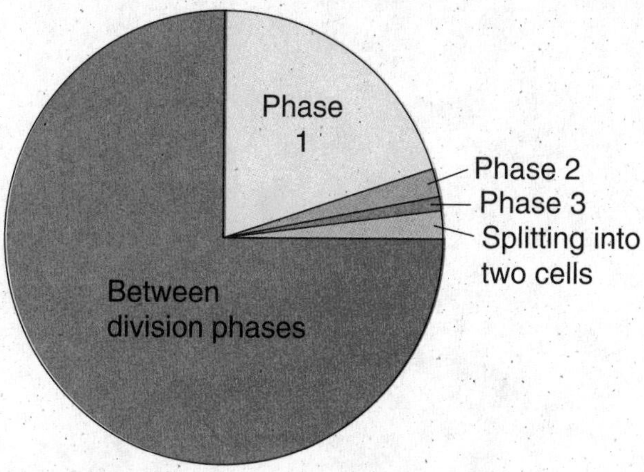

6. Which of the following statements is supported by the biologist's observations?

   Most of the cells she observed were

   (1) not actively dividing
   (2) in Phase 1
   (3) in Phase 2
   (4) in Phase 3
   (5) just completing cell division

7. Which of the following is a valid comparison based on the biologist's data?

   The plant cells spent

   (1) most of their time in Phase 1
   (2) most of their time in Phase 2
   (3) more time in Phase 1 than in Phase 2
   (4) more time in Phase 3 than in Phase 1
   (5) more time in Phase 3 than in Phase 2

Check your answers on pages 237–238.

Unit 2

Earth and Space Science
Earth and
Earth and Space Science
Space Science

Earth and Space Science

Earth and space science is the study of our world—from deep inside our planet, to Earth's surface where we live, to beyond the atmosphere and into outer space. Earth and space science covers topics as large as the universe and as small as a pebble.

Understanding Earth and space science can help you to better understand our planet and its place in the universe. It can also help you to take better care of yourself and the world you live in. Here are examples of very basic ways that Earth and space science is a part of everyday life.

Describe today's weather. ______________________________

Describe one way to use water wisely. ______________________________

List natural objects you've recently seen in the sky. ______________________________

____

Thinking About Earth and Space Science

You may not realize how often you use Earth and space science as you go about your daily life. Think about your recent activities.

Check the box for each activity you have done recently.

- ☐ Did you check a weather forecast?
- ☐ Did you use water?
- ☐ Did you turn over soil for a garden plot or dig a hole?
- ☐ Did you ride in an airplane?
- ☐ Did you go hiking, camping, or to the beach?
- ☐ Did you watch the sun rise or set?
- ☐ Did you look at the moon or the stars?

Write some other activities in which you used Earth and space science.

____

____

____

Previewing the Unit

In this unit, you will learn:

- how scientists predict and explain the weather
- how Earth is warmed
- how people can affect Earth
- how to conserve water
- how the planets, including Earth, are arranged in the solar system
- how scientists are learning about outer space

14 LESSON

Weather

Imagine what it would be like to have a hurricane or blizzard hit your area without warning. In the past—just decades ago—severe weather often took people by surprise. Today, thanks to weather satellites, global weather stations, and meteorologists, we can predict and prepare for all types of weather.

Weather maps also play a role in forecasting coming weather. Weather moves from one place to another. One day's snow in Buffalo may be the next day's snow in Boston. Weather maps show the weather over large areas and how it moves.

Vocabulary

air mass

continental polar air mass

continental tropical air mass

maritime polar air mass

maritime tropical air mass

front

stationary front

weather map

precipitation

meteorologist

forecast

Relate to the Topic

This lesson is about weather and weather maps. Think about a time when you experienced really bad weather.

Did you know in advance that bad weather was coming? If so, how did you know? ______________________________

____

Describe what happened. ______________________________

____

____

Reading Strategy

PREVIEWING A MAP A map is a picture that gives information about a place. Maps usually have a title, labels, and a key. The title tells the main idea of the map. The key tells what the colors or the symbols on the map represent. Refer to the map on page 106. Then answer the questions.

1. What is the topic of the map? ______________________________
   Hint: Look at the title.

2. What does a line of triangles represent? ______________________________
   Hint: Look at the map key.

Check your answers on page 238.

Weather Systems

You've probably noticed that weather can change dramatically overnight. One day is hot, humid, and drizzling, and the next day is clear and dry. It feels as if the air has changed. In fact, the air has changed. One large body of air has replaced another.

Air Masses

Large areas of air near Earth's surface take on the same temperature and moisture as the surface. For example, the air over a tropical ocean becomes warm and humid. A large body of air with a specific temperature and moisture is called an **air mass.** The term used to describe an air mass tells you where it came from. The word *continental* refers to a continent. The word *maritime* refers to the sea. There are four types of air masses:

- **Continental polar air masses** are cold and dry. They form over Canada and the northern United States.
- **Continental tropical air masses** are warm and dry. They form over the southwestern United States.
- **Maritime polar air masses** form over the northern Atlantic Ocean and the northern Pacific Ocean. These air masses are cold and moist.
- **Maritime tropical air masses** form over the Caribbean Sea, the middle of the Atlantic Ocean, and the middle of the Pacific Ocean. These air masses are warm and moist.

Air masses do not stay where they form. They may move thousands of miles. Think of a moving air mass as a large, flattened bubble of air. In the United States, air masses are usually pushed from west to east by winds. As the air mass moves, it may keep nearly the same temperature and moisture.

Fronts

The weather changes when one air mass moves out of an area and another moves in. The leading edge of a moving air mass is called a **front.** A cold front is at the front of a cold air mass. A warm front is at the front of a warm air mass. The weather can change quickly when a front passes through. A front often brings rain or snow to an area as it passes. When air masses stop moving for a while, the zone between them is called a **stationary front.**

Stormy weather often accompanies the passing of a front.

What Does a Weather Map Show?

Most newspapers print a **weather map** each day. A weather map shows where cold, warm, and stationary fronts are. It shows temperature and **precipitation,** such as rain, snow, and sleet.

Weather maps also show areas of high and low pressure. These areas of pressure are important because certain types of weather go with each. Most of the time, a high-pressure area means fair weather and no clouds. A low-pressure area is often cloudy with rain or snow.

High Temperatures and Precipitation for June 28

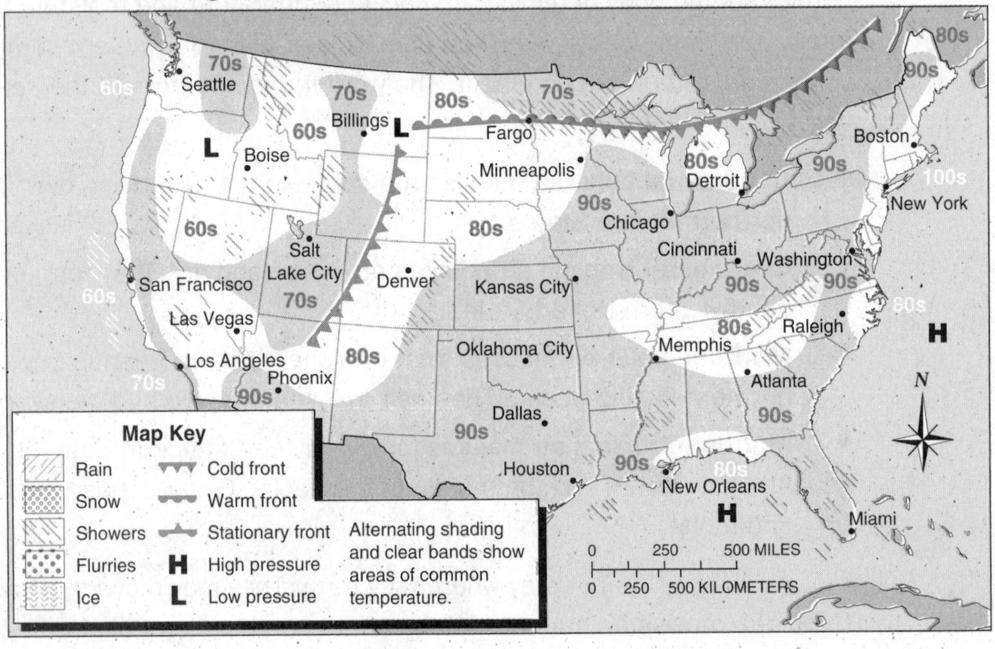

Reading a Map When you read a map, look at the title first. That gives you the main idea of the map. This map shows the weather for June 28, with high temperatures in degrees Fahrenheit, the temperature scale we usually use in the United States. It also shows precipitation. Next, look at the map **key** to see how information is shown. On this weather map, for example, cold fronts are shown by a line of triangles. The triangles point in the direction in which the front is moving. Finally, look at the map itself. Find details that will help you understand it. For example, look at Dallas. Dallas is in the shaded area that shows places with a high temperature in the 90s. There is no precipitation shading over Dallas. On this day Dallas is very hot and dry.

1. The symbol for a warm front looks like
   a. a row of semicircles. b. a row of triangles.

2. The city closest to a warm front is a. Fargo. b. Chicago.

3. A cold air mass is behind a cold front. The high temperature in the cold air mass over the western United States is in the
   a. 80s and 90s. b. 60s and 70s.

 Check your answers on page 238.

Weather Forecasts

Meteorologists are scientists who study the weather. Meteorologists study present weather conditions. Then they decide where the air masses and fronts will probably be the next day. From this data they **forecast,** or predict, the next day's weather. Suppose a meteorologist in Dallas studied the June 28 map. Her forecast for the next day might have said the high temperature would again be in the 90s and there would be no rain. Look at the map for June 29 below. Was the forecast correct?

High Temperatures and Precipitation for June 29

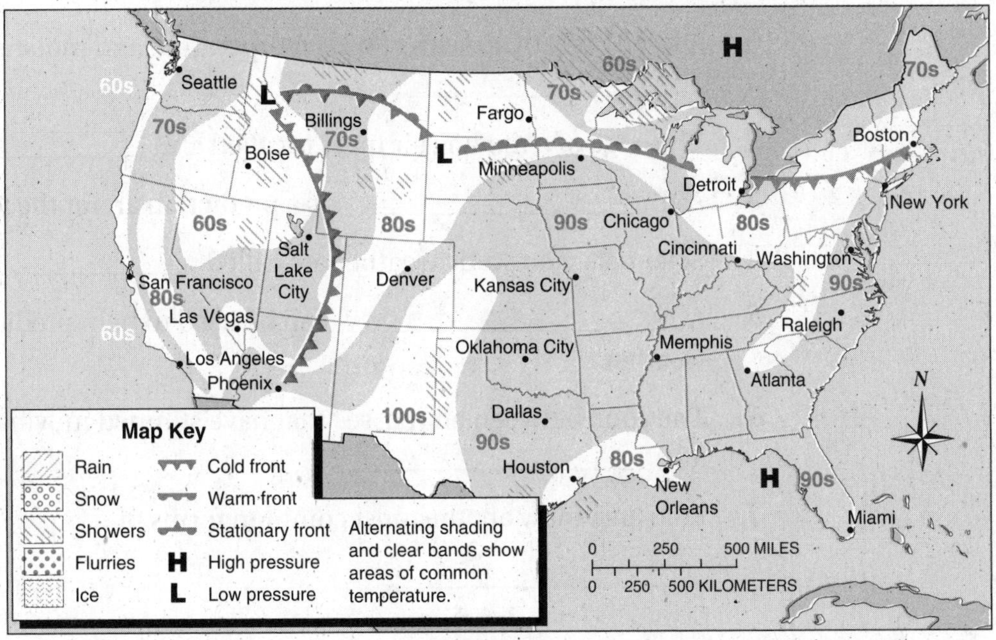

Making Predictions Like a meteorologist, you can use what you know to predict what will happen to the weather. Look at the map for June 28. In the upper right, there is a cold front moving south toward the northeastern United States. Now look at the map for June 29. The cold front has reached Boston. You can predict that soon the high temperature in the Boston area will drop from the 80s to the 70s. Use the map to answer these questions.

1. What is the weather like in New York City on June 29?
   a. high temperature in the 70s, rain
   b. high temperature in the 90s, dry

2. What kind of weather would you predict for New York City on June 30?
   a. high temperature in the 70s, dry
   b. high temperature in the 90s, rain

People often make jokes about the accuracy of weather forecasts. Yet meteorologists are pretty good at predicting tomorrow's weather. However, their long-range forecasts are not so accurate. Many factors can affect the weather. So forecasting more than a few days in advance involves guessing as well as predicting.

Check your answers on page 238.

Thinking About the Article

Practice Vocabulary

The words below are in the passage in bold type. Study the way each word is used. Then complete each sentence by writing the correct word.

air mass **stationary front** **front** **weather map**

precipitation **meteorologists** **forecast**

1. A large body of air with similar temperature and moisture is called a(n) ________________.
2. The edge of a moving air mass is called a(n) ________________.
3. A(n) ________________ is a prediction about the weather.
4. Scientists who study weather are called ________________.
5. A(n) ________________ can be used to help predict the coming weather.
6. The zone between air masses that have stopped moving is called a(n) ________________.
7. Rain and snow are the most common forms of ________________.

Understand the Article

Match the air mass with its characteristics. You may have more than one answer for each air mass.

	Air Mass	Characteristic
_____	8. continental polar	a. cold
_____	9. continental tropical	b. warm
_____	10. maritime polar	c. dry
_____	11. maritime tropical	d. moist

Write the answer to each question.

12. In what direction does weather in the United States generally move?

____

13. Why are long-range weather forecasts often inaccurate?

____

Apply Your Skills

Circle the number of the best answer for each question.

14. On a weather map, there is a line of alternating triangles and half circles pointing in opposite directions. Look at the map key on page 106. What does this symbol indicate?
    (1) cold front
    (2) warm front
    (3) stationary front
    (4) high-pressure area
    (5) precipitation

15. Refer to the map for June 28 on page 106. In which city are people most likely to be going to the beach to get relief from the heat?
    (1) Seattle
    (2) San Francisco
    (3) Los Angeles
    (4) New York
    (5) Detroit

16. Refer to the map for June 29 on page 107. What do you predict the next day's weather forecast for Salt Lake City is likely to be?
    (1) occasional showers, high temperature in the 60s
    (2) occasional showers, high temperature in the 90s
    (3) clear, high temperature in the 90s
    (4) clear, high temperature in the 50s
    (5) heavy rain, high temperature in the 80s

Connect with the Article

Write your answer to each question.

17. Refer to the map for June 28 on page 106. Which of the four types of air masses do you think is covering the western states? Give reasons for your answer.

____

____

____

18. Describe today's weather in your area. What kind of air mass is in your area now?

____

____

Check your answers on page 238.

15 LESSON

The Atmosphere

The Atmosphere
The Atmosphere
The Atmosphere

Vocabulary

atmosphere

radiant energy

infrared radiation

fossil fuels

photosynthesis

The air that surrounds Earth helps keep our planet warm. Like a blanket, the atmosphere holds in heat from the sun. Without the atmosphere, Earth would be very cold.

Human activities have changed the composition of the atmosphere. Many scientists think that these changes have caused Earth's temperature to increase. They are concerned that Earth will become even warmer—maybe too warm.

Relate to the Topic

This lesson explains how the atmosphere keeps Earth warm. It also describes global warming, a trend that many scientists think is caused by burning fossil fuels like oil and gas.

How do you and your family use oil and gas?

____

____

What can you do to use less oil and gas?

____

Reading Strategy

USING WHAT YOU KNOW Use what you already know about a topic to help you understand an article. Think about what you already know about increasing global temperatures. Then answer the questions.

1. What have you read about global warming?

____

____

Hint: Think about things you've seen or heard in the news.

2. What might happen if the Earth becomes warmer?

____

____

Hint: Think about how warm temperatures affect snow and ice.

Check your answers on page 238.

The Greenhouse Effect

The last 30 years have been unusually warm. Since the mid 1970s, the average global temperature has risen by about one degree Fahrenheit (abbreviated 1 °F). This is about 0.5 degrees Celsius (0.5 °C) as measured on the scale used by scientists. Is the recent heat wave part of a long-term rise in Earth's temperature? Or were the warm years just a matter of chance? Whatever caused this trend, the heat has focused people's attention on global, or worldwide, warming.

How Earth is Warmed

The air around us, called the **atmosphere,** plays a large role in the warming of Earth. When the gases in the atmosphere absorb energy, they become warmer. But from where does the energy come? It comes from two places, the sun and Earth.

Energy from the sun is called **radiant energy.** When you are outside on a bright day, the radiant energy of sunlight warms you. The atmosphere absorbs about 20 percent of the sun's radiant energy and reflects about 30 percent back into space. The remaining 50 percent of the sun's radiant energy is absorbed by Earth.

Earth radiates energy back into the atmosphere as **infrared radiation.** We feel infrared radiation as heat. You can feel heat rising from the pavement or from sand on a beach. These are examples of infrared radiation.

The infrared radiation reflected from Earth's surface does not escape into space. Instead, water vapor, carbon dioxide, and other gases in the atmosphere trap the heat. This is called the greenhouse effect because it is similar to what happens in a greenhouse. The gases that trap heat are called greenhouse gases.

Greenhouses use radiant energy from the sun to foster plants' growth.

Are People's Activities Increasing the Greenhouse Effect?

The greenhouse effect is a normal effect of the atmosphere. Without it, Earth would be much colder. But scientists say that the greenhouse gases in the atmosphere are increasing. This may cause Earth to become warmer, a trend called global warming. Such a change would be the result, or effect, of human activity.

In the last hundred years, people have burned more and more **fossil fuels.** Fossil fuels include coal, oil, gasoline, and wood. When these fuels burn, they increase the amount of carbon dioxide, a greenhouse gas, in the air. Also, people have destroyed many forests throughout the world. Plants absorb carbon dioxide during **photosynthesis.** Fewer plants means that more carbon dioxide remains in the atmosphere. More carbon dioxide in the atmosphere means that more heat is trapped close to Earth.

Carbon dioxide is the main greenhouse gas, but there are several others. Ozone, chlorofluorocarbons (CFCs), methane, and nitrogen oxide all absorb infrared radiation, trapping heat close to Earth. These greenhouse gases have increased as a result of pollution from cars, factories, and farms.

If greenhouse gas emissions continue at their present level or increase, many scientists think that Earth's temperature will increase 2.2 to 10 °F (1.4 to 5.8 °C) by 2100. Global warming could melt the ice caps at the North and South poles, flooding coastal areas and low-lying islands around the world. It could reduce the amount of land suitable for farming and change weather patterns, affecting crops.

Understanding the Relationships Among Ideas When you read, you are thinking all the time. Your mind is busy linking facts and ideas to one another and to things you already know. Reread the section of the article under the heading *Are People's Activities Increasing the Greenhouse Effect?* The main ideas are: (1) People are burning more fossil fuels. (2) People are destroying forests. (3) People are producing more air pollution. (4) Carbon dioxide and other greenhouse gases are increasing. (5) Global temperature is increasing. The first three main ideas are related. They are all things people do that affect the atmosphere.

1. How are Ideas 4 (increased greenhouse gases) and 5 (increased global temperature) related to one another?
   a. Idea 5 may be the result of Idea 4.
   b. Idea 4 may be the result of Idea 5.

2. What is the relationship of Ideas 1, 2, and 3 to Ideas 4 and 5?
   a. Ideas 1, 2, and 3 are the causes of Ideas 4 and 5.
   b. Ideas 4 and 5 are parts of Ideas 1, 2, and 3.

 Check your answers on page 238.

Reducing air pollution might help slow global warming.

What Can Be Done About Global Warming?

The problem of global warming may seem so large that no one can do anything about it. Still, many nations have agreed on a plan to cut the global emissions of greenhouse gases. Industrial nations have committed themselves to reducing their production of these gases. Individuals also can do many things that will help. Almost anything a person does that saves energy means that less fossil fuels are burned. If less fossil fuels are burned, there is less air pollution and less greenhouse gases are put into the air.

People can save energy at home by adding insulation and turning down the thermostat in the winter and turning it up in the summer. Conserving electricity, which is usually produced by burning fossil fuels, will also help. Driving a car that gets many miles per gallon of gasoline saves energy. Driving only when necessary will help, too. If your car is old, make sure its air conditioner is in good working order. The air conditioners of older model cars can leak CFCs into the air.

Recycling also saves energy. When recycled materials are used in manufacturing, less energy is used. Also, recycling can help reduce the amount of garbage in landfills and incinerators. Landfills produce methane gas when garbage breaks down. Garbage burned in incinerators produces carbon dioxide.

In addition, each person can plant a tree. A single tree may not do much, but it will help, especially if many people each plant one. Some cities, such as Los Angeles, even sponsor tree plantings.

Understanding Compound Words Science books are full of long words. Most of these words are compound words: long words that are made of smaller parts. Some familiar compound words are *baseball, sunshine,* and *supermarket.* Often you can figure out what a compound word means if you know what each part means. There are several compound words in the article you just read. *Sunlight* is light energy from the sun. A *landfill* is a place to bury trash (fill) in the ground (land).

1. What does *worldwide* mean (page 111, first paragraph)?

   ____

2. What does *greenhouse* mean (page 111, last paragraph)?

   ____

Check your answers on page 238.

Thinking About the Article

Practice Vocabulary

The words below are in the passage in bold type. Study the way each word is used. Then complete each sentence by writing the correct word.

fossil fuels **atmosphere** **greenhouse effect**

infrared radiation **global warming**

1. The air that surrounds Earth is called the ____________________.
2. The trend toward higher average temperatures worldwide is called ____________________.
3. The heat you feel rising from hot pavement is called ____________________.
4. Gases in the atmosphere absorb heat energy radiated from Earth. This is known as the ____________________.
5. Many scientists think that burning ____________________ contributes to the warming trend.

Understand the Article

Write the answer to each question.

6. What kind of energy warms you when you sit out in the sun?

____

7. How is the greenhouse effect like a blanket?

____

____

8. List the major greenhouse gases.

____

____

9. What did many nations agree to do to help slow global warming?

____

____

Apply Your Skills

Circle the number of the best answer.

10. The word *photosynthesis* has two parts. *Photo-* means light, and *synthesis* means combining parts into a whole. What does the word *photosynthesis* mean?
    (1) combining hydrogen and oxygen to make water
    (2) using light to combine substances into food
    (3) artificial light
    (4) artificial food made from light
    (5) the release of light

11. Carbon dioxide is a greenhouse gas. Planting trees may help reduce levels of greenhouse gases. Which statement links these two ideas?
    (1) Trees take in carbon dioxide during the process of photosynthesis.
    (2) The emissions of greenhouse gases are on the rise.
    (3) Burning fossil fuels releases carbon dioxide.
    (4) Cutting down trees may decrease the amount of carbon dioxide in the atmosphere.
    (5) Recycling saves energy.

12. Why would the sea level rise if the temperature on Earth becomes several degrees warmer?
    (1) Less ocean water would evaporate.
    (2) Some land would no longer be suitable for farming.
    (3) The ice caps at the North and South poles would melt.
    (4) There would be more waves.
    (5) The pull of Earth's gravity would decrease.

Connect with the Article

Write your answer to each question.

13. Why do industrialized nations produce more greenhouse gases than nonindustrialized nations?

____

____

14. What specific things can you do to help slow global warming?

____

____

____

Check your answers on pages 238–239.

LESSON 16

Resources

Most of us just turn on the faucet to get fresh water. We often take an endless supply of water for granted. But if you lived in a place where you had to haul water every day from a distant well, you would soon come to value water more. Fresh water is one of Earth's most precious resources.

Some communities can get all the fresh water they need from nearby lakes and rivers. But many other communities exist in areas that are far from any lake or river. These communities must go to a lot of extra effort to get fresh water.

Vocabulary

glacier

resource

groundwater

water cycle

renewable resource

reservoir

aqueduct

Relate to the Topic

This article is about the supply of fresh water. It describes what a water-poor area like California does to ensure fresh water for its farms, businesses, and homes. Think about the tap water in your own home.

Where does your tap water come from? ______________________

What would you do if you had no tap water? ______________________

____

Reading Strategy

SCANNING BOLDFACED WORDS Science materials often highlight technical terms in bold type—type which is darker than the type around it. Look at the boldfaced terms on pages 117 and 118. Then answer the questions.

1. What are glaciers?

   ____

   Hint: Look at the last paragraph on page 117.

2. What is the technical term for a lake created by a dam?

   ____

   Hint: Look under the heading Water Supplies.

Check your answers on page 239.

Supplying Fresh Water

California is well known for its extreme variations in weather and natural disasters. Storms, earthquakes, and mud slides in California often make the national news. But these are single events lasting a few days at most. In contrast, one of California's major everyday problems—its water supply—gets much less attention.

California, like many areas of the West, is mostly desert. But you would never guess this when touring the state. In the Central Valley, a low-lying area that runs more than half the length of the state, green orchards and crops are planted in neat rows, mile after mile. In the Los Angeles area, sprinklers water lush lawns and gardens, and swimming pools dot the backyards. Yet normal rainfall in Los Angeles is just 14 inches per year—about the same as Tripoli, Libya, another desert city.

Most of the precipitation that falls in California falls in the northern mountains. Yet most of the people and agriculture are in the southern part of the state. A complex system of trapping and moving water from the north and from other states allows California to supply water to its farm industry and more than 34 million people.

Some California farms depend on water that has been moved over great distances.

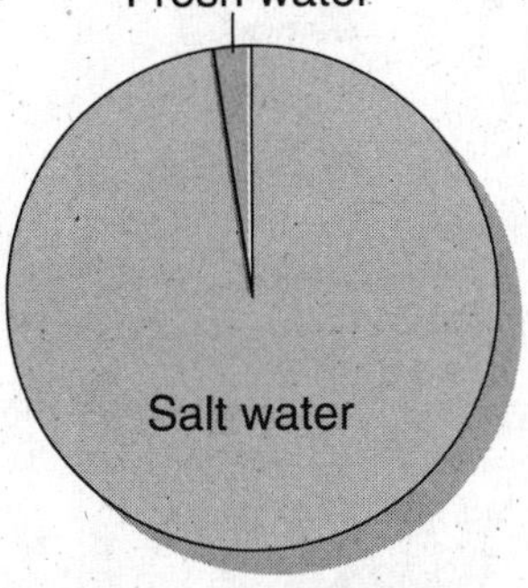

Earth's Water Resources

Water as a Resource

Astronauts often call Earth the blue planet because it is covered by water. Earth has plenty of water, but most of it is in the oceans. Ocean water is salty, and you cannot drink it. Less than three percent of Earth's water is fresh water. Most of this fresh water is frozen in ice at the poles and in **glaciers,** which are large masses of ice that form where more snow falls than melts. Only about one percent of all Earth's water is available as a resource. A **resource** is a substance that is needed for human life and activities. Usable fresh water is a resource that is found in rivers, lakes, and the atmosphere. Water is also found underground in **groundwater.**

The supply of fresh water is constantly being renewed in an endless **water cycle.** Water that evaporates from lakes, rivers, and the salty oceans falls as saltless precipitation. In this way, water can be considered a **renewable resource.** However, the amount of fresh water used worldwide continues to grow. As the population expands, more people need more water for drinking, cooking, sanitation, crops, livestock, factories, and power plants. At the same time more human activity means more water pollution. And last, water is often not present where it is most needed. Like California, some regions are water-poor, while others are water-rich.

Drawing Conclusions A conclusion is an idea that follows logically from the information you have. Conclusions must be supported by facts. For example, from the facts in the paragraph above you can conclude that the fresh water supply may eventually be too small to meet the world's needs.

You can conclude that water pollution cuts the supply of fresh water because

a. less of the available water is fit for drinking and cooking.

b. rivers with polluted water eventually dry up.

Water Supplies

The United States as a whole has more than enough water for everyone. Moving the water where it is needed is the problem. For example, most precipitation in the West falls in the mountains, such as the Rockies and the Sierra Nevada. It flows as surface water in rivers, such as the Sacramento and Colorado. **Reservoirs,** lakes created by dams, store water. Large pipes called **aqueducts** carry the water to Southern California, Arizona, and other dry areas of the West.

California's Water Supply System

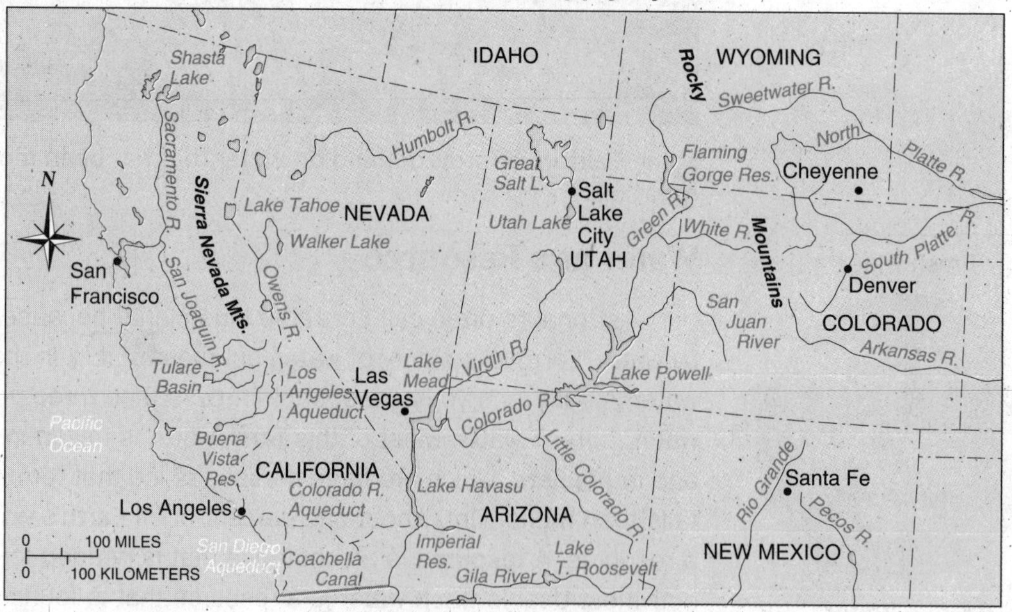

 Check your answer on page 239.

Another problem is that supplies of surface water depend on precipitation. If less than the normal amount of rain or snow falls over a long period of time, a drought occurs in that area. Groundwater, rivers, lakes, and reservoirs become low. During a drought, water use may have to be restricted.

Groundwater supplies are threatened by overuse and pollution. When a lot of water is taken from wells, the groundwater levels may go down. In West Texas, water for irrigating crops has been pumped for over 100 years. In that time the level of the groundwater has dropped about 100 feet. In other areas polluted wells have been shut down.

Finally, as the population of an area grows, competition for water increases. Southern California's population has been growing since the early 1900s. More and more people are moving to California's cities. Some people in California feel that the state has enough water. But they think that farms are getting more than their fair share. The farmers and their supporters argue that California supplies most of the country with food products. These people feel that irrigated open land adds to the quality of life for everyone in the country. While California tries to solve its long-term water problems, all Californians must conserve water.

Reading a Map A map is a picture that gives information about a place. To read a map, first look at the title. It tells you the main idea of the map. Then look at the labels. They point out different parts of the map. On the map on page 118, the orange labels are the names of rivers, aqueducts, lakes, and reservoirs. The black labels are the names of states, cities, and mountain ranges.

The map on page 118 shows that water is supplied to Southern California by the

a. Sacramento River
b. Colorado River Aqueduct

Conserving Water

Many areas, not just California, have problems with their water supply. That is why it's important to get into the habit of conserving water. Here are some things you can do.

- Take shorter showers and install a water-saving shower head.
- Fix leaks. A dripping faucet can waste 300 to 600 gallons of water per month.
- Put a brick in the toilet's tank to cut the amount of water used for each flush. Or install a new low-flow toilet: they use 1.6 gallons per flush, while older toilets use 3.5 to 7 gallons per flush.
- Run the washing machine and dishwasher only with full loads.
- If you're doing dishes in the sink, don't run the water. Use one basin to wash and another to rinse.
- Turn off the water when you're brushing your teeth or shaving. A bathroom faucet uses up to 5 gallons of water per minute.

 Check your answer on page 239.

Thinking About the Article

Practice Vocabulary

The words below are in the passage in bold type. Study the way each word is used. Then complete each sentence by writing the correct word.

glaciers **resource** **groundwater**

water cycle **renewable resource**

1. A ____________________ is one for which there is a replaceable supply.
2. Water that is found underground is called ____________________.
3. Water is a ____________________ that many of us take for granted.
4. ____________________ are large masses of ice that form where more snow falls than melts.
5. The endless movement of water from oceans to atmosphere to land is called the ____________________.

Understand the Article

Write the answer to each question.

6. Where does most of the water used in California come from?

____

7. Where is the world's supply of usable fresh water found?

____

____

8. What causes a drought?

____

____

9. List two ways to conserve water.

____

____

____

Apply Your Skills

Circle the number of the best answer.

10. When there is a drought in California, which conclusion can you make?
    (1) There is too little precipitation in the northern part of the state.
    (2) The reservoir levels are high all over the state.
    (3) There is too little precipitation in the southern part of the state.
    (4) The system of aqueducts is not transporting enough water.
    (5) Farm crops will not be affected by the lack of water.

11. Why are there water shortages in parts of the United States?
    (1) Not enough rain falls in the United States each year.
    (2) Most of the water in the United States is polluted.
    (3) Much of the water in the United States is groundwater.
    (4) Some areas get too much precipitation, while others do not get enough.
    (5) The United States does not have many glaciers.

12. Refer to the map on page 118. Which of the following statements about the Los Angeles Aqueduct is correct?
    (1) It carries water from Los Angeles to Las Vegas.
    (2) It carries water from the Owens River to Los Angeles.
    (3) It carries water from northern California to Los Angeles.
    (4) It delivers water to the Sacramento River.
    (5) It connects Great Salt Lake with Lake Powell.

Connect with the Article

Write your answer to each question.

13. If the world's supply of drinkable fresh water were running low, what alternative source of water can you think of to tap?

14. Describe ways in which you or someone you know has conserved water.

LESSON 17

The Solar System

The Solar System
The Solar System
The Solar Syst

Vocabulary

solar system

inner planets

silicon

erode

conglomerate

outer planets

space probe

People have been studying the solar system for centuries. Until fairly recently, observations of the solar system were made only from Earth.

Over the last 40 years, several unmanned space probes have explored the far reaches of the solar system. By sending photos and data back to Earth, these space probes have given us a closer look at Jupiter, Saturn, Uranus, and Neptune.

Relate to the Topic

This article describes some of the unmanned space missions that have been sent to the outer planets. Think about what it might be like to travel to another planet.

If you had the chance to visit another planet, would you go? Why or why not?

____

____

What would you hope to learn if you went to another planet?

____

____

Reading Strategy

USING HEADINGS TO ASK QUESTIONS A heading usually summarizes the information that follows it. Think of questions you might have about the heading topic. Look for answers as you continue reading. Read the headings on pages 123 through 125. Then answer the questions.

1. What is one question that is likely to be answered on page 123?

____

Hint: Read the heading.

2. Where would you expect to find information about Neptune?

____

Hint: Look for a heading that contains the word Neptune.

Check your answers on page 240.

The Planets

The first spacecraft to visit planets were launched in the 1960s. Since then, scientists have been learning new things about the solar system. The **solar system** is made up of the sun and the objects that revolve around the sun. These objects include the planets and their moons. Mercury, Venus, Earth, and Mars are called the **inner planets** because they are fairly close to the sun. They are all rocky planets. We know from the explorations of *Sojourner,* a robotic rover, that two of these rocky planets, Earth and Mars, have similar kinds of rocks. For example when *Sojourner* explored the surface of Mars in 1997, it found **silicon**, a common element found in Earth rocks. Also, the rounded shape of some Mars rocks suggests that they were **eroded,** or worn away. Some Mars rock is similar to **conglomerate,** rock formed when water rounds pebbles and larger stones that eventually become cemented together. Both processes have shaped rocks on Earth as well.

Jupiter, Saturn, Uranus, Neptune, and Pluto are called the **outer planets.** Except for rocky Pluto, the outer planets are huge balls of gas. They are much farther from the sun than the inner planets. The outer planets are so far away that only unmanned spacecraft, often called **space probes,** can be sent to explore them. It takes these spacecraft years to reach the outer planets.

Missions to the Outer Planets

Pioneer 10 was the first space probe to visit an outer planet. It was launched in 1972 and provided the first close-up pictures of Jupiter and its moons. The following year *Pioneer 11* sent back photos of Saturn and its rings.

Like *Pioneer 10* and *11,* most space probes are designed to visit only one planet. But scientists got a bonus with *Voyager 1* and *Voyager 2*. When these probes were launched in 1977, four of the outer planets were on the same side of the sun. These planets would not be in this position again for 175 years. So after reaching Jupiter, the *Voyager* space probes were able to fly on to Saturn, Uranus, and Neptune. They used the gravity of one planet to speed on to the next. Despite problems with radio reception, cameras, and computers, scientists on Earth guided *Voyager 1* and *Voyager 2* through an almost perfect grand tour.

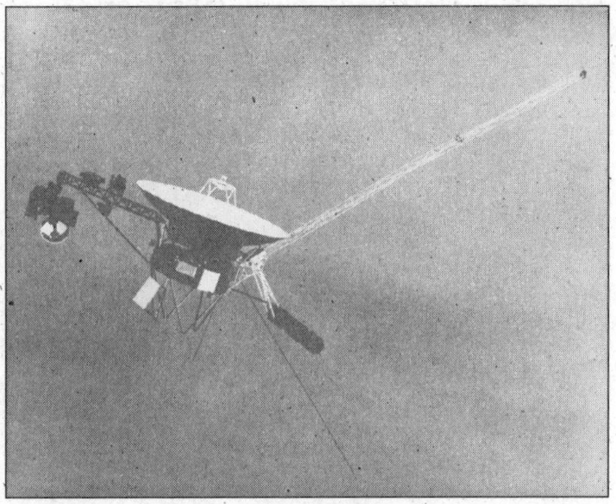

Each *Voyager* space probe had three computers, scientific instruments, and cameras mounted on a movable platform.

The *Pioneer* and *Voyager* probes flew by the outer planets and then continued out of the solar system. But the *Galileo* spacecraft was designed to orbit only its target planet, Jupiter. Launched in 1989, *Galileo* took pictures of the 1994 collision of comet Shoemaker-Levy with Jupiter. *Galileo* reached Jupiter in 1995 and began orbiting the planet. It lowered a separate probe into the atmosphere. Then it continued to circle Jupiter, sending back data about the planet and its moons.

All the space probes sent back spectacular photos. They also sent back data about Jupiter, Saturn, Uranus, Neptune, and their moons. Some basic data about these four planets and Earth are shown in the following table.

Earth and Four Outer Planets

	Earth	Jupiter	Saturn	Uranus	Neptune
Diameter (miles)	8,000	89,000	75,000	32,000	30,000
Mass (compared to the mass of Earth)	1	318	95	15	17
Distance from the sun (millions of miles)	93.5	486.4	892	1,790	2,810
Time of one revolution around sun (years)	1	12	29	84	165
Time of one rotation (length of day in hours)	24	10	11	17	16
Number of known moons	1	39	30	21	8

Reading a Table One way to present a set of facts is to organize them in a **table,** or chart. When you read a table, start with the title to get the main idea. From the title of this table, you know you will find information about Earth and four outer planets. The column headings ("Earth," "Jupiter," and so on) tell you which planet's information is in that column. The entries in each row of the left-hand column tell you what information appears in that row. For example, the first row of the table gives you information about diameter in miles. To find Saturn's diameter, you look along that row until you reach the Saturn column. Its diameter is 75,000 miles.

1. How many known moons does Jupiter have? ____________________

2. How long does it take Uranus to revolve around the sun? ____________________

Jupiter and Saturn

Photos sent back by the spacecraft showed that Jupiter has rings. Jupiter also has a swirling, stormy atmosphere into which *Galileo*'s probe parachuted. The atmosphere is made mostly of hydrogen and helium gases. The Great Red Spot of Jupiter is a storm several times larger than Earth.

 Check your answers on page 240.

Saturn's rings photographed by *Voyager 2* when it was 27 million miles away

Jupiter's four largest moons were first seen by the astronomer Galileo with a telescope in 1610. Ganymede, the largest moon in the solar system, looks similar to our moon. Io has active volcanoes, and its surface looks like pizza. Europa has a smooth surface of ice with a network of grooves. Callisto also has ice, but its surface has many deep craters.

Like Jupiter, Saturn is made mostly of hydrogen and helium. Saturn rotates quickly, causing bands of clouds to form in its atmosphere. Wind speeds of 500 miles per hour have been measured.

Galileo's biggest surprise for scientists was Saturn's rings. Scientists discovered that the planet has thousands of narrow rings, instead of a few very wide rings, Saturn's rings are made of particles ranging from specks of dust to large rocks. Some rings have "spokes" that appear and disappear. This new information has raised many questions about Saturn's rings.

Uranus and Neptune

It took almost five years for *Voyager 2* to travel the distance between Saturn and Uranus. Uranus is made mostly of hydrogen and helium. The temperature in the atmosphere is about −330 °F. At Uranus, *Voyager 2* found ten new moons.

The last planet *Voyager 2* flew by was Neptune. Neptune, made mostly of hydrogen, also has a stormy atmosphere. One feature seen by *Voyager 2* is the Great Dark Spot. This spot is a storm almost as big as Earth. Data sent back to Earth suggests that Neptune's winds, moving over 1,200 miles per hour, might be the fastest in the solar system. *Voyager 2* also discovered six new moons orbiting Neptune, bringing the total number of known moons to eight.

Drawing Conclusions Conclusions are ideas that are based on facts. They follow logically from the facts. This article describes four of the outer planets and some of their moons. From the fact that the author refers to the number of "known" moons of Uranus and Neptune, you can reach the conclusion that further exploration may lead to the discovery of more moons.

Refer to the table on page 124. What can you conclude about a planet's distance from the sun and the time it takes to revolve around the sun?

a. The farther away it is from the sun, the longer a planet takes to revolve around the sun.

b. The closer it is to the sun, the longer a planet takes to revolve around the sun.

The Missions Continue

A new space probe called *Cassini,* launched in 1997, is scheduled to reach Saturn and its largest moon, Titan, in 2004. Scientists continue to analyze *Galileo*'s data. *Voyager 1* and *Voyager 2* are still speeding out of the solar system. Some *Voyager* instruments will continue to send data until about 2015. If aliens ever come across one of the *Voyager* space probes, they will find a recording aboard. It has greetings from Earth in sixty languages.

 Check your answer on page 240.

Thinking About the Article

Practice Vocabulary

The words below are in the passage in bold type. Study the way the words are used. Then complete each sentence by writing the correct words.

solar system **inner planets** **outer planets** **space probes**

1. All of the ____________________ except Pluto are balls of gas.
2. ____________________ like *Pioneer, Voyager,* and *Galileo* send data about the planets and moons back to Earth.
3. The ____________________ consists of the sun and all the objects revolving around it.
4. Earth is one of the ____________________, which are small and rocky.

Understand the Article

Match each planet with its description. Write the letter of the planet in the space provided.

Description		Planet
______	5. Largest planet in the solar system	a. Earth
______	6. Planet with the most rings	b. Saturn
______	7. Has longest time of revolution	c. Jupiter
______	8. Rotates in 24 hours	d. Uranus
______	9. Has 21 known moons	e. Neptune

Write the answer to each question.

10. Name all of the planets in the solar system.

____

____

11. What was the mission of the *Pioneer, Voyager,* and *Galileo* spacecraft?

____

____

12. What is the most distinctive characteristic of Saturn?

____

Apply Your Skills

Circle the number of the best answer.

13. According to the table on page 124, which planet is about twice as far from the sun as Saturn?
    (1) Earth
    (2) Jupiter
    (3) Uranus
    (4) Neptune
    (5) Pluto

14. According to the table on page 124, which planet has the <u>most</u> known moons?
    (1) Earth
    (2) Jupiter
    (3) Saturn
    (4) Uranus
    (5) Neptune

15. Which of the following can be concluded from the fact that the *Voyager* probes had a movable camera platform?
    (1) The camera lenses could be switched from the control center on Earth.
    (2) The cameras took color photographs and radioed them to Earth.
    (3) The cameras were mounted on tripods on the platform.
    (4) The platform was used to steady the cameras.
    (5) The cameras could be pointed at specific objects.

Connect with the Article

Write your answer to each question.

16. Why do you think that it is not practical to send astronauts on missions to the outer planets at this time?

____

____

17. Do you think it is a good idea to spend tax dollars on missions to explore the solar system? Explain your answer.

____

____

____

Check your answers on page 240.

18 LESSON

Space Exploration

Space Exploration Space Exploration Space Explora

Vocabulary

solar cell

humidity

filtration

electrolysis

microgravity

freefall

colloid

What comes to mind when you hear the term *space station?* Perhaps you think of a huge city in space that is visited by spacecraft as they travel through the galaxy. Your mental image may have been shaped by movies you have seen, such as the *Star Wars* movies or *2001: A Space Odyssey.*

Right now, scientists and engineers from around the world are building a real space station. It will play an important role in space exploration in the future.

Relate to the Topic

This lesson is about the International Space Station. It describes the different parts of the space station. It also explains how the space station meets the needs of the people who live and work on it.

What are some basic things you need to live?

____

How do you take care of your basic needs when you are far from home?

____

____

Reading Strategy

PICTURING AN EVENT When you read about an event or experience, it can help if you try to imagine what is happening by forming a picture of something in your mind. Look at the first paragraphs on pages 129 and 131. Then answer the questions.

1. What does the first paragraph on page 129 ask you to picture?

____

Hint: Look for a sentence with the word picture *in it.*

2. What does the first paragraph on page 131 ask you to imagine?

____

Hint: Look for a sentence with the word imagine *in it.*

Check your answers on page 240.

The International Space Station

Picture what it would be like to carry out experiments while traveling at 17,500 miles per hour. That is exactly what people are doing on the International Space Station (ISS). The ISS is a research center that is being built more than 200 miles above the surface of Earth. Its purpose is to allow scientists to perform experiments in space. The ISS will provide knowledge useful for space exploration in the twenty-first century.

The ISS is being built by the United States and 15 other nations. Its construction began in 1988 and is scheduled to be finished by 2004. Like a skyscraper on Earth, the ISS is being built piece by piece. Each piece is carried from Earth to the construction site by a spacecraft, such as a space shuttle. The pieces are connected in space.

The International Space Station orbits more than 200 miles above Earth.

Inside the International Space Station

When the ISS is fully assembled, it will be almost 300 feet long and more than 350 feet wide. It will have a long, bridge-like frame. Ten cylinder-shaped structures called modules will be attached to the frame. Six of the modules will be laboratories, two will be living quarters, and two will be for activities such as control and communication.

Wings that extend from the frame carry a huge group of solar cells. A **solar cell** is a device that converts sunlight into electricity. The electricity that is generated by the solar cells provides power for all of the activities on the ISS. Batteries store some of the electricity for use when the ISS is on the dark side of Earth.

A crew of six to seven people can occupy the ISS at one time. Spacecraft that carry the crewmembers to and from the ISS park at one of several docking stations. The spacecraft also bring in supplies for the crew and materials for new experiments.

Supporting Life on the International Space Station

Humans cannot live without food, water, and oxygen. If people are to explore space by traveling away from Earth, they must meet these basic needs. Early spacecraft were used for short flights. They carried enough food, water, and oxygen to last for one flight. But the ISS will stay in space for many years. Supplies of food still have to be brought to the ISS from Earth, but water and oxygen can be recycled.

Water on the ISS is recycled from many sources. Wastewater from the sinks and showers is one source. Another source is excess **humidity** in the air, which is condensed to liquid water. Even the water in the crewmembers' urine is saved. Water from all these sources is screened to remove other materials. This screening process is called **filtration.** The water is then purified at high temperatures. The pure water is stored so that it can be reused.

Like people on Earth, crewmembers on the ISS take in oxygen and give off carbon dioxide when they breathe. On the ISS, oxygen is replaced through a process called electrolysis. **Electrolysis** involves using electricity to produce chemical changes. Electricity is passed through a tank of water, splitting the water molecules into hydrogen and oxygen. The oxygen is added to the air in the ISS. The hydrogen is released into space. Excess carbon dioxide in the air is also released into space.

Recycling Water and Oxygen on the International Space Station

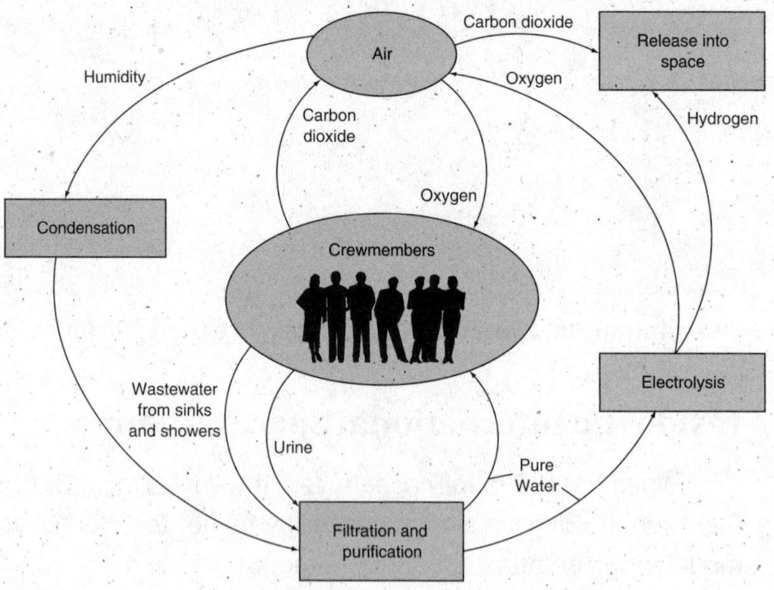

Reading a Diagram A diagram is a picture that shows how something is put together or explains how something works. Some diagrams have arrows that show the order of steps in a process. Labels tell you what happens in each step. In the diagram above, the arrow that points from the crewmembers to the air indicates that crewmembers exhale carbon dioxide into the air.

According to the diagram, which is a source of water to be purified?

a. condensation   b. electrolysis

 Check your answer on page 240.

Experiments on the International Space Station

Why do scientists conduct experiments on the ISS instead of doing them on Earth? The answer is that the ISS has something that no laboratory on Earth has: microgravity. **Microgravity** is another term for apparent weightlessness. Everything in the ISS appears to be weightless because it is all moving toward Earth at the same rate. This condition is called **freefall.** Can you imagine what it is like to be in freefall? A person bungee-jumping from a bridge is in freefall until the bungee cord slows his or her fall.

Microgravity helps scientists learn about certain physical and chemical changes. For example, in microgravity it is easier to study how crystals grow, metals form, and fires burn. One experiment on the ISS studied how colloids form in microgravity. A **colloid** is a mixture of fine particles suspended in another substance, such as a liquid. Paint and ink are examples of colloids.

On the ISS, scientists can conduct long term experiments in microgravity because the ISS does not have to return to Earth. It is a permanent laboratory in space. The situation is different on the Space Shuttle. The Space Shuttle missions are relatively short. Microgravity experiments that are done on the Space Shuttle do not last longer than about two weeks.

Many of the experiments being done on the ISS are designed to help people prepare for future space exploration. Space explorers will spend a long time in microgravity, so it is important to know how their bodies will be affected. Scientists are using the ISS to look at the effects of microgravity on nerves, muscles, lungs, and bones.

To study how microgravity affects bones, scientists measure the density of crewmembers' bones after they return from the ISS. The density is compared with measurements made before the crewmembers went to the ISS. If the bone density of crewmembers is always less after a mission, scientists can conclude that microgravity contributes to a loss of bone density.

Evaluating Support for Conclusions A conclusion is an idea that follows logically from other information. Conclusions must be supported by facts. For example, the statement *long experiments in microgravity are possible on the ISS* is a conclusion. It is supported by two facts: *the ISS has microgravity* and *the ISS does not have to return to Earth.*

Which facts would support the conclusion that microgravity causes a loss of bone density?

a. The ISS has microgravity, and bone density is less before a crewmember goes to the ISS.

b. The ISS has microgravity, and bone density is less after a crewmember returns from the ISS.

Check your answer on page 240.

Thinking About the Article

Practice Vocabulary

The words below are in the passage in bold type. Study the way each word is used. Then match each word to its meaning. Write the letter.

_____ 1. solar cell

_____ 2. filtration

_____ 3. electrolysis

_____ 4. microgravity

_____ 5. freefall

_____ 6. colloid

a. screening a substance to remove other materials

b. apparent weightlessness

c. moving toward Earth at equal rate

d. mixture of fine particles suspended in another substance

e. a device that makes electricity from sunlight

f. using electricity to produce chemical changes

Understand the Article

Write or circle the answer to each question.

7. What is the purpose of the International Space Station (ISS)?

____

8. How does the ISS get the electricity it needs to operate?
   a. It runs entirely on batteries that are replaced each time a spacecraft visits.
   b. It uses solar cells to convert sunlight into electricity.

9. What sources of water are recycled on the ISS?

____

____

10. How does the ISS replace the oxygen that crewmembers use?
   a. It uses electricity to produce oxygen from water.
   b. It collects oxygen from outside the International Space Station.

11. How does the ISS differ from laboratories on Earth?
   a. The ISS has microgravity, which laboratories on Earth do not.
   b. Long term experiments can be done on ISS but not in laboratories on Earth.

Apply Your Skills

Circle the number of the best answer for each question.

12. Refer to the diagram on page 130. According to the diagram, which two substances are released into space from the ISS?
    (1) humidity and urine
    (2) urine and pure water
    (3) pure water and oxygen
    (4) oxygen and carbon dioxide
    (5) carbon dioxide and hydrogen

13. Refer to the diagram on page 130. According to the diagram, which process makes pure water out of wastewater from sinks and showers?
    (1) condensation
    (2) hydrolysis
    (3) electrolysis
    (4) filtration and purification
    (5) microgravity

14. Which statement supports the conclusion that the ISS does a better job of conserving water and oxygen than early spacecraft did?
    (1) Early spacecraft brought water and oxygen from Earth.
    (2) Early spacecraft stored human wastes and brought them back to Earth.
    (3) The ISS recycles water and oxygen, but early spacecraft did not.
    (4) The ISS has shower facilities, but early spacecraft did not.
    (5) The ISS releases hydrogen into space, but early spacecraft did not.

Connect with the Article

Write your answer to each question.

15. How is being on the ISS similar to riding a roller-coaster with a long, steep drop?

16. In your opinion, is it a good idea that the ISS is being built by more than one nation? Explain your answer.

Check your answers on pages 240–241.

Science at Work

Building Trades: Construction Worker

As you walk or drive around your city or town, you will see construction workers. Construction workers work on a variety of projects. Some help build highways and roads. Others work on huge projects like skyscrapers or smaller projects like houses. Regardless of the size of the project, construction workers must be in good physical shape, have a good working knowledge of Earth's forces and materials, be able to read blueprints, and have strong measurement and visual skills.

Construction workers learn to use a wide variety of tools and machines. The equipment must be operated safely and correctly. Workers must also be concerned with the safety of others working at the job site. Working with the forces of nature and Earth materials such as sand, dirt, rock and water can be dangerous. Depending on the type of project on which they are working, construction workers must wear protective clothing such as hard hats, goggles, boots, and durable pants and shirts.

Look at the Some Careers in Building Trades chart.

- Do any of the careers interest you? If so, which ones?
- What information would you need to find out more about those careers? On a separate piece of paper, write some questions that you would like answered. You can find more information about those careers in the *Occupational Outlook Handbook* at your local library or online.

Some Careers in Building Trades

Carpet Installer
removes any existing carpet and lays new padding and carpeting

Electrician
installs and repairs electrical systems in buildings

Painter
prepares walls for painting and applies paint to surface

Tilesetter
prepares floors and walls for new tile; lays tiles in specific pattern

Construction workers must be able to follow directions to ensure that a project is done safely and correctly. They also need to use their knowledge about different forces and materials in the earth.

Read the directions below for constructing a swimming pool. Then answer the questions.

Building an In-ground Swimming Pool

1. ***Pick and Prepare the Pool Site.*** Pick a level area a good distance away from any structures. The pool site should be a little higher than the surrounding area to allow for drainage. Make sure the area directly around the pool is sloped downward from the pool itself. Too much rain and splash water around the pool causes slipperiness, which is a safety hazard.

2. ***Dig the Hole.*** Plot out the area for the pool by connecting stakes one foot wider and one foot longer than the actual size of the pool itself. Dig the hole 2–4 inches deeper than the pool itself. Dig another 4-ft. x 6-ft. hole in the middle of the deep end of the pool. Make it one foot deep. This is where the pool's drainage equipment will be placed.

3. ***Prepare the Hole to Receive the Pool Shell.*** Fill and level the base of the hole with 2–4 inches of sand or rock dust, as they do not absorb much water. This bed will support the pool. A bed is needed for consistent, unchanging support and drainage underneath the pool. Do not use dirt because it absorbs too much water. If too much water collects beneath the pool, the shell may crack or shift.

1. Which materials are acceptable for making the pool shell's support base?
   (1) dirt and sand
   (2) dirt and rock dust
   (3) stakes and water
   (4) sand and rock dust
   (5) sand and water

2. Why is it important to grade the area around the pool?
   (1) to make the pool look attractive and expensive
   (2) to make sure the water stays in the pool and not on the land
   (3) to make sure rain and splash water don't collect around the pool
   (4) to make sure the construction worker does his or her job correctly
   (5) to make sure that the pool can be drained for the winter

3. Have you seen construction workers on the job? Use a separate piece of paper to describe the job they were doing. What safety, weather, or pollution issues did they need to consider?

Check your answers on page 241.

UNIT 2

Unit 2 Review: Earth and Space Science
Unit 2 Review: Earth and Space Science

Unit 2 Review
Earth and Space Science

Weather Maps

Most daily newspapers print a weather map. The heavy lines show fronts. The symbols point in the direction in which the front is moving. The terms *warm front* and *cold front* describe the temperatures that are behind the front. Temperatures on U.S. weather maps are shown in degrees Fahrenheit. A stationary front is the area between two air masses that have stopped moving for awhile.

High Temperatures and Precipitation for July 22

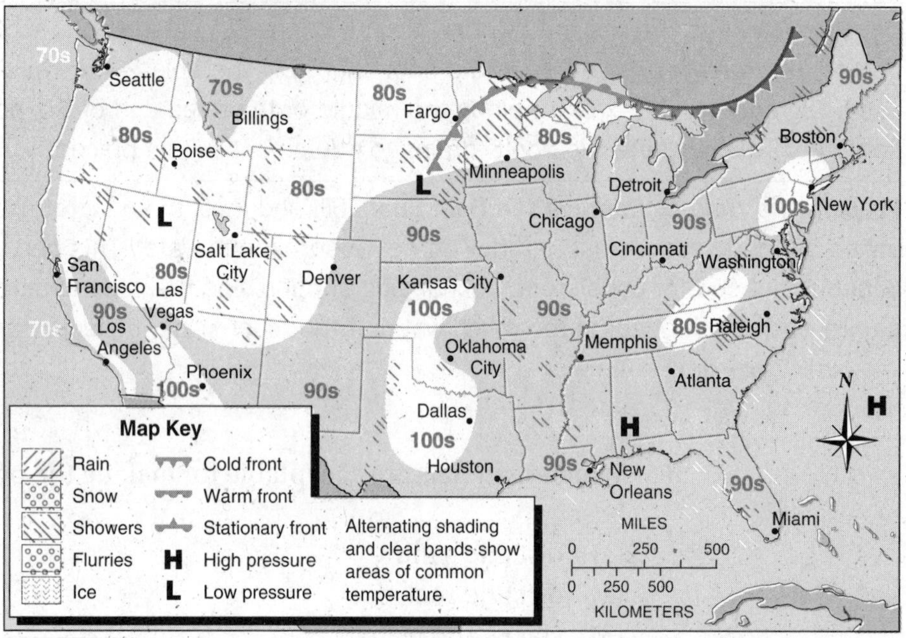

Fill in the blank with the word or words that best complete each statement.

1. According to the map, the high temperature in degrees Fahrenheit for Oklahoma City is in the ____________________.

2. The type of precipitation for July 22 in the United States is ____________________.

Circle the number of the best answer.

3. What is the weather like along the stationary front?
   (1) hot, with sunshine
   (2) hot, with showers
   (3) cold, with sunshine
   (4) cold, with snow flurries
   (5) moderate temperatures, with high winds

The Ozone Hole

Ozone is a form of oxygen. A layer of ozone is found 6 to 30 miles above Earth's surface. Scientists measure the thickness of the ozone layer in Dobson Units. They have discovered that the ozone layer has become thinner in the last 30 to 40 years. It becomes especially thin over Antarctica between August and December each year. The area where the ozone layer is very thin is known as the ozone hole.

Gases called chlorofluorocarbons (CFCs) are the main cause of the ozone hole. CFCs were used in aerosol spray cans for many years. CFCs escape into the atmosphere and destroy ozone. The destruction of ozone is a serious problem because the ozone layer absorbs ultraviolet light from the sun. The energy from ultraviolet light, called **ultraviolet rays,** is very harmful to plants and animals, causing sunburn and skin cancer. Thinning of the ozone layer allows more ultraviolet rays to get through to Earth's surface. As a result, skin cancer is likely to increase worldwide.

Average Thickness of Ozone Layer over Antarctica

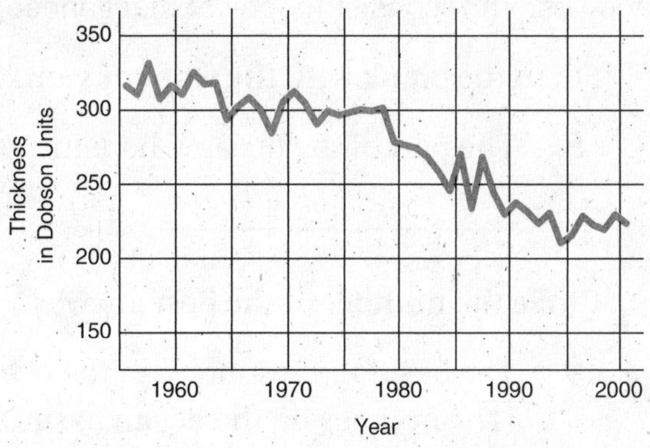

Fill in the blank with the word or words that best complete each statement.

4. Ozone is a form of ____________________.

5. ____________________ rays are dangerous rays from the sun.

Circle the number of the best answer.

6. If the use of CFCs were to increase, more people would probably die of
   (1) oxygen poisoning
   (2) CFC poisoning
   (3) skin cancer
   (4) sunburn
   (5) all of the above

7. Based on the graph, what can you conclude about the ozone layer over Antarctica?
   (1) Since the 1950s, it has gradually increased in thickness.
   (2) It was thickest in the 1980s.
   (3) Its thickness decreased most rapidly between 1960 and 1978.
   (4) Its thickness decreased most rapidly between 1978 and 1989.
   (5) By 2010 it is likely to be as thick as it was in 1960.

Go on to the next page.

The Oceans

Oceans cover nearly three-fourths of Earth's surface. The water is relatively shallow where the oceans meet the continents. The bottom of the ocean has a gentle slope in this area. It is called the **continental shelf** because the ocean bottom is almost flat. Since the water is shallow, sunlight can reach the bottom. There are many plants here. There are also many animals. We get shellfish, such as clams and lobsters, from the continental shelf. This is also the richest part of the sea for fishing.

Along the world's coastlines, the continental shelf can extend from just a few miles to as much as a thousand miles from the shore. Then the bottom slopes more steeply. This is the **continental slope.** The slope levels out to form the **ocean basin,** the bottom of the sea. The resources from these regions come mostly from the upper layers of the water in the open ocean. Large fish, such as tuna, are caught here.

The ocean gives us more than food resources. The rock layers of the continental shelf are sources of oil and natural gas. On the ocean basin are lumps of minerals, called nodules. They consist mostly of manganese, iron, copper, and nickel.

Fill in the blank with the word or words that best complete the statement.

8. The part of the ocean where the water meets dry land is the

_____________________.

Circle the number of the best answer.

9. The best food resources in the ocean are in
   (1) nodules on the ocean basin.
   (2) nodules on the continental shelf.
   (3) waters of the open ocean.
   (4) waters of the continental-shelf region.
   (5) waters of the continental-slope region.

10. If you sailed away from a continent, in which order would you pass over the different areas of the ocean bottom?
   (1) ocean basin, continental shelf, continental slope
   (2) ocean basin, continental slope, continental shelf
   (3) continental slope, continental shelf, ocean basin
   (4) continental shelf, ocean basin, continental slope
   (5) continental shelf, continental slope, ocean basin

11. Polluting the water over the continental shelf has negative economic consequences. Which statement supports this conclusion?
   (1) The continental shelf has a gentle slope.
   (2) The water over the continental shelf is shallow.
   (3) Sunlight can reach the bottom of the continental shelf.
   (4) Shellfish are harvested from the continental shelf.
   (5) The continental shelf can extend as far as a thousand miles from shore.

The Sun

The sun is the nearest star to Earth. The sun appears very large and bright. However, it is not especially large or bright when compared to other stars. The sun appears large and bright because it is so much closer to Earth than any other star. The next nearest star is more than 250,000 times farther away.

Huge amounts of heat energy and light energy are given off by the sun. The energy comes from nuclear reactions in the sun. These reactions take place in the **core,** which is the center of the sun. The temperature there is believed to be about 27 million degrees Fahrenheit. A large portion of the heat energy is changed into light energy on the surface of the sun. As a result, the temperature of the surface is only about 10,000 degrees Fahrenheit.

Parts of the Sun

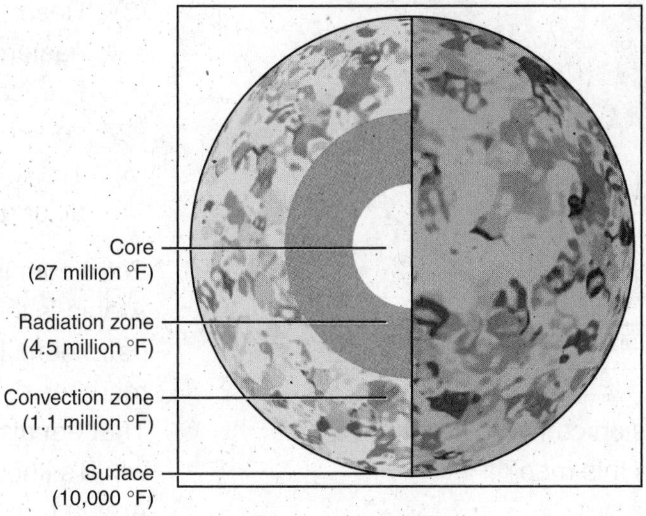

Fill in the blank to complete each statement.

12. The nearest star to Earth is the ________________.

13. The hottest part of the sun is the ________________.

Circle the number of the best answer.

14. Altair is a star similar in size and age to the sun. Based on the diagram, which part of Altair would you expect to have the lowest temperatures?
    (1) the core
    (2) the radiation zone
    (3) the convection zone
    (4) the surface
    (5) Not enough information is given.

Science Extension

Select one natural disaster or type of bad weather that your area sometimes experiences. Then make a list of things you could do to prepare yourself and your family for such an event.

Check your answers on pages 241–242.

Mini-Test • Unit 2

GED PRACTICE

This is a 15-minute practice test. After 15 minutes, mark the last number you finished. Then complete the test and check your answers. If most of your answers were correct but you did not finish, try to work faster next time.

Directions: Choose the one best answer to each question.

Questions 1 and 2 refer to the following map.

Average Annual Precipitation in Oregon

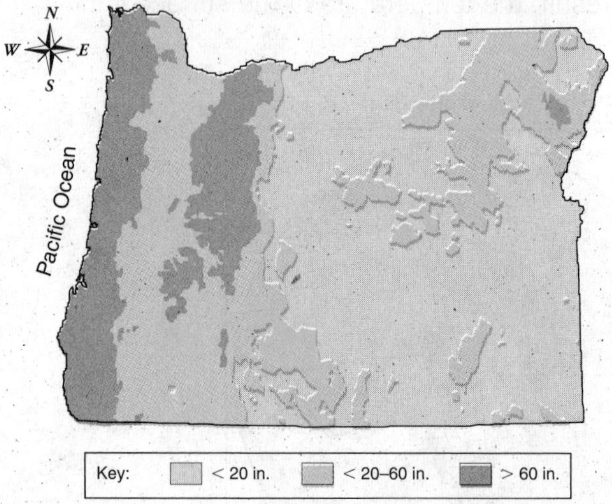

1. Which conclusion can you draw from the information on this map?

   Annual precipitation is

   (1) greater in the southern half of Oregon than in the northern half of Oregon
   (2) greater in the western half of Oregon than in the eastern half of Oregon
   (3) highest in the southeastern part of Oregon
   (4) lowest along the coast of Oregon
   (5) about the same in all parts of Oregon

2. What inference can you make from the information on this map?

   (1) Northwestern Oregon has more sunny days than other parts of the state.
   (2) Central Oregon has temperate rain forests.
   (3) Desert plants are found mostly in the eastern half of Oregon.
   (4) Hurricanes are common in the southeastern part of Oregon.
   (5) The temperature is nearly the same in all parts of Oregon.

3. Petroleum is a valuable resource. Saudi Arabia is the world's largest exporter of petroleum. It has known petroleum reserves of more than 260 billion barrels. That equals more than one-quarter of the world's known petroleum. In 1996 Saudi Arabia removed three billion barrels of petroleum from the ground.

   Which information supports the prediction that Saudi petroleum reserves will be depleted within a century?

   (1) Saudi Arabia is too close to the equator.
   (2) Every year Saudi Arabia removes about one-ninetieth of its petroleum reserves.
   (3) Saudi Arabia has known petroleum reserves of less than 300 billion barrels.
   (4) Saudi Arabia has about one-quarter of the world's known petroleum.
   (5) The country that exports the most petroleum is Saudi Arabia.

4. Sandstone is formed when sand is carried to a spot by wind, a river, ocean currents, or a glacier. As the sand builds up in the area, the weight of the upper layers compacts the lower layers. Minerals in the water between the sand grains bind the grains together like glue.

   Which process is most similar to the formation of sandstone?

   (1) the formation of volcanic glass from molten rock that cools on Earth's surface
   (2) the formation of diamond from carbon under extremely high heat
   (3) the formation of petroleum from the breakdown of ancient marine organisms
   (4) the formation of limestone from remains of coral and plankton that are cemented together on the ocean floor
   (5) the formation of petrified wood from dead trees that become buried and take up minerals from water

5. A scientist releases a balloon into the atmosphere. The balloon carries instruments that measure altitude and temperature. As the balloon rises, it sends data back to the scientist on the ground. The scientist analyzes the data and concludes that the temperature of the atmosphere decreases as the altitude increases.

   Which data would support this conclusion?

   (1) 25 °F at 1,000 feet, 29 °F at 2,000 feet, and 32 °F at 3,000 feet
   (2) 32 °F at 1,000 feet, 32 °F at 2,000 feet, and 35 °F at 3,000 feet
   (3) 32 °F at 1,000 feet, 29 °F at 2,000 feet, and 32 °F at 3,000 feet
   (4) 32 °F at 1,000 feet, 35 °F at 2,000 feet, and 32 °F at 3,000 feet
   (5) 32 °F at 1,000 feet, 29 °F at 2,000 feet, and 25 F at 3,000 feet

Questions 6 and 7 refer to the following table.

The Inner Planets

Planet	Diameter (in miles)	Mass (compared to Earth's mass)	Distance from Sun (in millions of miles)	Time of Rotation (in Earth days)
Mercury	3,000	0.06	36.5	58.7
Venus	7,600	0.82	67.3	243
Earth	8,000	1	93.5	1
Mars	4,200	0.11	142	1

6. Which statement about the inner planets is an opinion?

   (1) Mercury has the smallest diameter.
   (2) Venus has the longest time of rotation.
   (3) Earth is the most beautiful planet.
   (4) Earth has the largest mass.
   (5) Mars is the farthest from the sun.

7. Imagine you could travel to one of the inner planets. If you wanted to experience a day-night cycle least like Earth's, which planet should you visit?

   (1) Mercury
   (2) Venus
   (3) Mars
   (4) All of the inner planets have a day-night cycle very similar to that of Earth.
   (5) All of the inner planets have a day-night cycle very different from that of Earth.

Check your answers on page 242.

Unit 3

Chemistry

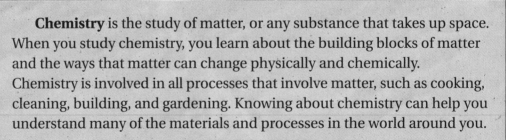

Chemistry is the study of matter, or any substance that takes up space. When you study chemistry, you learn about the building blocks of matter and the ways that matter can change physically and chemically. Chemistry is involved in all processes that involve matter, such as cooking, cleaning, building, and gardening. Knowing about chemistry can help you understand many of the materials and processes in the world around you.

Describe how you cooked or cleaned something recently. ____________

____

Describe what you observe when something burns. ______________

____

Chemistry

Thinking About Chemistry

You may not realize how often you use chemistry as you go about your daily life. Think about your recent activities.

Check the box for each activity you have done recently.

- ☐ Did you clean your house or car?
- ☐ Did you do the laundry?
- ☐ Did you ride in a car, truck, bus, or other motorized vehicle?
- ☐ Did you cook on a stovetop, oven, or grill?
- ☐ Did you light a candle?
- ☐ Did you maintain or repair an engine?
- ☐ Did you use cologne, lotion, or other cosmetics?
- ☐ Did you shampoo, condition, or color your hair?

Write some other activities in which you used chemistry.

____

____

____

Previewing the Unit

In this unit, you will learn:

- what matter is and how it behaves
- how chemistry is used to clean things
- what kinds of chemicals are in household cleaners
- how substances can combine to form new substances
- how chemistry is used in cooking
- how food changes when it is cooked
- how different kinds of matter can mix together
- how a gas heater works

Lesson 19	**Matter**
Lesson 20	**Changes in Matter**
Lesson 21	**Mixtures and Solutions**
Lesson 22	**Combustion**

LESSON 19

Matter

Vocabulary

substance

mixture

element

compound

atom

molecule

chemical symbol

chemical formula

chemical reaction

reactants

products

chemical equation

Supermarkets usually have an entire aisle full of different kinds of cleaning products. There are cleaners for the kitchen and cleaners for the bathroom. There are cleaners for white laundry and cleaners for colored laundry.

Many of these cleaners contain the same few chemicals in different combinations. They work in similar ways to clean. It's interesting to look at some basic ideas about matter, using cleaning products and processes as examples.

Relate to the Topic

This lesson describes the types of matter in some common cleaning products. Think about the different kinds of cleaning products in your home.

List some household cleaning products that your family uses.

____

____

What types of things do you clean with these products?

____

____

Reading Strategy

PREVIEWING A TABLE A table organizes information into rows and columns. A table usually has a title and headings. The title tells you the general topic of the table. The headings tell you the kind of information each column in the table contains. Skim the table on page 145. Then answer the questions.

1. What is the topic of the table? ____

____

Hint: Look at the title.

2. What kind of information does each column in the table contain?

____

Hint: Look at the headings above each column.

Check your answers on page 242.

The Chemistry of Cleaning

Almost everyone has run into the laundry problems of "ring around the collar" or stubborn yellow stains. Makers of detergents and bleaches claim their products can remove the toughest stains. Detergents can remove many stains. But recently scientists figured out why some oily yellow stains won't go away.

If the clothing is washed right away, the oily stain can be removed. But what happens if the stain sits for a week? The aging oil can combine with oxygen from the air. This process changes the colorless oil to a yellow substance. The yellow substance reacts with the fabric. In effect, the clothing is dyed yellow.

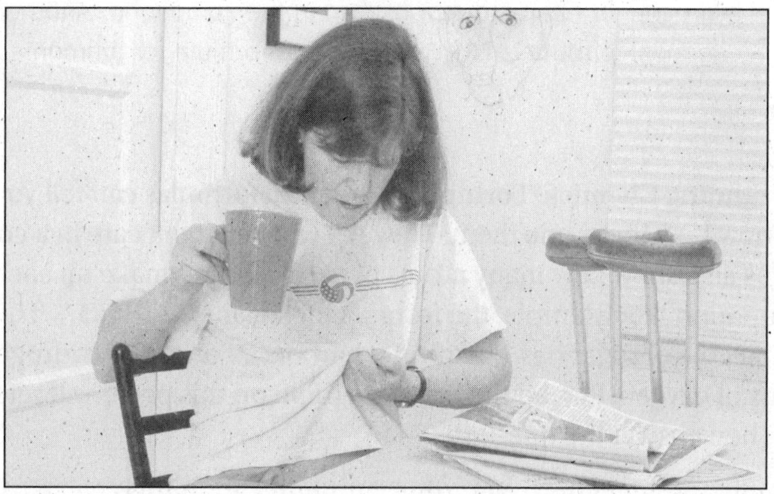

The sooner stained clothing is washed, the easier it is to get it clean.

Substances and Mixtures

Solving laundry problems is just one practical application of chemistry. Knowing about chemistry can help you make better use of the products you buy for cleaning and other jobs around the house.

Everything is made up of matter. Matter can be divided into two groups—substances and mixtures. All the matter in a **substance** is the same. A **mixture** is a combination of two or more substances that can be separated by physical means.

There are two kinds of substances. An **element** is a substance that cannot be broken into other substances by ordinary means. Two or more elements can combine chemically to form a **compound,** another type of substance. The smallest unit of an element is an **atom.** The smallest unit of a compound is a **molecule.** Each molecule in a compound is made up of atoms from each of the elements in the compound.

Forms of Matter

Mixtures	Substances	
	Compounds	Elements
lemonade	salt	oxygen
granola	sugar	carbon
salad	water	iron
soil	ammonia	gold
cement	bleach	nitrogen

Chemical Symbols and Formulas

When they write about matter and its changes, chemists use a kind of code. A **chemical symbol** of one or two letters stands for each element. The symbols for some common elements are shown in the table on this page. When elements combine to form a compound, the symbols are grouped together in a **chemical formula.** For example, H_2O is the chemical formula for water. The formula shows that the elements hydrogen (H) and oxygen (O) make up the compound water. The formula also shows there are two atoms of hydrogen for each atom of oxygen in the compound. Another chemical formula is NH_3, which is the formula for ammonia.

Symbols of Common Elements

Element	Symbol
Hydrogen	H
Carbon	C
Nitrogen	N
Oxygen	O
Sodium	Na
Magnesium	Mg
Sulfur	S
Chlorine	Cl
Iron	Fe
Calcium	Ca

Understanding Chemical Formulas Chemical formulas can tell you a great deal if you know how to decode them. They tell what elements are in a compound. Formulas also show how many atoms of each element make up each molecule of the compound. For example, the formula for sugar is $C_{12}H_{22}O_{11}$. This means that each molecule of sugar has 12 atoms of carbon, 22 atoms of hydrogen, and 11 atoms of oxygen. Reread the first paragraph on this page, and refer to the table above. Then answer the questions.

1. Name the elements in NH_3 (the compound ammonia).

____

2. How many atoms of each element are in each molecule of ammonia?

____

Chemical Reactions

In a **chemical reaction,** elements are combined into compounds or compounds are changed into other substances. For example, iron is a gray solid. Oxygen is a colorless gas. When iron and oxygen combine, they form a new substance. This substance is iron oxide, or rust. It is a brownish red or orange solid. In a chemical reaction, the substances that you start with are called the **reactants.** In this example, iron and oxygen are the reactants. The substances that result from the reaction are called the **products.** In this example, there is one product—iron oxide.

Scientists use equations to describe reactions. A **chemical equation** shows the reactants and products of a reaction. This equation shows how rust forms:

$$\text{iron} + \text{oxygen} \rightarrow \text{iron oxide}$$

Rust stains are hard to remove from clothing. However, you can remove the stain if you reverse the chemical reaction. The acid in lemon juice reacts with rust to form a water-soluble iron compound. When you rinse the treated stain, the iron washes away.

Compounds in Household Cleaners

NH_3 $NaOCl$ $NaOH$ $NaHCO_3$

Another example of a chemical reaction is the effect of bleach on clothing. The formula for chlorine bleach is NaOCl. In water, this compound produces salt and oxygen. The release of oxygen causes the whitening of the fabric. Nonchlorine bleaches use other sources of oxygen. One source is hydrogen peroxide, H_2O_2. Another source is calcium carbonate, $CaCO_3$.

Understanding Chemistry Roots, Suffixes, and Prefixes The name of a compound tells you what's in it. The root names of the elements are in the name of the compound. For example, table salt, NaCl, is called sodium chloride. It consists of sodium (Na) and chlorine (Cl). But why is it called sodium chlor*ide* and not sodium chlorine? When the suffix *-ide* is added to the end of the root name of the second element of a compound, it has a special meaning. It means the compound consists of just two elements. Another special suffix in chemistry is *-ate*. For example, calcium carbon*ate* is $CaCO_3$. The suffix *-ate* is used when the second element of a compound has the element oxygen with it.

1. What elements are in the compound barium chloride? Circle the letter of each correct answer.
   a. barium b. calcium c. chlorine d. oxygen
2. What elements are in the compound calcium chlorate? Circle the letter of each correct answer.
   a. barium b. calcium c. chlorine d. oxygen

Prefixes are used when more than one compound can be made from the same elements. For example, CO and CO_2 are both made from carbon and oxygen. Prefixes are used to distinguish the two compounds. So CO is carbon *mon*oxide. *Mon-* means "one," and it tells you there is one atom of oxygen in each molecule of carbon monoxide. CO_2 is carbon *di*oxide. *Di-* means "two," and it tells you there are two atoms of oxygen in each molecule of carbon dioxide. Some common prefixes are shown in the table at the right.

Prefix	Meaning
mono-	one
di-	two
tri-	three
tetra-	four

3. How many chlorine atoms are in the compound carbon tetrachloride? ____________
4. What is the name of the compound that has one aluminum atom and three oxygen atoms? Circle the letter.
   a. aluminum monoxide b. aluminum dioxide c. aluminum trioxide

 Check your answers on page 243.

Thinking About the Article

Practice Vocabulary

The words below are in the passage in bold type. Study the way each word is used. Then complete each sentence by writing the correct word.

mixture	**substance**	**element**
compound	**atom**	**chemical reaction**

1. A(n) ______________________ such as iron or oxygen is a pure substance that cannot be broken down into other substances by ordinary means.
2. Salad dressing is a(n) ______________________, a combination of two or more kinds of matter that can be separated by physical means.
3. When elements or compounds change into one or more different substances, a(n) ______________________ takes place.
4. All the matter in a(n) ______________________ is the same.
5. The smallest particle of an element is a(n) ______________________.
6. The elements sodium and chlorine combine chemically to form a(n) ______________________ commonly called table salt.

Understand the Article

Circle the letter of the correct answer.

7. The chemical symbol for the element calcium is
   a. C   b. Ca
8. The chemical formula for the compound called chlorine bleach is
   a. NaOCl   b. Cl
9. Chemists show the reactants and products in a chemical reaction by writing a
   a. chemical symbol.   b. chemical equation.
10. Which two elements combine to form rust?
    a. oxygen and iron
    b. hydrogen and oxygen
    c. iron and calcium
11. The products of a chemical reaction have
    a. the same characteristics as the reactants.
    b. different characteristics than the reactants.

Apply Your Skills

Circle the number of the best answer for each question.

12. Which elements are in hydrogen peroxide (H_2O_2)?
    (1) helium and potassium
    (2) helium and boron
    (3) hydrogen and chlorine
    (4) hydrogen and oxygen
    (5) hydrogen and phosphorus

13. What is the name of the compound MgS?
    (1) magnesium sulfur
    (2) magnesium sulfide
    (3) magnesium disulfide
    (4) sulfur magnesiate
    (5) magnesium sulfate

14. The compound calcium carbonate has the elements calcium and carbon. The suffix *-ate* tells you that the compound also has which element?
    (1) iron
    (2) chlorine
    (3) nitrogen
    (4) oxygen
    (5) hydrogen

Connect with the Article

Write your answer to each question.

15. The body of an automobile is made mostly of steel, which contains iron. Paint protects these steel parts from rusting. If the paint wears away, the auto body may start to rust. How does painting the steel help prevent it from rusting?

____

____

____

16. Name a common household cleaning compound and describe how you or someone you know uses it.

____

____

____

Check your answers on page 243.

LESSON 20

Changes in Matter

Changes in Matter

Changes in Ma

Changes in Matter

Vocabulary

solid

liquid

gas

melting

freezing

boiling

evaporation

condensation

physical change

chemical change

oxidation

All cooks use chemistry, even cooks who can only boil water or fry an egg. When you cook, you often change matter from one state to another. For example, heating water changes it from a liquid to a gas—steam—if you leave it boiling long enough. This is one kind of a physical change.

You also change matter when you cook. One example is cooking an egg. Adding heat to an egg causes chemical changes in the proteins the egg contains. You can see that a chemical change has occurred by observing how a scrambled egg is different from a raw egg. The properties of the egg have changed.

Relate to the Topic

This lesson explains the difference between physical and chemical changes. Think about your favorite cooked food.

What is the food like when it is raw? ______________________________

____

What is it like when it is cooked? ______________________________

____

Reading Strategy

PREVIEWING PHOTOS Science articles often have photos that show real-life examples to illustrate scientific concepts. A photo can help you understand a concept that might otherwise take many words to explain. A photo usually has a caption that tells you how the photo relates to the rest of the article. Look at the photos on pages 151 and 153. Then answer the questions.

1. What do the photos on page 151 show? ______________________________

   ____

   Hint: Look at the photos and caption.

2. What does the photo on page 153 show? ______________________________

   ____

   Hint: Look at the caption under the photo.

Check your answers on page 243.

Cooking with Chemistry

Ice cubes, water, and steam are used by cooks. Ice cubes are used to chill liquids. Water is used to boil food and as an ingredient in many recipes. Steam, which is actually water vapor, is used to cook vegetables. What do ice, water, and steam have in common? They are three forms, or states, of the same compound, H_2O.

Each state of matter has its own properties, or characteristics. A **solid** has a definite shape and takes up a definite amount of space. A **liquid** takes up a definite amount of space, but it doesn't have a definite shape. A liquid flows and takes the shape of its container. A **gas** does not have a definite size or shape. It expands to fill its container. If you remove the lid from a pot of steaming vegetables, water vapor escapes and spreads throughout the kitchen.

Changes of State

Matter changes state when energy, in the form of heat, is added to or removed from a substance. When you leave an ice cube tray on the counter, the ice absorbs heat from the air. Eventually the ice cubes melt. **Melting** is the change from a solid to a liquid. If you put the tray back in the freezer, the water will change back into ice. **Freezing** changes a liquid to a solid by removing the heat from it.

When you heat water, bubbles of gas form. They rise and burst on the surface of the water. **Boiling** is the rapid change from a liquid to a gas. A liquid can also change to a gas slowly through **evaporation.** If a glass of water is left out for a long time, the water evaporates from its surface. The reverse of boiling or evaporation is **condensation.** This is the change from a gas to a liquid. If a soft drink bottle is taken from the refrigerator, water vapor in the air will condense on the cold surface of the bottle.

Melting and boiling are two changes in state.

Physical Changes and Chemical Changes

A **physical change** is one in which the appearance of matter changes but its make-up and most of its properties stay the same. The boiling of water, the melting of butter, the dissolving of sugar in tea, and the smashing of a plate are physical changes. No new substances are formed. Matter is changed from one state to another in boiling and melting. When sugar dissolves, matter is mixed. When a plate breaks, it changes size and shape.

Unlike a physical change, a **chemical change** causes new substances to form. Some people make a beverage called a lemon fizz with baking soda and lemonade. This involves a chemical change. Baking soda mixed with an acid, like lemonade, gives off the gas carbon dioxide. This is a new product.

Many activities involve both physical and chemical changes. Making an omelet is an example. Breaking and beating the eggs cause physical changes. The chemical make-up of the eggs has not changed. You have just mixed the parts together. Cooking the eggs causes a chemical change. The heat changes the chemical make-up of the proteins in the eggs and makes them harden.

Finding the Main Idea The main idea of a paragraph tells what the paragraph is about in general. It is often stated in a topic sentence. The main idea of the first paragraph on this page is that the chemical make-up of matter stays the same during physical change. The main idea is stated in the first sentence of the paragraph, the topic sentence. Reread the second paragraph on this page. Look for the main idea and topic sentence.

What is the main idea of the second paragraph on this page?

a. A chemical change causes new substances to form.

b. Making a lemon fizz involves a chemical change.

Cooking a Hamburger

Cooking and eating a hamburger involves both physical and chemical changes. When a butcher grinds beef to make hamburger meat, the meat is ground into small pieces. No new substances are made, so grinding beef is a physical change.

Until the meat is packaged in plastic, the surface of the meat reacts with oxygen in the air. Myoglobin, a chemical in the beef, combines with oxygen. This chemical change is called **oxidation.** This change turns the surface of the meat bright red.

The next step is to form hamburger patties. In this step, you are changing the shape of the ground beef. There aren't any chemical changes, just a physical change.

 Check your answer on page 243.

Changes in Matter

Cooking hamburgers involves both physical and chemical changes.

Now the hamburgers are ready for cooking. Many cooks quickly sear one side and then the other on a very hot surface. Searing causes a chemical change in the surface proteins, and they form a crust. The crust keeps too much water from evaporating. It also keeps some of the fat from melting and seeping out of the hamburger. By preventing these physical changes, the crust keeps the hamburger from becoming dry.

Applying Knowledge to Other Contexts Information becomes more valuable when you use it. This article describes the physical and chemical changes in a hamburger as it is prepared and cooked. You can apply your knowledge of physical and chemical changes to other foods. For example, baking brownies causes a chemical change. The proteins in the liquid batter undergo chemical changes and become firm. On the other hand, cutting up brownies is a physical change. You are just changing the shape of the brownies when you cut them. Label each of the following as a *chemical change or a physical change.*

1. A piece of apple turns brown when it is exposed to the oxygen in air.

____

2. A tray of ice cubes melts when left outside of the freezer.

____

As a hamburger cooks, the inside loses its red color. This is caused by another chemical change in myoglobin. At the same time, chemical changes in the proteins make the meat become firmer.

When you eat the hamburger, more physical and chemical changes occur. Your teeth cut and grind the hamburger. This is a physical change. The hamburger is broken down chemically by substances in your digestive system. Digestion is another series of physical and chemical changes.

Check your answers on page 243.

Thinking About the Article

Practice Vocabulary

The words below are in the passage in bold type. Study the way each word is used. Then complete each sentence by writing the correct word.

gas **chemical change** **solid**

physical change **liquid**

1. A ____________________ is a state of matter that has a definite shape and takes up a definite amount of space.
2. A ____________________ is a state of matter that takes up a definite amount of space but doesn't have a definite shape.
3. A ____________________ is a state of matter that will spread out to fill all the available space.
4. A ____________________ is one in which the appearance of matter changes, but its make-up and most of its properties remain the same.
5. A ____________________ causes new substances to form that were not present before the change.

Understand the Article

Write the answer to the question.

6. Name the three states of matter of H_2O.

____

Match the process with its description.

______ 7. boiling		a.	change from liquid to solid
______ 8. evaporation		b.	rapid change from liquid to gas
______ 9. freezing		c.	change from gas to liquid
______ 10. condensation		d.	slow change from liquid to gas

Identify each of the following as a *chemical change* or *physical change.*

11. Chopping onions ____________________
12. Baking cookies ____________________

Apply Your Skills

Circle the number of the best answer for each question.

13. Which title best describes the main idea of this article?
    (1) Chemical Changes
    (2) Physical Changes
    (3) Chemical Changes in Cooking
    (4) Chemical and Physical Changes in Cooking
    (5) Cooking a Hamburger

14. Jason leaves a bar of chocolate on the dashboard of his car. When he comes back, he finds it has melted in the sun. This is an example of
    (1) a chemical reaction
    (2) condensation
    (3) a chemical change
    (4) a physical change
    (5) oxidation

15. Which of the following is an example of a chemical change?
    (1) melting a bowl of ice cream
    (2) freezing a popsicle
    (3) mixing a milk shake
    (4) baking a cake
    (5) bringing soup to a boil

Connect with the Article

Write your answer to each question.

16. Think about one of the changes of state, such as freezing or evaporating. What is an example of it from everyday life?

17. Describe an experience you or someone you know has had while cooking a meal or snack. What physical or chemical changes occurred in the food as it was cooked?

Check your answers on page 243.

Mixtures and Solutions

LESSON 21

Mixtures and Solutions

Most of the foods we eat are mixtures of two or more substances. Chocolate chip cookies and tossed salad are two examples. You can actually see the different parts of these mixtures. This is not the case for all mixtures.

For example, have you ever added sugar to a cup of tea? As you stir the sugar and tea, the sugar disappears—it dissolves in the tea. This type of mixture is called a solution. The sugar is evenly distributed in the tea. Orange soda and hot chocolate drinks are also solutions.

Vocabulary

mixture

distillation

solution

solvent

solute

solubility

Relate to the Topic

This lesson is about common types of substances called mixtures and solutions. Most of the beverages we drink are mixtures. Think about the beverages you drink.

List two beverages you like to drink. ______________________

Do you think these beverages are mixtures? Why or why not?

____

____

Reading Strategy

PREVIEWING A LINE GRAPH A **line graph** shows how one thing changes as a second thing changes. Instead of telling you in words, the graph shows you with a line. The title and labels help you read the line graph. The title tells you the main idea. The labels along the side and bottom tell you what two things are being compared. Skim the line graph on page 159. Then answer the questions.

1. What is the main idea of the line graph on page 159?

____

Hint: Look at the title.

2. What two things are being compared in the graph? ______________________

____

Hint: Look at the labels of the graph.

Check your answers on page 244.

Mixing It Up

Mixtures are all around you. The paper in this book is a mixture of fibers. The inks with which it is printed are mixtures of colored substances. Even the air around you is a mixture. It contains nitrogen, oxygen, carbon dioxide, and other gases.

What is a mixture? A **mixture** is made up of two or more substances that can be separated by physical means. The properties of a mixture are the properties of its ingredients. That is why sugar water is sweet and wet. Neither the sugar nor the water loses its properties when they are mixed together. Another characteristic of a mixture is that the amounts of its ingredients can vary.

Mixtures can be solids, liquids, or gases. A penny is a solid mixture of the elements copper and zinc. Blood is a mixture of liquids, such as water; solids, such as cells, sugar, and proteins; and gases, such as oxygen and carbon dioxide. A soft drink is a mixture of flavored liquid and the gas carbon dioxide.

The substances in a mixture can be separated by physical means. A mixture of red and blue blocks can be sorted by hand. A filter can be used to separate sand from water. A magnet can separate a mixture of steel and plastic paper clips. Liquid mixtures can be separated by distillation. **Distillation** is the process of boiling a mixture of liquids so that they will separate from one another. Since the different liquids boil at different temperatures, the gases formed can be condensed and the condensed liquids collected as they boil out of the mixture one at a time. That's how alcohol is obtained from fermented juices and brewed grains.

Sterling silver is a mixture of silver and copper.

Milk is a mixture of water, proteins, fat, and sugar.

What Is a Solution?

A solution is a special type of mixture. In a **solution,** the ingredients are distributed evenly throughout. All samples taken from a solution have the same amount of each substance. That's why the first and last sip from a soft drink taste the same. Solutions can be made of solids, liquids, or gases. Brass is a solid solution. Tea is a liquid solution. Seltzer is a solution of carbon dioxide gas in water.

In a solution, the substance that is present in a greater amount is called the **solvent.** Water is the most common solvent. The substance present in a smaller amount is called the **solute.** The solvent and solute may be in different states before the solution is formed. However, the final state of the solution will be that of the solvent. So a solution of water and powdered fruit drink is a liquid, not a solid.

Comparing and Contrasting When learning about things that are related, it is helpful to compare and contrast them. Comparing is pointing out how two things are alike. Contrasting is showing how two things are different. This article compares solutions and other mixtures. They are alike in that both can be separated by physical means. This article also contrasts solutions and other mixtures. One way they are different is that the ingredients of a solution are distributed evenly throughout. In other mixtures the ingredients can be mixed unevenly.

1. How are mixtures and solutions alike?
   a. Both are only liquids or gases.
   b. Both consist of two or more substances mixed together.

2. How are mixtures and solutions different?
   a. A solution is always liquid, and a mixture can be solid, liquid, or gas.
   b. A mixture can be in any state of matter, but a solution is always in the state of matter of the solvent.

How Solutions Form

When a solute dissolves, its particles spread evenly throughout the solution. How quickly the solute dissolves depends on several things. The smaller the particles of solute, the more quickly they dissolve. That's why instant coffee is made of small grains, not large chunks.

Stirring or shaking make a solute dissolve faster. The movement brings the solvent in contact with more of the solute. Stirring a cup of instant coffee makes the coffee dissolve more quickly.

Heat also makes a solute dissolve faster. Molecules move more quickly when they are hot. You can make instant coffee more quickly with boiling water than with cold water.

 Check your answers on page 244.

Solubility of Some Solids in Water

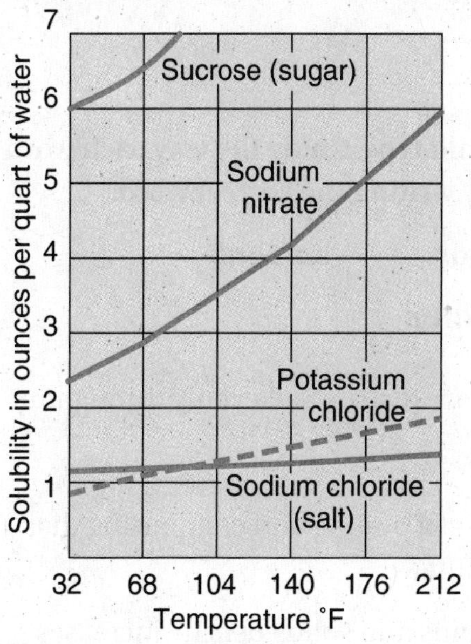

Solubility

The amount of a solute that will dissolve in a given amount of solvent at a given temperature is called its **solubility.** The effect of temperature on solubility is shown in the graph on this page. Each line on the graph is called a solubility curve. You can use this graph to find the solubility of substances in water at various temperatures.

The solubility of solids and liquids usually increases as the temperature rises. However, the opposite is true of gases. As the temperature rises, dissolved gas particles gain energy. They escape from the surface of the solution. That's why an opened bottle of soda goes flat more quickly at room temperature than in the refrigerator.

Reading a Line Graph Line graphs show information instead of presenting it in words. The title tells you the main idea of the graph. This graph shows the solubility of some solids in water. The labels along the side show how many ounces of the solid will dissolve in one quart of water. The labels along the bottom show the temperature of the water. To find out how much sodium nitrate will dissolve in a quart of water heated to 176 °F, first find the line that shows sodium nitrate. Then find the point on that line that intersects with the grid line for 176 °F on the bottom temperature scale. From that point on the sodium nitrate line, look along the horizontal grid line to the left-hand scale. There you will see that about 5 ounces of sodium nitrate will dissolve in 1 quart of water heated to 176 °F.

1. How many ounces of salt will dissolve in one quart of boiling water (212 °F)?
   a. about 1.5 b. about 6
2. Which of the following substances is more soluble in water?
   a. potassium chloride b. sugar

What happens if you add more solute than the solvent can hold? Extra solute settles to the bottom. That is why there is a limit to how sweet you can make iced tea. Once you reach the solubility limit of sugar, no more dissolves. The sugar on the bottom doesn't make the tea sweeter.

If the temperature of a sugar solution changes, the solubility of sugar changes. Suppose you dissolve all the sugar you can in hot water. Then you let the water cool. Sugar crystals will come out of the solution. If you let the water evaporate, the sugar crystals will be left behind. This is how rock candy is made.

Check your answers on page 244.

Thinking About the Article

Practice Vocabulary

The words below are in the passage in bold type. Study the way each word is used. Then complete each sentence by writing the correct word.

distillation **solution** **solvent**

solute **solubility**

1. A mixture in which the substances are distributed evenly throughout is called a ______________.
2. ______________ is a process of boiling and condensing that is used to separate liquids in a mixture.
3. The ______________ of liquids and solids usually increases with increases in temperature.
4. The substance present in the smaller amount in a solution is called the ______________.
5. Because so many substances dissolve in it, water is often called the universal ______________.

Understand the Article

All of the items listed below are mixtures. In each pair of items, however, one of the mixtures is a solution. For each pair, write the name of the solution.

6. ______________ chocolate chip cookie dough/hot chocolate
7. ______________ instant coffee/chicken noodle soup
8. ______________ brass/gravel

Circle the letter of the correct answer.

9. Refer to the line graph on page 159. The solubility of which of the following solids is less affected by changes in temperature?
   a. sodium chloride b. sodium nitrate
10. Why does adding heat make a solid or liquid solute dissolve more quickly?
    a. The heat melts the solute.
    b. The heat makes the molecules move more quickly so they mix together faster.

Apply Your Skills

Circle the number of the best answer for each question.

11. What is the difference between a solvent and a solute?
    (1) A solvent is part of a mixture, and a solute is part of a solution.
    (2) A solvent is always a liquid, and a solute is always a solid.
    (3) A solvent is always a gas, and a solute is always a liquid.
    (4) A solvent is present in a greater amount in a solution, and a solute in a lesser amount.
    (5) A solvent can be separated out by chemical means, and a solute can be separated out by physical means.

12. How are soil, cement, and air alike?
    (1) They are all in the same state of matter.
    (2) They are all solutions.
    (3) They are all mixtures.
    (4) They are all elements.
    (5) They are all compounds.

13. Refer to the line graph on page 159. Approximately how much sugar will dissolve in 1 quart of water at 32 °F?
    (1) 1 ounce
    (2) 2 ounces
    (3) 4 ounces
    (4) 6 ounces
    (5) 7 ounces

Connect with the Article

Write your answer to each question.

14. Suppose you mixed a fruit drink from grape-flavored powder, sugar, and water. Identify the solvent and the solutes. What happens when you combine them?

___

___

___

15. What is an experience you or someone you know has had with a mixture or solution?

___

___

___

Check your answers on page 244.

LESSON 22

Combustion

You may not be familiar with the word *combustion*. But you use this process every day. Combustion refers to chemical reactions that involve burning, or fire.

You may use combustion to heat your home in the winter by burning wood, gas, or oil. These are examples of combustion reactions. You also use a combustion reaction to get to work every day if you travel by car or bus.

Vocabulary

combustion

hydrocarbons

activation energy

kindling temperature

Relate to the Topic

This lesson is about combustion. Think about your experiences with an accidental fire or a fire that could have become dangerous.

Describe an experience you've had with fire. ______________________

____

____

____

How did you put the fire out? ______________________

____

____

____

Reading Strategy

SCANNING BOLDFACED WORDS Science materials often highlight technical terms in bold type. Words are highlighted this way in order to draw attention to terms that are likely to be new to the reader. Look at the boldfaced terms on page 163. Then answer the questions.

1. What are hydrocarbons made of? ______________________
   Hint: Scan the second paragraph.
2. What is a kindling temperature? ______________________

   ____

   Hint: Scan the last paragraph.

Check your answers on page 244.

The By-Products of Burning

Humans first used fire in prehistoric times. Ever since then, people have been burning fuels to produce heat. At first, people burned wood for warmth and then for cooking. During the 1700s, the first engines were invented. In an engine, a fuel is burned and heat energy is produced. This energy is then captured and used to produce motion. Today, fuels are used to provide heat and to power engines.

Combustion Reactions

Burning is a chemical change that chemists call **combustion.** In combustion, oxygen reacts with a fuel. Heat and light energy are released. An example of combustion is the burning of a fuel such as kerosene, oil, or gas. These fuels are **hydrocarbons,** or compounds made only of hydrogen and carbon. When they burn, the hydrogen and carbon combine with oxygen from the air. Carbon dioxide and water vapor are produced.

Combustion reactions need a little energy to get them started. This energy is called **activation energy.** To start a twig burning, you must light a match to it. Once combustion starts, no additional energy is needed.

Each substance has its own **kindling temperature.** That's the temperature to which the substance must be heated before it will burn. The form of a substance affects its kindling temperature. For example, sawdust catches fire faster than a log. Vaporized gasoline ignites more easily than liquid gasoline.

The burning of gasoline in this motorcycle's engine is an example of combustion.

How a Combustion Heater Works

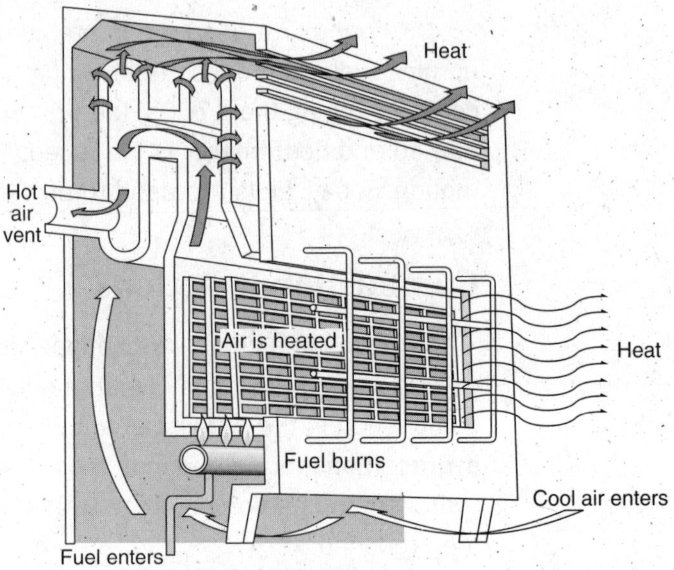

A Gas Heater

A small kerosene or natural gas heater can be used to warm one or two rooms. A kerosene heater has a small built-in fuel tank. Some natural gas heaters have fuel tanks, too. Other gas heaters are connected to the gas lines of the house. The fuel is piped to the burners. Most heaters use an electric spark to start the combustion reaction. Cool air from the room enters at the base of the heater. The heat from combustion warms the air. Warmed air then flows into the room. With a gas heater, the waste products of combustion leave the house through a vent. With a kerosene heater, all of the hot air flows into the room.

Kerosene heaters have many advantages. A kerosene heater is not very expensive. It does not have to be attached to a chimney, so it can be moved from room to room. These heaters warm up quickly and provide heat for up to 30 hours without refueling.

Kerosene heaters also have some disadvantages. If not used properly, they can be unsafe. If the heater is close to drapes, they may catch fire. The outside of the heater is very hot and can cause burns. The heater may tip over, causing injury or a fire. These are all obvious hazards. Less obvious is the hazard caused by the release of pollutants into the air.

Making Predictions Active readers think about what they read. They make predictions about what will come next. Sometimes the predictions are based only on what they have just read. Sometimes they look ahead for clues about what's coming. Reread the second and third paragraphs above. The second paragraph discusses the advantages of kerosene heaters. When you read that, you can predict that the next paragraph will discuss the disadvantages of kerosene heaters. Based on what you have read about the advantages and disadvantages of kerosene heaters, which of the following topics is more likely to come next? Circle the letter of your prediction.

a. The low cost of running combustion heaters.

b. The hazards of pollutants produced by combustion heaters.

 Check your answer on page 244.

Indoor Air Pollution

Complete combustion produces carbon dioxide and water vapor. Combustion is complete only if the fuel is pure and there is plenty of oxygen. Often the fuel is not pure. Also, there may be too little oxygen. Then combustion is incomplete. When combustion is incomplete, other substances are released along with carbon dioxide and water vapor. These substances pollute the air.

Incomplete combustion can cause a high level of pollutants to develop in the air. These may include carbon monoxide, nitric oxide, nitrogen dioxide, or sulfur dioxide. These substances can harm the eyes, throat, and lungs. Carbon monoxide is especially dangerous. You can't smell it or see it. Yet high levels of carbon monoxide can cause death.

Understanding the Implied Main Idea Sometimes a writer does not actually state the main idea of a paragraph in a topic sentence. You have to "read between the lines" and add up the details to figure out the main idea. The first paragraph above has no topic sentence. Instead, it describes complete combustion and incomplete combustion. The main idea is that complete combustion produces harmless products, and incomplete combustion produces pollutants. Reread the second paragraph above. Circle the letter of its implied main idea.

a. Indoor air pollutants can be harmful to health and can even cause death.

b. Indoor air pollutants can collect even when a room is not airtight.

Both natural gas and kerosene heaters can give off pollutants. Natural gas burns more cleanly than kerosene. But makers of kerosene heaters claim that these heaters can burn cleanly, too. If high-quality kerosene is used, the combustion reaction is 99.5 percent complete, meaning that only 0.5 percent of the reaction is incomplete.

Kerosene and natural gas heaters are not the only producers of indoor air pollution. Wood stoves, fireplaces, gas stoves, and tobacco smoke are other sources. Leaking chimneys and furnaces also produce indoor air pollution.

Safety Precautions

People using kerosene heaters or other types of combustion devices indoors should always follow the manufacturer's instructions. The heater should always be in a safe place. It should be placed away from materials that might burn and away from places where children play.

To reduce indoor pollution, use only high-quality kerosene in a kerosene heater. Keep the doors to other rooms open for ventilation. Remember that combustion uses oxygen from the air. It is a good idea to open a window slightly to let more oxygen in and allow pollutants to escape.

Check your answer on page 244.

Thinking About the Article

Practice Vocabulary

The words below are in the passage in bold type. Study the way each word is used. Then complete each sentence by writing the correct word.

combustion	**kindling temperature**
activation energy	**hydrocarbon**

1. Chemists call burning ______________.

2. A(n) ______________ is a compound, such as kerosene or natural gas, made only of hydrogen and carbon.

3. The energy required to start a combustion reaction is called ______________.

4. Before it will burn, a substance must be heated to its ______________.

Understand the Article

Write or circle the answer to each question.

5. Which gas from the air is needed for combustion?

____

6. What happens during a combustion reaction?
   a. Oxygen reacts with a fuel, producing heat, light, carbon dioxide, and water vapor.
   b. Carbon dioxide, water vapor, and carbon monoxide combine to form heat, oxygen, and carbon by-products.

7. Which pollutants can be produced when combustion is incomplete? Circle the letter of each correct answer.
   a. oxygen
   b. sulfur dioxide
   c. carbon monoxide
   d. kerosene
   e. nitrogen dioxide
   f. nitric oxide

8. Why is it important to provide oxygen to a kerosene or gas heater?
   a. Without enough oxygen, combustion is incomplete, producing pollutants.
   b. Without enough oxygen, the heater costs more to run.

Apply Your Skills

Circle the number of the best answer for each question.

9. On the basis of the information in the article, which of the following can you predict about small kerosene and gas heaters?
   (1) Wood-burning stoves produce more air pollution than do small heaters.
   (2) Sales of small heaters have increased since the fuel shortages of the 1970s.
   (3) High-quality kerosene produces more pollutants than low-quality kerosene.
   (4) More fires are caused by small heaters than by built-in heating systems.
   (5) A shortage of kerosene and natural gas makes small heaters too expensive.

10. Which of the following would you predict might happen if kerosene were used in a small heater in an airtight room?
   (1) Only carbon dioxide and water vapor would be produced, making the room warm and damp.
   (2) The pollutants released by incomplete combustion would eventually overcome the people in the room.
   (3) Oxygen from outdoors would be used to keep the combustion reaction going to heat the room.
   (4) The combustion reaction would speed up, eventually causing the heater to explode.
   (5) The heater would become so hot that the drapes would ignite, causing a fire in the home.

11. What is the implied main idea of the first paragraph on page 163?
   (1) The first fuel was wood, used to provide heat.
   (2) Over time, people have burned fuels for many purposes.
   (3) Engines change heat energy into the energy of motion.
   (4) Fire was discovered in prehistoric times.
   (5) Air pollution is caused by burning fuels.

Connect with the Article

Write your answer to each question.

12. How can the hazards of using a kerosene or gas heater be reduced?

____

13. Describe something you have that uses combustion. What type of fuel is used? Do you think it is producing any air pollutants?

____

____

Check your answers on pages 244–245.

Science at Work

Service: Beautician/ Cosmetologist

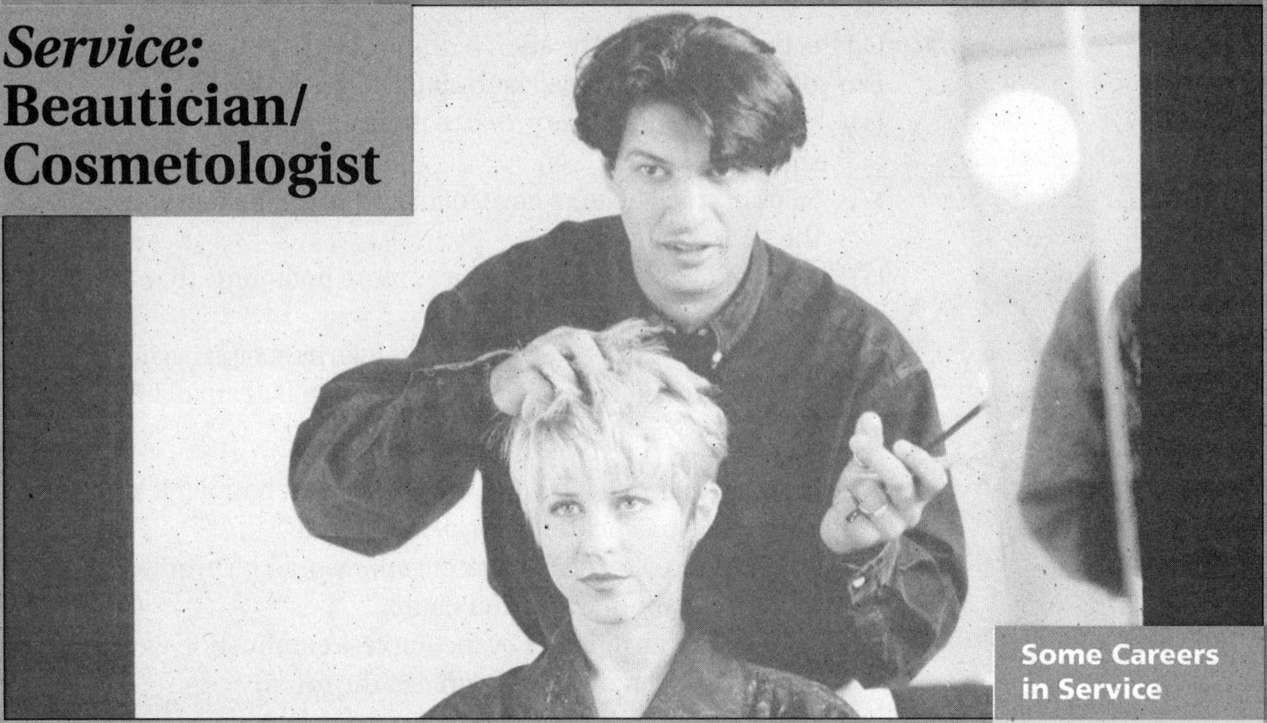

Do you like to help people look their best? Do you have a good sense of style? If so, you may be interested in becoming a beautician or cosmetologist. Helping people look their best involves careful analysis of their individual physical traits.

Beauticians shampoo, cut, style, and treat hair. This often involves the use of chemicals to curl, straighten, or color hair. If not used properly, these chemical products may prove harmful. Treating clients' skin with chemical products must also be done with great care. Leaving a product on too long or using it in sensitive areas may result in burns or infection.

Beauticians and cosmetologists need excellent oral communication skills and pleasant personalities. Because they often are on their feet for long periods of time, beauticians should be in good physical health.

Look at the chart showing some of the careers in service.

- Do any of the careers interest you? If so, which ones?
- What information would you need to find out more about those careers? On a separate piece of paper, write some questions that you would like answered. You can find out more information about those careers in the *Occupational Outlook Handbook* at your local library or online.

Some Careers in Service

Barber
cuts and styles men's and children's hair

Cosmetology Instructor
trains students in the use of beauty aids and products

Make-up Consultant
works with customers to select colors and facial care products

Manicurist
treats customers' cuticles and nails by shaping, polishing, and applying decorations

Read the following information and look at the figure. Then answer the questions.

When Ramon's customers ask about how to care for their hair, he tells them about pH values. He explains the **pH scale** ranges from 0–14. Products with a pH value under 7 are called acids. Products on the acidic side of the scale make hair look shinier but not as thick. Distilled water has a value of 7 and is neutral. Those products with a pH value above 7 are called bases or alkaline products. They make hair thicker, but they are also harder on hair because they dry it out and make it swell.

Ramon's Shampoo Choices

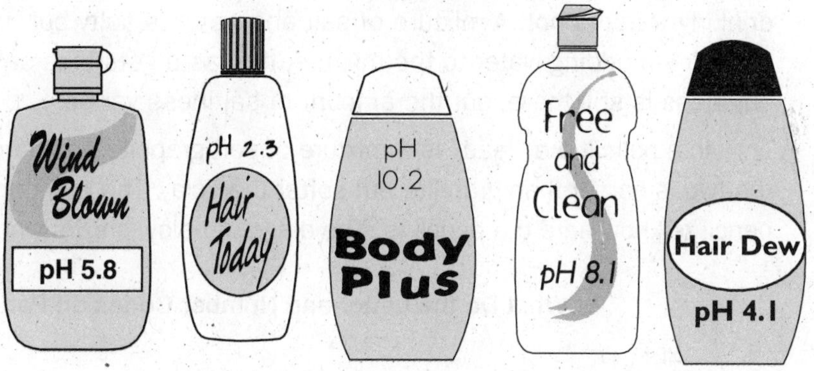

1. Ramon's customer Renee wants her hair to look thicker. Which shampoo will make her hair look the thickest?
   (1) Wind Blown
   (2) Hair Today
   (3) Body Plus
   (4) Free and Clean
   (5) Hair Dew

2. Which shampoo is closest to neutral in pH value?
   (1) Wind Blown
   (2) Hair Today
   (3) Body Plus
   (4) Free and Clean
   (5) Hair Dew

3. Which sequence below ranks the shampoos from most acidic to most alkaline?
   (1) Wind Blown; Hair Today; Body Plus; Free and Clean; Hair Dew
   (2) Hair Dew; Free and Clean; Body Plus; Hair Today; Wind Blown
   (3) Hair Today; Hair Dew; Free and Clean; Wind Blown; Body Plus
   (4) Body Plus; Free and Clean; Wind Blown; Hair Today; Hair Dew
   (5) Hair Today; Hair Dew; Wind Blown; Free and Clean; Body Plus

Check your answers on page 245.

Unit 3 Review: Chemistry

UNIT 3

Unit 3 Review
Chemistry

Mixtures

The "lead" in your pencil is not actually made of the metal lead. It is made mostly of a form of carbon called graphite. Graphite is very soft. As a result, anything you write with graphite will easily smudge. To solve this problem, graphite is mixed with clay.

A **mixture** is a combination of two or more substances. The properties of a mixture vary depending on the make-up of the mixture. For example, salt is salty and drinking water is not. A mixture of salt and water is salty but not as salty as salt alone. If you keep adding water to the mixture, the taste gets less salty. The property of saltiness is still there, but the amount of saltiness varies.

In a pencil, the "lead" is a mixture of soft graphite and harder clay. The mixture of the two is harder than graphite but softer than clay. The number or letters stamped on a pencil tell how hard the pencil is. The diagram below shows what the pencil codes mean.

What Do the Letter and Number Codes on Pencils Mean?

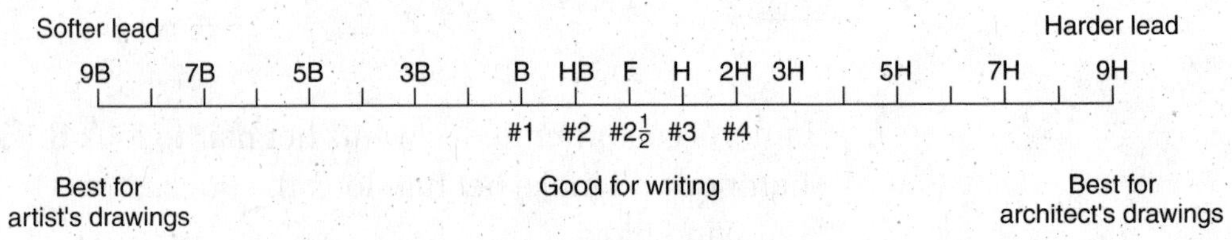

Fill in the blank with the word or words that best complete each statement.

1. A(n) ____________________ is a combination of two or more substances that are combined in varying proportions.

2. The lead in a pencil is a combination of ____________________ and ____________________.

Circle the number of the best answer.

3. How is the lead in a pencil marked 9H different from the lead in a pencil marked 9B?
   (1) The 9H lead is softer.
   (2) The 9H lead is better for drawing.
   (3) The 9H lead contains more clay.
   (4) The 9H lead contains more graphite.
   (5) There is no difference between the two.

Energy and Chemical Reactions

In a **chemical reaction,** one substance or set of substances is changed into another substance or set of substances. In this process, energy may be given off or taken in. An **exothermic reaction** gives off energy. Burning, or **combustion,** is an example of an exothermic reaction. When wood is burned, energy is given off in the form of light and heat.

Photosynthesis is a chemical reaction that takes place in plants. In this reaction, plants use the energy in sunlight to turn carbon dioxide and water into glucose, a type of sugar, and oxygen. This is an example of an **endothermic reaction,** or one that takes in energy.

You may have used an instant hot pack for first aid. These plastic pouches contain chemicals. When you break the seal inside the pouch, the chemicals come together and react. The reaction is exothermic and gives off heat. Once the reaction is finished, no additional heat is given off.

There are also instant cold packs used for first aid. When the chemicals in these pouches react, they do not give off heat. Instead, they take in heat. Because the reaction absorbs heat, the pouch feels cold when placed against the skin.

Fill in the blank with the word or words that best complete each statement.

4. A(n) ____________________ gives off energy.

5. A(n) ____________________ takes in energy.

6. In a(n) ____________________, substances are changed into other substances.

7. One type of exothermic reaction that gives off heat and light energy is ____________________, or burning.

Circle the number of the best answer.

8. What is the implied main idea of the last paragraph on this page?
   (1) Instant cold packs are more useful than instant hot packs.
   (2) Instant cold packs feel cold when placed against the skin.
   (3) The reaction in instant cold packs is exothermic.
   (4) The reaction in instant cold packs is endothermic.
   (5) Exothermic reactions usually feel cold to the touch.

9. Which chemical process produces the heat given off by a gas heater?
   (1) a physical reaction
   (2) combustion
   (3) an endothermic reaction
   (4) photosynthesis
   (5) an instantaneous reaction

Go on to the next page.

Putting Out Fires

Fire, or **combustion,** is a useful chemical reaction. However, sometimes a fire gets out of control and must be put out. There are several ways to do this. All methods of putting out a fire work by removing something the reaction needs in order to continue.

One way of putting out a fire is to take away one of the substances that is used in the reaction. The simplest way to do this is to remove the **fuel,** or the material that is burning. You do this when you turn off the gas on the stove.

In a raging fire, it is hard to remove the fuel. It is easier to remove the oxygen that is needed to keep the reaction going. A small fire can be smothered. Baking soda can be poured on a small grease fire on a stovetop. The layer of baking soda keeps oxygen away from the grease, which is the fuel. Smothering a campfire with dirt works the same way.

Another way to put out a fire is to take away some of its heat. Materials do not burn until they are heated to their **kindling temperature.** Once a fire is burning, it continues to heat its fuel to the kindling temperature. If you can take enough heat away from the fuel, it will be below the kindling temperature and will not burn. This is how water puts out a campfire.

A carbon-dioxide fire extinguisher uses two methods at once. The carbon dioxide is heavier than oxygen. It makes a layer below the oxygen but above the fuel, smothering the fire. As the carbon dioxide comes out of the extinguisher, it expands rapidly. This process absorbs heat. So the carbon dioxide also cools the burning material.

Circle the number of the best answer.

10. If you place a burning candle in a glass jar and seal the lid, the flame goes out after a few seconds. Why does this happen?
    (1) The air in the jar becomes too hot.
    (2) The burning candle has used up all of the oxygen in the jar.
    (3) Too much carbon dioxide has built up in the jar.
    (4) Not enough carbon dioxide is available.
    (5) Glass is not flammable.

11. A heavy blanket thrown on a small fire puts out the fire by
    (1) adding carbon dioxide
    (2) removing oxygen
    (3) removing fuel
    (4) removing heat
    (5) cooling the fuel

Fusion Reactions

Nuclear reactions are changes in the nucleus, or center, of an atom. One kind of nuclear reaction that is being studied by many scientists is fusion. **Nuclear fusion** is the reaction in which two nuclei combine. In the process, the nucleus of a larger atom is formed.

In nuclear fusion, hydrogen nuclei fuse, or join, and form a helium nucleus. A huge amount of energy is released. This reaction takes place only under conditions of great pressure and high temperature. Such conditions are found on the sun. Fusion reactions are the source of the energy that the sun gives off.

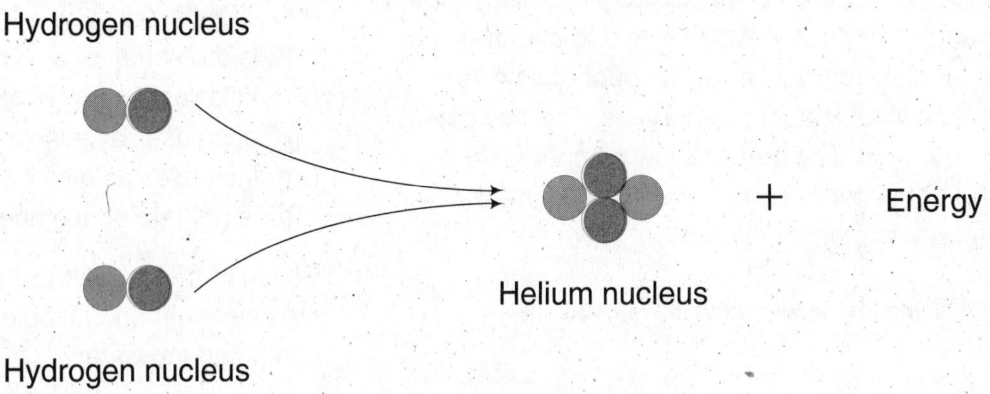

Fusion reactions do not take place naturally on Earth. There is no place on the planet as hot as the sun. Scientists are looking for ways to make fusion occur at lower temperatures. If scientists could make such "cold fusion" reactions work, they would have a powerful energy source.

Fill in the blank with the word or words that best complete each statement.

12. A nuclear reaction in which two nuclei combine is called a ______________________.

13. Fusion reactions take place naturally on the ______________________.

14. In a nuclear fusion reaction, hydrogen nuclei combine to form the nucleus of a(n) ______________________ atom.

Science Extension

Check your refrigerator and make a list of the mixtures and solutions you find there. Remember, mixtures and solutions can be solid, liquid, or gas, or a combination of these.

Check your answers on page 245.

Mini-Test • Unit 3

GED PRACTICE

This is a 15-minute practice test. After 15 minutes, mark the last number you finished. Then complete the test and check your answers. If most of your answers were correct but you did not finish, try to work faster next time.

Directions: Choose the one best answer to each question.

Questions 1 through 4 refer to the following information and graph.

Some types of bottled water contain minerals and some do not. One way to measure the amount of minerals in water is to add a known amount of water to a known amount of a white powder called sodium polyacrylate. This powder absorbs water. The graph below compares the amount of water absorbed from four different samples of water.

Mineral Concentration in Water Samples

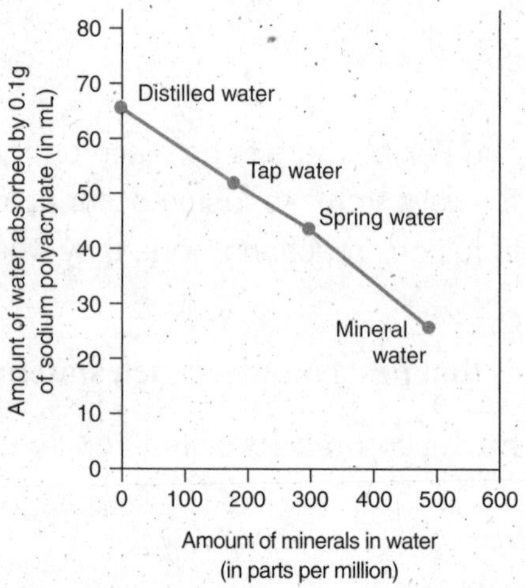

1. Compare the samples of water tested. Based on the graph, which sample contained the least amount of minerals?
   (1) distilled water
   (2) tap water
   (3) spring water
   (4) mineral water
   (5) Not enough information is given.

2. Which of the following can you infer from the graph?

   The amount of water absorbed by sodium polyacrylate
   (1) is the same for all types of water
   (2) is lowest for tap water
   (3) decreases as mineral content increases
   (4) increases as mineral content increases
   (5) is not related to mineral content

3. Which of the following would provide evidence that an unlabeled bottle of water contained tap water?

   One-tenth of a gram of sodium polyacrylate
   (1) absorbs 65 mL of this water
   (2) absorbs 50 mL of this water
   (3) absorbs 42 mL of this water
   (4) releases 65 mL of this water
   (5) releases 50 mL of this water

4. Which of the following might be a good use for sodium polyacrylate?
   (1) to flavor mineral water
   (2) to purify distilled water
   (3) to clean up polluted water
   (4) to soak up urine in disposable diapers
   (5) to give off perfume in disposable towelettes

5. A student placed two solid chemicals at room temperature in a test tube and shook the test tube. After a few minutes, the test tube contained a slushy liquid and felt cold. The student concluded that the chemical reaction took in heat.

   Which of the following supports this conclusion?

   (1) The test tube contained both chemicals.
   (2) The two chemicals mixed together.
   (3) The solid chemicals became liquids.
   (4) The test tube cooled off after the reaction.
   (5) The chemicals melted from the heat.

Questions 6 through 9 refer to the following information and diagram.

Calories tell us how much energy is in food. Calories are measured using an instrument called a calorimeter, shown below. The food is placed inside the calorimeter and burned. The increase in the temperature of the water surrounding the metal container indicates how much energy the food contained.

A Calorimeter

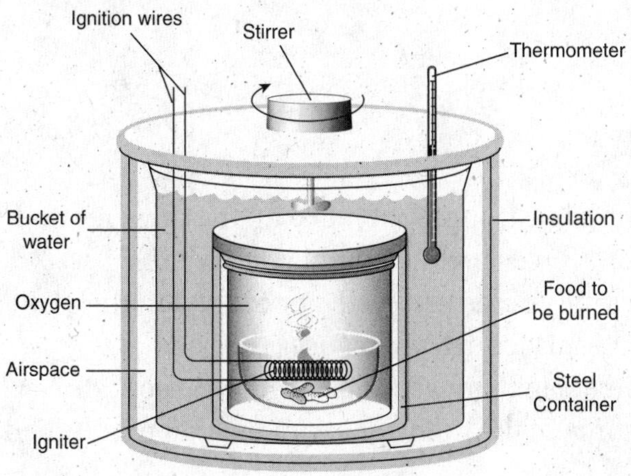

6. What inference do you need to make to fully understand this paragraph?

   (1) Calories are a measure of food energy.
   (2) A calorimeter is used to calculate the number of calories in food.
   (3) Eating too many calories can cause a person to gain weight.
   (4) A calorimeter burns food the same way that the body does.
   (5) The amount of heat produced by burning food is used to calculate calories.

7. What causes the food in the calorimeter to catch on fire?

   (1) the insulation
   (2) the igniter
   (3) the stirrer
   (4) the air in the air space
   (5) the heated steel container

8. Which of these people would be most likely to use data collected with a calorimeter?

   (1) a farmer
   (2) a restaurant owner
   (3) a nutritionist
   (4) a pediatrician
   (5) a building safety specialist

9. Which statement is a valid conclusion about high-calorie foods placed in a calorimeter?

   (1) They will not catch fire in the calorimeter.
   (2) They will not float in the calorimeter.
   (3) They will not cause the water in the calorimeter to change temperature.
   (4) They will cause the same temperature change as will low-calorie foods.
   (5) They will cause a greater temperature change than will low-calorie foods.

Check your answers on pages 245–246.

4 UNIT

Physics

Physics is the study of the basic things that make up the universe and what happens when they exert forces on one another. Every time something moves or changes, physics is involved. For example, when you strike a match against a rough surface, friction causes the head of the match to ignite, producing heat, light, and sound. Heat, light, sound, motion, and electricity are some of the many phenomena that are studied in physics.

What happens when a tennis player hits the ball?

____

____

Physics

Thinking About Physics

You may not realize how often you use physics in your daily life. Think about your recent activities.

Check the box for each activity you have done recently.

- ☐ Did you turn a doorknob?
- ☐ Did you lift something?
- ☐ Did you play a sport?
- ☐ Did you use lights or a computer powered by electricity?
- ☐ Did you use a magnet to attach a picture or note to a refrigerator door?
- ☐ Did you use a tool to fix something that was broken?
- ☐ Did you use a solar-powered calculator?
- ☐ Did you listen to music on a CD?

Write some other activities in which you used physics.

____

____

____

Previewing the Unit

In this unit, you will learn:

- how machines make it easier to do work
- what happens when moving objects collide
- how electronic devices work
- what light is
- how lasers work
- how sound waves produce music

Lesson 23	**Machines**
Lesson 24	**Momentum**
Lesson 25	**Electricity**
Lesson 26	**Light and Lasers**
Lesson 27	**Sound Waves**

LESSON 23

Machines

Vocabulary

- force
- gravity
- friction
- work
- effort
- resistance
- simple machine
- lever
- pivot
- mechanical advantage
- wheel and axle
- gear
- compound machine

Walk into a bicycle store and you'll see an amazing assortment of bikes. There are racing bikes, mountain bikes, and bikes with training wheels. There are one-speed bikes and 21-speed bikes. There are even bikes that let you pedal while you lie on your back.

Despite their differences, all bicycles have certain things in common. They all let you get around more quickly than you can by walking or running. And all bikes—even ones with many complicated parts—are really just a collection of simple machines that work together.

Relate to the Topic

This lesson is about force and work. It describes some simple machines, which are devices that help us do work. It also describes a more complex machine—the bicycle. Think about the last time you rode a bicycle.

Why did you ride the bicycle? ______________________________

____

How many speeds did the bicycle have? ______________________________

Reading Strategy

RELATING TO WHAT YOU KNOW When you read, think about what you already know about the topic. The topic of this lesson is machines, including levers and gears. Think about what you already know about levers and gears. Then answer the questions.

1. When would you use a lever? ______________________________

   ____

   Hint: Picture a lever and think about how you would use it.

   ____

2. Where are you likely to find gears? ______________________________

   ____

   Hint: Think about where you have seen gears or a gearshift.

Check your answers on page 246.

How a Bicycle Works

In many large cities, businesses use messengers to carry documents across town. These messengers can be seen speeding past clogged traffic. Are they running? Are they driving? No, they're riding bicycles.

A bicycle is a good way to get around. You don't have to be very strong to go at a moderate speed. If you have a bicycle with 3, 10, or 21 speeds, it can help you ride easily up most hills. By riding a bicycle, you can get your exercise on the way to work.

A bicycle is a good means of transportation.

Force and Work

When you push down on the pedal of a bicycle, you are applying a force to it. A **force** is a push or a pull. There are many kinds of forces. The pull of one magnet on another is a force. The pull that Earth has on you and all other objects is the force of **gravity**. A force between surfaces that touch each other is known as **friction.** Friction between the brake pads and the wheel of a bicycle or automobile stops the wheel from turning.

Work is done when a force causes an object to move. Lifting a bag of groceries is work. Your upward force of lifting overcomes the downward force of gravity. The force you exert is called the **effort.** The force you overcome is the **resistance.**

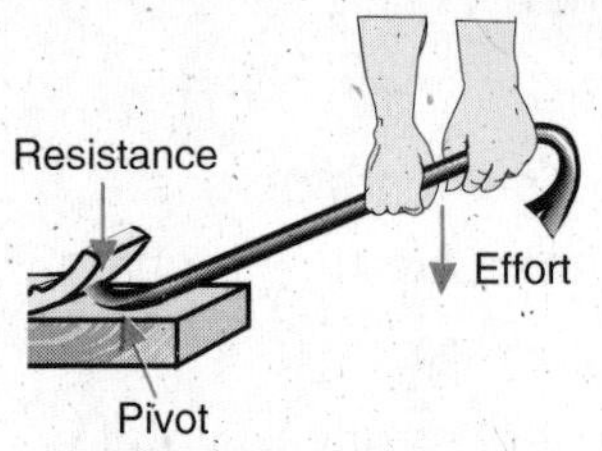

Lever

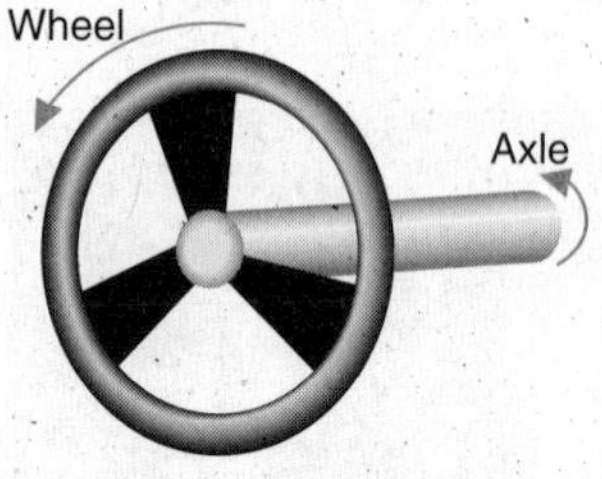

Wheel and Axle

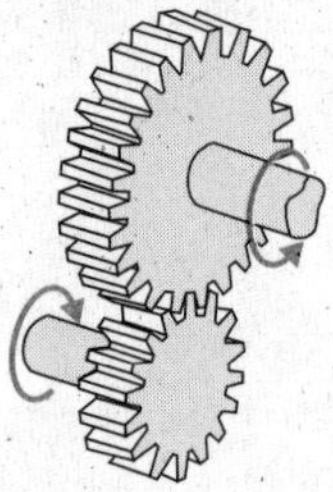
Gears

Simple Machines

Sometimes your effort cannot overcome the resistance. Then you need the help of a machine. If you have ever used a screwdriver to pry the lid off a paint can, you have used a machine. A **simple machine** is a device used to do work. There are several kinds of simple machines. A bicycle has three of them: a lever, a wheel and axle, and gears.

A **lever** is a bar that turns on a pivot. A **pivot** is an object on which another object turns. When you open the paint can, you are using the screwdriver as a lever. The lever transfers the force from your hand to the lid. The lever also multiplies your effort. The greater force overcomes the friction holding the lid on the can.

The number of times a machine multiplies your effort is the **mechanical advantage** of the machine. You may have noticed that a longer screwdriver is a better lever than a shorter screwdriver. That is because a longer lever gives a greater mechanical advantage.

A **wheel and axle** is another type of simple machine. It is made of two objects that turn in a circular motion on the same center. A wheel and axle doesn't always look like a wheel. A crank handle is a wheel and axle.

Gears are wheels with teeth. Unlike a wheel and axle, gears do not turn on the same center. The gears are arranged so that the teeth meet, and each gear turns on its own center. If you turn one gear, you cause any gear it touches to turn.

Understanding a Diagram A diagram is a picture that shows how something is put together or explains how something works. Some diagrams use arrows. To understand these diagrams, you have to look carefully at where the arrows point. In the diagram of a lever above, the arrow for the word *Resistance* shows the direction of the resistance force. The arrow for the word *Effort* shows that you have to push down on the lever to overcome the resistance.

1. The diagram of the lever indicates that when you push down on one end of a lever, the other end of the lever does what?
   a. also moves down b. moves up to overcome the resistance
2. In the diagram of gears, the arrows show that the two gears turn
   a. in the same direction b. in opposite directions

A Compound Machine

Sometimes it takes more than one machine to get a job done. A **compound machine** is made up of several simple machines. A bicycle is a compound machine. The brake handles and gearshifts are levers. The wheels and pedals are wheel and axle machines. Bicycles also contain gears. The number of "speeds" a bicycle has equals the number of front gears multiplied by the number of back gears. If a bike has many "speeds," you can get the mechanical advantage you need for any situation.

A bicycle is a compound machine.

A machine can multiply your effort. It can also multiply your speed. However, it cannot do both at once. When you ride a bicycle on a level path, you use the higher "speeds." The highest "speed" on a bicycle combines the largest front gear—at the pedals, which are a crank—with the smallest gear on the rear wheel. You have to pedal hard but not very quickly. Yet the bicycle moves quickly. The only resistance is friction, which is a small force. The bicycle is not multiplying your force. Instead, it is using your force to multiply your speed.

You use the lower "speeds" to climb hills. In the lowest "speed," you combine the smallest front gear at the pedals with the largest rear gear. You don't need to pedal hard. However, you do have to pedal quickly, even though the bike moves slowly. The bicycle is multiplying your effort to move you against a large force—gravity.

Drawing Conclusions Conclusions are ideas that are based on facts. They follow logically from the facts. The previous paragraph describes pedaling a bicycle on a hill at the lowest gear speed. The low gear speed multiplies your effort. From the facts in the paragraph you can conclude that pedaling uphill is easier on a 21-speed bike than on a one-speed bike, because the 21-speed bike multiplies your effort much more.

Based on the information in the first two paragraphs on this page, which can you conclude?

a. Gravity exerts a larger force when you ride up a hill than friction does on level ground.

b. Higher gear speeds result in more force on a level path than lower gear speeds do.

 Check your answer on page 247.

Thinking About the Article

Practice Vocabulary

The words below are in the passage in bold type. Study the way each word is used. Then complete each sentence by writing the correct word.

force **work** **simple machine**

mechanical advantage **compound machine**

1. A ____________________ is a push or a pull.
2. A basic device used to do work is called a ____________________.
3. A ____________________ like a bicycle contains several simple machines.
4. The number of times a machine multiplies your effort is the ____________________ of the machine.
5. In physics, ____________________ is done when a force causes an object to move.

Understand the Article

Circle the letter of the answer to each question.

6. Gravity, magnetism, and friction are all examples of
   a. forces
   b. energy
7. When effort force is greater than resistance force, what happens?
   a. movement, or work
   b. nothing
8. Why does it take less effort to pry up the lid of a paint can with a longer screwdriver than with a shorter screwdriver?
   a. The longer screwdriver provides a greater mechanical advantage.
   b. The longer screwdriver fits better under the lid of the can.

Match each simple machine with its example.

______ 9. lever

______ 10. wheel and axle

______ 11. gears

a. a doorknob

b. a crowbar

c. the wheels that turn the blade of a can opener

Apply Your Skills

Circle the number of the best answer for each question.

12. Refer to the diagram of a wheel and axle on page 180. What do the arrows in the diagram show?
    (1) The wheel and the axle turn in opposite directions.
    (2) The wheel and the axle turn in the same direction.
    (3) The wheel turns but the axle does not turn.
    (4) The axle turns but the wheel does not turn.
    (5) Neither the wheel nor the axle turns.

13. When gears turn, the teeth rub on each other. This adds extra resistance, which is due to which force?
    (1) friction
    (2) gravity
    (3) magnetism
    (4) motion
    (5) advantage

14. What happens when the resistance force is larger than the effort force?
    (1) The effort force will overcome the resistance force.
    (2) The effort force will stop.
    (3) The effort force will continue.
    (4) The resistance force will decrease.
    (5) No work will be done.

Connect with the Article

Write your answer to each question.

15. When you ride a bicycle up a hill, you can stand up as you pedal. How would this help you get up a hill?

____

____

____

16. What is one experience you or someone you know has had riding or repairing a bicycle? Discuss simple machines, effort, resistance, or work in your description.

____

____

____

Check your answers on page 247.

LESSON 24

Momentum

Vocabulary

energy

collision

momentum

elastic

At a baseball game, the sound of a bat colliding with a ball is unmistakable. This collision sends the ball flying. A well-hit baseball has a lot of momentum. That means it will travel a long distance through the air before it hits the ground. If the ball has enough momentum and takes the right path, it could leave the field for a home run.

There are several ways that batters can give a baseball more momentum when they hit it. One way is to swing the bat faster. Another way is to use a heavier bat. Some baseball players break the rules to give the ball more momentum.

Relate to the Topic

This lesson is about momentum. It explains what momentum is and how it is transferred when one object collides with another, such as when a bat hits a ball. Think about other sports you have played or watched.

When is momentum transferred in golf? ______________________

____

When is momentum transferred in bowling? ______________________

____

Reading Strategy

INTERPRETING PHOTO CAPTIONS A **caption** is a short sentence that accompanies a photo or other illustration. The caption explains what is shown in the illustration or gives more information about it. Captions help you understand what is pictured and how it relates to the surrounding text. Read the caption beneath the photo on page 187. Then answer the questions.

1. Who is the person shown in the photo? ______________________
   Hint: Look for a person's name in the caption.

2. Why does the article have a photo of that person?

   ____

   ____

   Hint: Look for at the headings on pages 186 and 187.

Check your answers on page 247.

Breaking the Rules

A major league pitcher can throw a fastball at more than 90 miles per hour. At this speed, the ball reaches the batter in less than half a second. The batter has only a bit more than one tenth of a second to decide if the pitch looks good. The batter must swing quickly. The swing cannot be early or late by more than a few thousandths of a second. If it is, what might have been a home run becomes a foul ball.

Even good batters get hits only about three out of ten times at bat. So batters are always looking for ways to improve their chances. Practice helps. Physical conditioning is also important. However, some batters look for ways that are outside the rules. Most of these ways involve changing the bat.

Collisions

A moving baseball has **energy,** the ability of matter to do work. A catcher can feel this energy as the pitched baseball slams into the mitt. In a **collision,** a moving object strikes another object. The second object may or may not be moving. A catcher's mitt is not moving at the time the ball collides with it. A bat, on the other hand, is moving as the ball collides with it.

These players have just collided.

All moving objects have momentum. **Momentum** is a measure of the motion of an object, and it depends on the object's weight and speed. When two objects collide, momentum is transferred from one object to the other. Suppose you stand still with your arm extended to the side. If someone throws a baseball into your hand, this collision will push your hand back. The ball transfers some of its momentum to your hand. The effect of the ball on your hand is greater if the ball has more momentum. This would be true if the ball were either heavier or moving faster.

The transfer of momentum is more complicated when both objects are moving. When the moving bat hits the moving ball, they are traveling in opposite directions. The bat is not moving as fast as the ball, but it is much heavier. Therefore, the bat has more momentum than the ball. When the two collide, the ball moves off in the direction in which the bat was swinging.

The transfer of momentum also depends on how elastic the objects are. Something that is **elastic** can be stretched or compressed and will return to its original shape. In many collisions much of the momentum is lost. If the colliding objects are very elastic, only a little momentum is lost. If you drop a golf ball and a Super Ball, the Super Ball will bounce higher. This is because the Super Ball is more elastic than the golf ball, so it loses much less momentum.

Drawing Conclusions A conclusion is an idea that follows logically from the information you have. Conclusions must be supported by facts. You have just read that a hit baseball moves in the direction in which the bat is swinging. You have also read that the bat has more momentum than the ball. From these facts, you can conclude that two colliding objects will move in the direction of the object that has more momentum.

Reread the third paragraph above. What can you conclude about the materials that Super Balls are made of?

a. Super Balls are made of materials that return to their original shape after being compressed.

b. Super Balls are made of materials that do not return to their original shape after being compressed.

Corking Bats

Some baseball players "cork" their bats. They cut off the top of the bat and hollow it out. They fill the space with cork, sawdust, or even Super Balls. Then they glue the top back on. Baseball players feel that this kind of change makes a bat springy. They think the bat becomes more elastic.

Corking bats is against the rules of professional baseball. If a player who hasn't been hitting well suddenly hits a string of home runs, the bat may be taken by the umpires. The bat is x-rayed or cut open. If the bat is corked, the player may be suspended from playing.

 Check your answer on page 247.

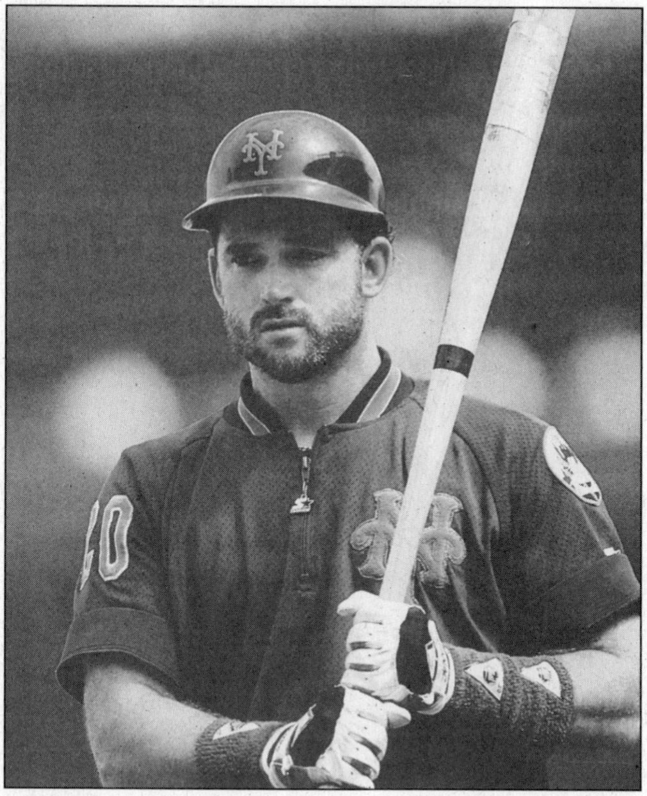
When Howard Johnson's hitting suddenly improved, he was accused of corking his bat. The bat was x-rayed and found to be solid wood.

Players who cork their bats are cheating. Yet there is so much money in professional baseball that some players are willing to cheat in order to play better. After retiring, one player admitted to using a corked bat for years. He believed that it enabled him to hit a lot of home runs. The player who used Super Balls got caught when his bat cracked. The balls bounced out right in front of the umpire!

What Does Corking a Bat Do?

Scientists have analyzed what happens when a bat is corked. They have found that the bat gets lighter. A batter can swing a lighter bat more quickly. In the opinion of some scientists, this is the reason that the corked bat is better. If the batter can swing more quickly, the swing can be started a bit later. This gives the batter a little more time to decide whether or not to swing at the ball.

Distinguishing Fact from Opinion Facts can be proven true. Opinions, on the other hand, are what someone believes, thinks, or feels. They may or may not be true. When reading about science topics, it is important to distinguish fact from opinion. Reread the previous paragraph. One fact in the paragraph is that a corked bat is lighter than a solid wood bat. One opinion is that a corked bat is better because a lighter bat requires less time to swing, giving the player extra time to decide whether to swing.

Reread the first paragraph above. Write *fact* or *opinion* next to each statement.

1. The player who used Super Balls got caught when his bat cracked. __________
2. Using a corked bat is the best way to hit more home runs. __________________

There may be one more advantage to the corked bat. This one is in the player's mind. If the batter thinks that the bat gives him an advantage, it may improve the batter's confidence. The batter steps up to the plate believing that he is about to hit a home run.

Check your answers on page 247.

Thinking About the Article

Practice Vocabulary

The words below are in the passage in bold type. Study the way each word is used. Then complete each sentence by writing the correct word.

energy **collision** **momentum** **elastic**

1. In a(n) ______________________, a moving object strikes another object.
2. An object's ______________________ depends on its weight and speed.
3. An object that is ______________________ returns to its original shape after being stretched or compressed.
4. ______________________ is the ability of matter to do work.

Understand the Article

Circle the letter of the best answer.

5. Why does a moving baseball bat have more momentum than the ball?
   a. The bat is much heavier than the ball.
   b. The bat is moving much faster than the ball.
6. How can you increase an object's momentum? Circle the letters of each correct answer.
   a. increase its weight
   b. make it more elastic
   c. increase its speed
   d. decrease its speed
7. Why do some baseball players cork their bats?
   a. They think it makes the bat more elastic, giving a hit ball more momentum.
   b. They think solid wood bats are too heavy to swing properly.
8. Which of the following items is more elastic?
   a. a golf ball
   b. a Super Ball
9. When a moving object collides with a standing one, what decides if the standing object will be moved? Circle the letter of each correct answer.
   a. the speed of the moving object
   b. the weight of the moving object
   c. the weight of the standing object

Apply Your Skills

Circle the number of the best answer for each question.

10. Based on the information about collisions in the article, which conclusion can you make?
    (1) Collisions occur only when two objects are moving.
    (2) Collisions occur only when one object is moving.
    (3) All momentum is lost in collisions.
    (4) The momentum of a moving object increases after a collision.
    (5) A standing object will move if enough momentum is transferred.

11. Which of the following statements describes a fact?
    (1) A corked bat helps batters hit the ball better.
    (2) A corked bat can make a poor hitter into a good hitter.
    (3) A corked bat is lighter than a solid bat.
    (4) A corked bat will help a player hit more home runs.
    (5) A corked bat is better than a solid bat.

12. From the appearance of a car after a collision, what can you conclude about cars?
    (1) Cars have little momentum.
    (2) Cars have more momentum than trucks.
    (3) Cars usually collide with moving objects.
    (4) Cars are not very elastic.
    (5) Cars return to their original shapes after a crash.

Connect with the Article

Write your answer to each question.

13. Your friend is in a compact car and you are in a sport utility vehicle. Both vehicles are moving at the same speed along a highway. Which has more momentum? Explain your answer.

14. Think about a time when you collided with something while riding in a car, walking, or playing a sport. What was the collision and the transfer of momentum like?

Check your answers on page 247.

Lesson 25

Electricity

Vocabulary

electronics

electron

transistor

diode

integrated circuits

printed circuit board

microprocessor

software

The contest between humans and machines is part of American folklore. According to legend, John Henry, the strongest man working on the railroads in the mid-1800s, died after he outperformed a steam powered machine that drilled through rock. The steam engine could do the work of many people, but in less time.

A modern version of that contest took place between a chess master and a masterpiece of electronics, a computer named Deep Blue. Like a steam engine, a computer allows people to do certain things faster than they could by other means.

Relate to the Topic

This lesson is about electricity and electronic devices. It describes how electronic devices work and what some of them can be used for. Think about an electronic device you have used.

What kind of electronic device was it? ______________________

How did the device change the way you perform a task?

____

____

Reading Strategy

SCANNING BOLDFACED WORDS Science materials often highlight technical terms in bold type—type which is darker than the type around it. Look at the boldfaced terms on pages 191 and 192. Then answer the questions.

1. What are electrons? ______________________

   ____

   Hint: Look at the last paragraph.

2. What device allows current to flow in one direction only?

   ____

   Hint: Look under the heading Electronic Components.

Check your answers on page 248.

Computers and Electronics

It was a dramatic battle between a human and a machine—the world's greatest chess player against a computer. The battleground was a chessboard. Garry Kasparov represented humankind. IBM's Deep Blue supercomputer was the challenger. Chess is a game with clear and strict rules, yet it is complex enough to challenge some of the finest human minds. Until Deep Blue, no machine had been able to beat a reigning chess champion.

In 1996 Deep Blue and Kasparov met for their first six-game match. Much to his surprise, Kasparov lost the first game. But he was able to adjust his playing style to take advantage of Deep Blue's weaknesses. Kasparov went on to win the match. For the time being, humankind had prevailed.

How Deep Blue Plays Chess

Deep Blue's approach to chess is very different from that of a human being. A chess master like Kasparov plays by recognizing patterns, forming concepts, and creating plans based on experience. In contrast, Deep Blue relies primarily on its ability to calculate quickly. It can analyze the consequences of 200 million chess positions per second. This speed is made possible by advances in **electronics,** a branch of engineering. Electronics is concerned with controlling the motion of electrons to generate, transmit, receive, and store information. **Electrons** are tiny particles of matter with a negative electrical charge.

Garry Kasparov used his wits to defeat Deep Blue's calculating power in their first match.

A printed circuit board.

Electronic Components

When electrons flow, they create an electric current. This current can be controlled by devices called electronic components. There are many types of electronic components, and each affects electric current in different ways. For example, a **transistor** is a device that can be used to amplify, detect, or switch electric current on and off. A **diode** allows current to flow in one direction only.

Components can be linked together in a circuit to perform specific tasks. For example, the circuits in a TV remote control unit allow you to change channels and turn the TV on and off. Today **integrated circuits** are so tiny they fit on a small silicon chip. Each chip can contain several hundred thousand components. Many chips can be connected to form even more complex circuits. Electronic components, including integrated circuits, are attached to a **printed circuit board.** They are connected by a pattern of metal tracks along which electrons flow. Printed circuit boards are found in many types of machines, from digital watches to cars to computers like Deep Blue.

Restating or Paraphrasing To **paraphrase** a passage means to restate the passage in a different way while keeping the same meaning. Paraphrasing can be done by using different words or by rearranging most of the same words. For example, the first sentence on this page can be paraphrased as, "Electrons create an electric current when they flow." The new sentence has the same meaning as the original sentence.

Which sentence paraphrases the second sentence on this page?

a. Devices called electronic components can control an electric current.
b. Devices called electric currents can control electronic components.

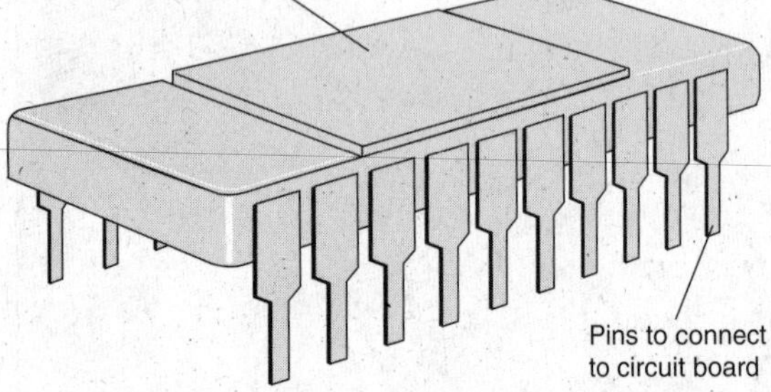

Microprocessor

Microprocessors

The most complex and advanced integrated circuits are the **microprocessors** of computers. These devices function as the computer's central processing unit, controlling the computer and performing calculations. First developed by Intel in the early 1970s, the microprocessor made small personal computers possible. Before the microprocessor, computers were very large, often taking up several rooms.

 Check your answer on page 248.

The central processing unit of a personal computer is usually on one microprocessor. In contrast, Deep.Blue has 32 microprocessors, all working at the same time. Each coordinates the work of 16 special-purpose "chess chips." This combination of microprocessors and special chips designed for a particular use is the basis for superior problem-solving computers.

Kasparov Versus Deep Blue, Round Two

After Kasparov's 1996 win, the computer scientists and chess experts on IBM's Deep Blue team went back to work to improve its performance. They doubled Deep Blue's speed by adding new microprocessors to its central processing unit. They doubled the number of special-purpose chess chips. These changes increased Deep Blue's calculation power tremendously.

The team made Deep Blue approach chess more as a human being does. They gave it more chess knowledge by redesigning the chess chips. And they gave it a limited ability to adjust to Kasparov's playing. They did this by designing **software,** instructions to the computer, that enabled them to change Deep Blue's playing between games.

Recognizing Cause and Effect Situations in which one thing makes another thing happen are cause-and-effect relationships. For example, the IBM team gave Deep Blue more chess knowledge and software that enabled them to adjust its playing. These causes led to an effect—Deep Blue was able to play chess more like a human being. What was the effect of adding new microprocessors to Deep Blue's central processing unit?

a. Deep Blue's speed doubled.
b. Deep Blue had better decision-making capabilities.

Kasparov also prepared for the 1997 rematch. He decided to use unusual opening moves, hoping that Deep Blue would not be prepared for them. He also decided to use odd playing styles. By doing this he hoped to confuse Deep Blue's ability to evaluate the positions of pieces on the chess board.

Kasparov's strategy worked for the first game, and he won. But Deep Blue's team changed the computer's strategy for the second game. Instead of trying to take Kasparov's pieces, it began to "crowd" him, limiting the moves he could make. Kasparov was so rattled by Deep Blue's change in strategy that he lost the second game. By the sixth game, Kasparov gave in to the pressure. He resigned the game after just 19 moves, making Deep Blue the match winner. It was the first time a computer had won a chess match against a reigning world champion.

To most people, Kasparov's battle with Deep Blue was mainly a contest between a man and a machine. But to the people at IBM who designed Deep Blue, it was an opportunity to test a complex computer system. The knowledge gained from these two chess matches can be applied to a variety of complex tasks, including analyzing financial data and predicting the behavior of molecules.

Check your answer on page 248.

Thinking About the Article

Practice Vocabulary

The words below are in the passage in bold type. Study the way each word is used. Then match each word to its meaning. Write the letter.

_____ 1. electronics

_____ 2. transistor

_____ 3. diode

_____ 4. integrated circuit

_____ 5. microprocessor

a. an electronic circuit that fits on a small silicon chip

b. an electronic device that allows current to flow in only one direction

c. a complex integrated circuit that serves as a computer's central processing unit

d. an electronic component that can be used as an amplifier, detector, or switch

e. a branch of engineering concerned with devices that control the flow of electric current

Understand the Article

Write or circle the answer to each question.

6. When playing chess, Deep Blue relied primarily on its ability to do what?
   a. make calculations fast b. imitate its human opponent

7. What is an electronic component? Give one example.

   ____

   ____

8. What is the purpose of the metal tracks on a printed circuit board?
   a. They connect the electronic components on the board, allowing electrons to flow along them.
   b. They prevent the board from cracking after heavy use.

9. What development in electronics made personal computers possible?
   a. transistors b. microprocessors

10. What is the chief difference between an ordinary personal computer and IBM's Deep Blue?
   a. An ordinary personal computer has transistors and diodes, and Deep Blue did not.
   b. An ordinary personal computer has one microprocessor, and Deep Blue had at least 32.

Apply Your Skills

Circle the number of the best answer for each question.

11. Refer to the first paragraph on page 191. Which of the following sentences best paraphrases the last sentence in that paragraph?
    (1) Even Deep Blue had been unable to beat a reigning chess champion.
    (2) No machine, not even Deep Blue, has been able to beat a reigning chess champion.
    (3) No reigning chess champion or machine had been able to beat Deep Blue.
    (4) No machine had beaten a reigning chess champion until Deep Blue did it.
    (5) No reigning chess champion had beaten a machine until Deep Blue did it.

12. What was one result of the development of the microprocessor? Computers
    (1) were able to make calculations
    (2) had central processing units that took up several rooms
    (3) were able to play chess
    (4) no longer needed printed circuit boards
    (5) became much smaller

13. What was the effect of the new software that Deep Blue's designers developed before the second chess match?
    (1) It increased Deep Blue's ability to evaluate chess positions.
    (2) It gave Deep Blue more chess knowledge.
    (3) It enabled Deep Blue's playing to be adjusted between games.
    (4) It enabled Deep Blue to remember previous moves.
    (5) It cut the time between games in half.

Connect with the Article

Write your answer to each question.

14. What are at least three machines that you or your family own that have electronic components?

____

____

15. After Kasparov lost to Deep Blue, some people concluded that computers were smarter than people. Do you agree? Why or why not?

____

____

Check your answers on page 248.

Lesson 26

Light and Lasers

Vocabulary

laser

light

frequency

wavelength

What do you think of when you hear the word *laser?* Perhaps you think of a laser light show at a concert or planetarium. Or you might imagine a laser printer connected to a computer. You might even picture science fiction characters fighting with laser weapons.

Does the word *laser* make you think of medical tools? It could, because lasers and the light that they produce are often used as tools in surgery. Lasers are ideal for the delicate skin treatments needed in some types of cosmetic surgery.

Relate to the Topic

This lesson is about light and lasers. It explains how laser light is different from ordinary light. It also describes how lasers are used in cosmetic surgery. Think about the idea of using cosmetic surgery to change your appearance.

If you could change one feature with cosmetic surgery, what would you change? ______________________________

____

Why would you change that feature? ______________________________

____

____

Reading Strategy

PREVIEWING DIAGRAMS Two of the most important elements of a diagram are the title and the labels. The title tells you the main idea of the diagram. The labels identify important details. Look at the diagram on page 199. Then answer the questions.

1. What is the main idea of the diagram? ______________________________

   ____

   Hint: Read the title.

2. What is the first step in producing laser light? ______________________________

   ____

   Hint: Look for a label marked with the number 1.

Check your answers on page 248.

Laser Surgery

On the morning of her 44th birthday, Paulette examined her face in the mirror. The bags under her eyes were dark and huge. A few age spots clustered on her cheeks. Wrinkles and frown lines were everywhere. Paulette thought about getting a chemical peel to improve her skin, but she didn't like the idea of putting strong chemicals on her face. She briefly considered a face lift, but it was too expensive. Finally, Paulette decided to go for the latest treatment—a laser peel.

Cosmetic surgeons perform laser peels, also called laser resurfacing, using a special type of laser. A **laser** produces a narrow beam of light that is strong and hot. Older lasers produced a continuous beam of intense light, making them ideal for cutting. The new lasers used for most cosmetic surgery produce short bursts of light. They pulse on and off in less than a thousandth of a second. These fast pulses are strong enough to burn off surface skin cells. Yet the pulsing prevents the heat from burning deep into the skin. This keeps the laser from hurting the deeper layers of skin that produce new cells and healthy looking skin. The pulsing laser has another benefit. It shrinks the skin, making sagging skin look tight and young.

Paulette's laser peel took about half an hour. Her surgeon had a computerized system that allowed him to map areas of her face and adjust the laser's energy. He used less energy near her eyes, where the skin is thin. He used more energy near her mouth, where the skin is thicker.

The surgery was short, but the recovery was long. Paulette had to treat her face to keep it moist and free from infection. Her skin was swollen, red, and tender for four weeks. Yet Paulette thinks the treatment was worth it. Six months after her laser peel, she loves the way her face looks—young, clear, and smooth.

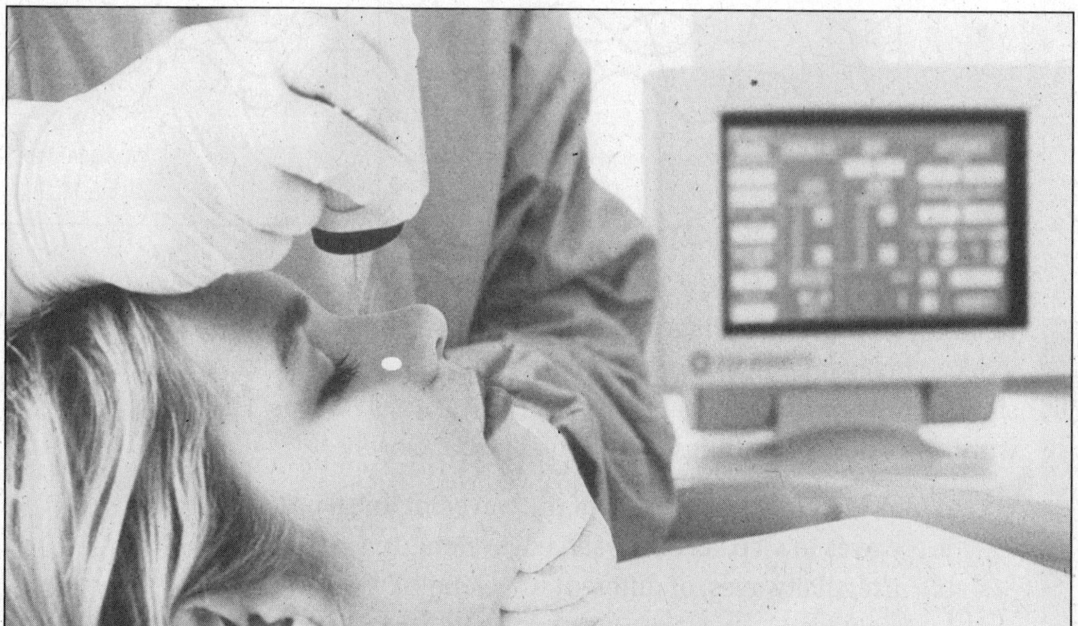

A cosmetic surgeon uses a laser to remove wrinkles and tighten the skin.

Removing wrinkles and age spots is not the only use of lasers in cosmetic surgery. Lasers can remove birthmarks, warts, scars, and tattoos. They are also used in other types of surgery in which precise, delicate control is needed. For example, they are used by eye surgeons to correct vision. Different kinds of lasers are used for each purpose. However, they all have the same basic design.

Getting in Step

Light is a form of energy that travels in waves. Other kinds of waves include sound waves, radio waves, and X rays. A wave has a regular pattern. It is usually drawn as a curved line that goes up and down. If you drop a stone into a pond, ripples of water move out in a circle. Each ripple is a wave. The energy of the wave makes the water move up and down. The **frequency** is the number of waves that pass a point in a certain amount of time. The **wavelength** is the distance from the top of one wave to the top of the next wave.

What we see as ordinary white light is made up of all the colors of a rainbow. Each color of light has its own frequency and wavelength. Imagine a crowd of people moving forward at the same speed. The people are not trying to walk in step. This is what ordinary light is like. Now imagine the crowd all marching in step. This is what laser light is like. All the waves have the same frequency and wavelength.

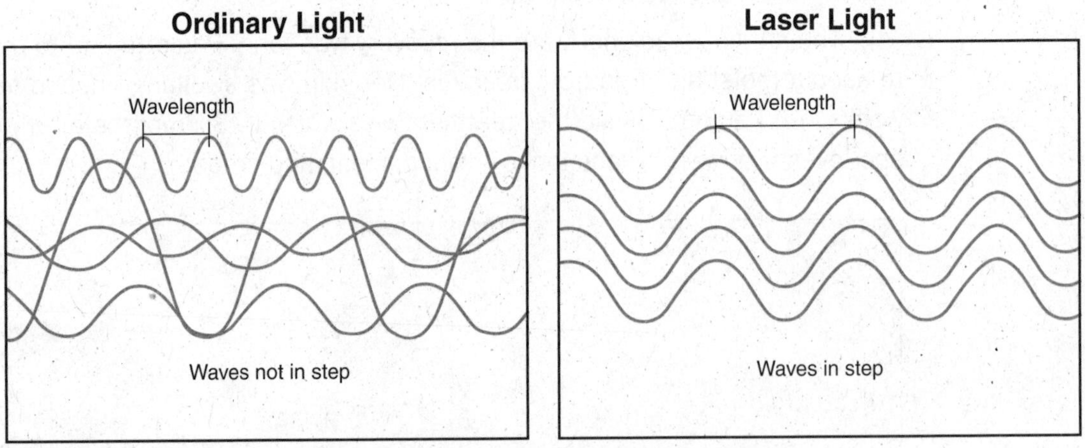

Reading a Diagram A **diagram** can help you see how something looks or works. This helps you follow what the author is describing. The diagrams above show how ordinary light waves differ from laser light waves. The labels are words that point out things you should look at closely.

1. Which is a good description of the wavelengths of ordinary light?
   a. waves in step, all of the same wavelength
   b. irregular waves, of different wavelengths

2. What is an important characteristic of laser light?
   a. Its wavelengths are all the same.
   b. Its waves are irregular.

 Check your answers on page 248.

How a Laser Works

A laser contains a material that will give off light waves that are all in step. A burst of electrical or light energy is applied to a tube. This energy is absorbed by the atoms in the tube. The atoms then give off the energy in the form of light. All the light given off has the same wavelength and frequency. A mirror at one end of the tube reflects light completely. A mirror at the other end reflects only some light. The light is reflected back and forth between the mirrors. The light gets stronger and stronger as this happens. When the light becomes strong enough, it passes through the partially reflecting mirror. This light is the laser beam.

How a Laser Produces Light

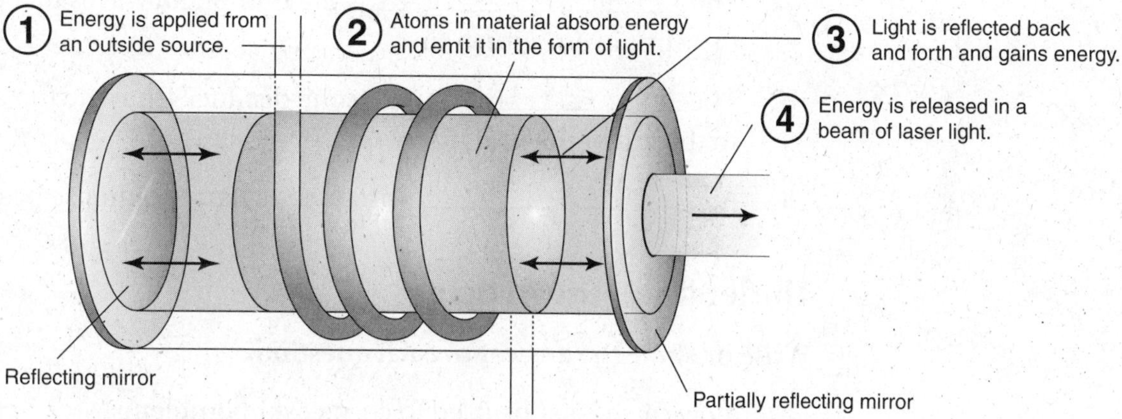
1 Energy is applied from an outside source.
2 Atoms in material absorb energy and emit it in the form of light.
3 Light is reflected back and forth and gains energy.
4 Energy is released in a beam of laser light.
Reflecting mirror
Partially reflecting mirror

Understanding Sequence The order in which things happen is called sequence. Understanding sequence helps you understand how things like lasers work. For example, the paragraph above explains the sequence of events that leads to the production of the laser beam. The diagram helps you visualize this sequence. The first step in producing a laser beam is applying energy to the laser. What happens after the light reflects back and forth between the mirrors?

a. The light is strong enough to pass through the partially reflecting mirror.
b. Energy is absorbed by the atoms in the tube.

Lasers with Different Wavelengths

What makes one kind of laser different from another is the material in the tube. Each type of material gives off a different wavelength of laser light. And different substances in the body absorb different wavelengths of light. Thus lasers of different wavelengths can be used on different types of tissue in laser surgery.

For example, removing a tattoo is similar to removing wrinkles and spots. The wavelength of the laser must be matched to the wavelength absorbed by the tattoo, which depends on its color. If a tattoo has more than one color, more than one laser treatment is needed. Removing some professional tattoos requires six to ten treatments. This is something to consider before getting a tattoo!

Check your answer on page 248.

Thinking About the Article

Practice Vocabulary

The words below are in the passage in bold type. Study the way each word is used. Then complete each sentence by writing the correct word.

laser **light** **frequency** **wavelength**

1. ______________ is a form of visible energy that travels in waves.
2. The ______________ is the number of waves that pass a point in a certain amount of time.
3. The ______________ is the distance from the top of one wave to the top of the next wave.
4. A ______________ produces a narrow, intense beam of light.

Understand the Article

Write or circle the answer to each question.

5. How can a laser be used to correct skin problems?
   a. The laser is used to make an incision, and then the surgeon uses other tools to correct the problem.
   b. The laser burns off the thin upper layer of skin, allowing new skin to form from the healthy layers below.
6. How are light, sound, and X rays similar?

   ____

   ____
7. Which is the correct description of laser light?
   a. All the waves are in step with one another.
   b. All the waves have different frequencies.
8. What determines the type of light produced by a laser?
   a. the material inside the laser tube
   b. the length of the laser tube
9. Why are lasers of different wavelengths useful in surgery?
   a. Different substances absorb different wavelengths of laser light, so a particular substance can be targeted, leaving other nearby substances alone.
   b. The different wavelengths are absorbed by many layers of skin, enabling surgeons to make deeper incisions.

Apply Your Skills

Circle the number of the best answer for each question.

10. According to the diagrams on page 198, what is a wavelength?
    (1) the time it takes for one wave to pass a given point
    (2) the number of waves that pass a given point in a given time
    (3) the distance between the highest and lowest part of a wave
    (4) the distance between the top of one wave and the top of the next
    (5) the midpoint of a wave

11. What is the first thing that happens when energy is applied to a laser tube?
    (1) The atoms in the tube absorb the energy.
    (2) The atoms in the tube give off the energy in the form of light.
    (3) Mirrors reflect the light back and forth to increase its energy.
    (4) The material in the tube changes state.
    (5) The laser light passes through one end of the tube.

12. According to the diagram on page 199, what do the mirrors in a laser do?
    (1) provide technicians with a way to see what is happening inside
    (2) direct a beam of light at the targeted object
    (3) reflect the light back and forth
    (4) change the angle at which light hits the sides of the tube
    (5) focus the light on the energy source inside the laser

Connect with the Article

Write your answer to each question.

13. When he was 18, Jim had his arm tattooed with his girlfriend's name in blue inside a dark red heart. Now Jim is getting married to another woman and his fiancee wants him to have the tattoo removed. How many treatments will he need?

____

____

____

14. Suppose you had a skin spot that could be removed either by applying a chemical or by laser. Would you try the laser? Why or why not?

____

____

____

Check your answers on pages 248–249.

LESSON 27

Sound Waves

Sound Waves

Sound Waves

Sound Waves

Vocabulary

pitch

pure tone

overtones

timbre

amplitude

resonance

Music is performed throughout the world for many different purposes. It's enjoyed as a source of entertainment. It is an important part of rituals in many religions. Music can be used to calm emotions, to rouse patriotism, and to stir people to action.

No matter why it is performed or how it is created, all music involves sound. Musical sounds have the same properties as other kinds of sound.

Relate to the Topic

This lesson is about music. It describes the basic features of musical sounds. It also explains why different instruments produce different sounds. Think about the music you listen to.

What kinds of music do you enjoy listening to most?

____

____

What instruments are usually played to make that music?

____

____

Reading Strategy

RELATING TO WHAT YOU KNOW When you read, try to relate what you are reading to what you already know about the topic. The topic of this lesson is the physics of the sounds we call music. Then answer the questions.

1. How do the sounds of a foghorn and a referee's whistle differ?

   ____

   Hint: Think about times when you heard each sound.

2. How do the sounds of an exploding firecracker and a snapping twig differ?

   ____

   ____

   Hint: Think about how you reacted when you heard each sound.

Check your answers on page 249.

The Physics of Music

Suppose someone asked you, "What is music?" What answer would you give? Everyone knows music when they hear it, but coming up with a definition of music is not an easy thing to do. Music usually involves an organized series of sounds with a definite pattern or rhythm. It may help to think of music as both art and physics. The art involves combining different sounds in a way that makes listeners feel a certain way—relaxed, excited, happy, or sad. The physics of music has to do with how the sounds are produced and controlled.

Sound is produced whenever an object, such as a guitar string, vibrates. A vibrating guitar string moves back and forth many times. Each time it moves out, it compresses the air in a small region next to it. Each time it moves back, it makes a small region of less compressed air. The alternating regions of compressed and less compressed air travel out from the string. These are the **sound waves** you hear when the guitar is strummed. You can imitate a sound wave by stretching a spring toy and then tapping one end of it. The tap will compress the coils near that end, and the compression will move through the coils to the other end.

When a sound wave reaches your ears, it makes your eardrums vibrate. The vibration passes to your inner ear. Nerves in your inner ear convert the sound wave to an electrical impulse and send the impulse to your brain. In your brain, the electrical impulse is interpreted as sound. The type of sound that you hear depends mainly on three physical characteristics of the sound wave: its frequency, its harmonics, and its amplitude.

The faster an object vibrates, the more regions of compressed and decompressed air the object produces in a certain amount of time. A pair of alternating regions of compressed and decompressed air is called a cycle. The number of cycles produced each second is the frequency of the sound. Frequency is measured in hertz, abbreviated Hz. One hertz equals one cycle per second.

Most people with good hearing can hear sounds that have frequencies ranging from about 15 Hz to 20,000 Hz. A tuba can make sounds with frequencies as low as 40 Hz, and a piano can go as low as 30 Hz. At the high end, piccolos, violins, and some other instruments can make sounds with frequencies as high as 15,000 Hz. You perceive the frequency of a sound wave as its **pitch.** A high-pitched sound, such as one made by a piccolo, has a higher frequency than a low-pitched sound, such as one made by a tuba.

Sound Wave Frequency

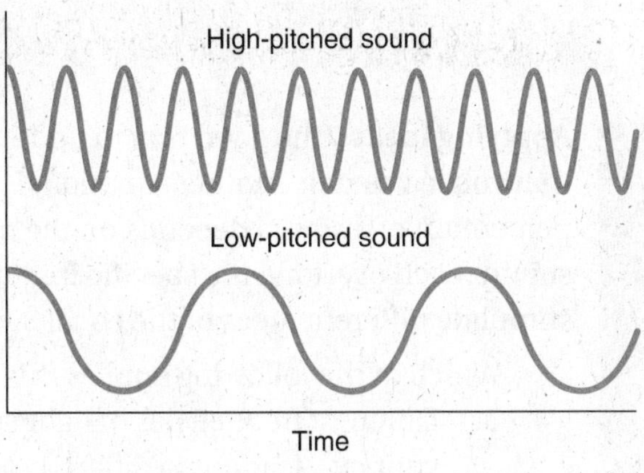

Many factors affect the pitch of sounds made by an instrument. One factor is its size. Usually, larger instruments can make lower-pitched sounds than smaller instruments of the same type. For example, the lowest note on a violin has a frequency of 190 Hz. The lowest note on a cello, which is shaped like a violin but is much larger, has a frequency of 70 Hz. Another factor that affects pitch is the amount of tension, or stiffness, in the part that vibrates. On a stringed instrument, the tension in each string can be adjusted by turning a screw that the string is wrapped around. Turning the screw one way increases the tension in the string, raising the pitch. Turning the screw the other way decreases the tension, lowering the pitch.

Harmonics

Sound Wave Harmonics

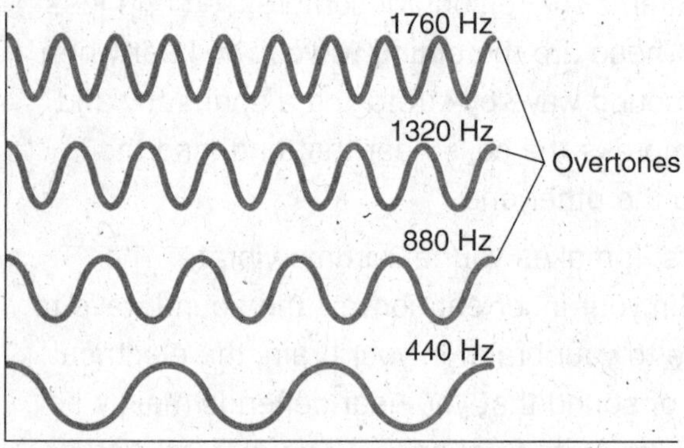

A tuning fork produces a sound made up of a single frequency. Such a sound is known as a **pure tone.** In contrast, all musical instruments produce sounds that consist of more than one frequency, even when a single note is played. For instance, when the note A above middle C is played on a piano, the main frequency of the sound that is produced is 440 Hz, but other frequencies are produced at the same time. The other frequencies, called harmonics, or **overtones,** are exact multiples of 440 Hz: 880 Hz (two times 440), 1320 Hz (three times 440), 1760 Hz (four times 440), and so on.

The number and strength of overtones determines the quality, or **timbre,** of a note. That's because different sound frequencies stimulate different areas of the cochlea—a structure in your inner ear. When a particular point in the cochlea is stimulated, nerve signals are sent to the brain. The brain interprets the signal, and you perceive a certain pitch. The combination of signals caused by overtones of a note determines how you perceive that note. You can tell whether the note is being played on a piano or a trumpet because the overtones from each instrument have different strengths.

Applying Ideas One good way to understand a new situation is to apply an idea that you learned in another situation. For example, you just read that your perception of a sound depends on the number and strength of overtones in the sound. Each overtone is a specific frequency, and different frequencies stimulate different areas of the cochlea in the inner ear.

Which of the following applies this model of perception to a new situation?

a. Different frequencies of light stimulate different light-sensitive cells in your eye, leading to different perceptions of color.

b. Some animals have eyes that are very sensitive to light, so they can see better at night than other animals can.

 Check your answer on page 249.

Amplitude

The more forcefully something vibrates, the more it compresses the air next to it. The extent to which the air is compressed in a sound wave is the called the **amplitude** of the wave. When a sound wave is drawn on a graph, the amplitude is shown by the height of the wave. The greater the amplitude of a sound wave, the harder the wave strikes your eardrums and the louder the sound that you hear. As a result, you perceive the amplitude of a sound wave as loudness. Loudness is measured in units called decibels.

Sound Wave Amplitude

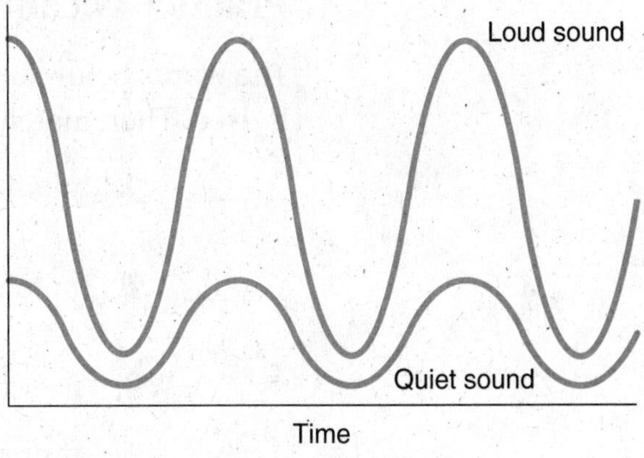

Loudness of Some Common Sounds

Sound	Decibels	Sound	Decibels
Quiet whisper	20	Lawn mower	85
Rustling leaves	40	Chain saw	115
Conversation	60	Rock concert	120
Hair dryer	75	Jet plane taking off	150

Reading Charts A chart is a simple table that presents information in rows and columns. Information is often easier to find when it is listed this way than when it is written in a paragraph. In the chart above, different kinds of sounds are listed under the column headings "Sound." The loudness of each sound is listed to the right in the same row, under the column heading "Decibels." For example, the chart shows that the loudness of a quiet whisper is 20 decibels.

According to the chart, which is louder?

a. lawn mower b. chain saw

Some small things that vibrate don't make very loud sounds by themselves because they don't compress much air. For example, if you strike a tuning fork, it will make a noise that you can barely hear unless you hold the tuning fork close to your ear. But if you strike the tuning fork again and touch the end to a hollow box of the right size, the noise will be louder. The vibrating tuning fork makes the box vibrate at the same frequency. This process is called **resonance.** Many musical instruments use resonance to make their sounds louder. For example, the body of an acoustic guitar, the bell of a trumpet, and the shell of a drum are all hollow structures that vibrate, or resonate, when another part of the instrument vibrates.

 Check your answer on page 249.

Thinking About the Article

Practice Vocabulary

The words below are in the passage in bold type. Study the way each word is used. Then match each word to its meaning. Write the letter.

______ 1. pitch	a.	the quality of a musical note based on the number and strength of overtones
______ 2. pure tone	b.	how the frequency of a sound wave is perceived
______ 3. overtone	c.	a measure of the height of a wave
______ 4. timbre	d.	when something that vibrates makes something else vibrate at the same frequency
______ 5. amplitude	e.	a frequency of sound that is an exact multiple of another frequency
______ 6. resonance	f.	a sound that consists of a single frequency

Understand the Article

Write or circle the answer to each question.

7. What creates a sound wave? ________________________________

____

8. Which is the frequency of a sound wave?
   a. the extent to which air is compressed in the wave
   b. the number of alternating regions of compression and decompression (cycles) that occur each second

9. If two musical instruments are of the same type, which one can usually produce lower-pitched sounds?
   a. the larger instrument   b. the smaller instrument

10. Why does a note played on a harmonica sound different from the same note played on a clarinet?
    a. The note lasts longer on the clarinet than on the harmonica.
    b. The overtones of each instrument have different strengths.

11. What physical characteristic of sound waves is perceived as loudness?

____

Apply Your Skills

Circle the number of the best answer for each question.

12. When you pluck a rubber band while stretching it, it will make a higher sound the farther you stretch it. Which idea does this illustrate?
    (1) Larger objects make lower-pitched sounds than smaller objects.
    (2) The number of overtones determines the quality of a note.
    (3) Pitch depends on the amount of tension in the part that vibrates.
    (4) Resonance enhances the sounds produced by many musical instruments.
    (5) Sound waves with greater amplitude strike your eardrums harder.

13. The sounds made by a music box will be louder if you set the music box on a table than if you hold it in the air. What causes this increase in loudness?
    (1) resonance
    (2) harmonics
    (3) timbre
    (4) frequency
    (5) compression

14. Refer to the chart on page 205. According to the chart, which sounds are both quieter than the sound of a hair dryer?
    (1) quiet whisper and lawn mower
    (2) chain saw and rustling leaves
    (3) conversation and rock concert
    (4) lawn mower and jet plane taking off
    (5) rustling leaves and conversation

Connect with the Article

Write your answer to each question.

15. Why do most men have lower-pitched voices than most women?

____

____

16. Exposure to loud sounds can cause permanent hearing loss. What can you do to protect your hearing?

____

____

Check your answers on page 249.

Science at Work

Construction: Insulation Contractor

Have you ever wondered what helps keep your home warm in the winter and cool in the summer? Through the use of insulation materials, homes and workplaces are kept at appropriate temperatures all year round. Selecting and installing the proper insulation materials are the responsibility of insulation contractors.

Insulation contractors pick the type of insulation material best suited for specific places in a building. Basements, walls, attics, water heaters, and ceilings are just some of the places where they apply their knowledge of insulation material selection and installation.

Insulation contractors must understand basic physics principles such as energy and heat transfer, condensation, and evaporation. They must also have good math and measurement skills and be able to read blueprints and other diagrams. The frequent introduction of new building materials and building safety codes requires that insulation contractors keep up to date about new developments in their field.

Look at the Some Careers in Construction chart.

- Do any of the careers interest you? If so, which ones?
- What information would you need to find out more about those careers? On a separate piece of paper, write some questions that you would like answered. You can find more information about those careers in the *Occupational Outlook Handbook* at your local library or online.

Some Careers in Construction

Carpenter
frames, finishes, and remodels buildings and furniture

Drywall Installer
measures, installs, and finishes drywall or sheetrock surfaces in homes and buildings

Plumber
installs and repairs water pipes and drains

Roofer
repairs leaks and problems in roofs; removes old material and installs new roofs

Use these guidelines to answer the questions that follow.

Insulation Installation Guidelines

1. Before installing any insulation material, check for and seal any air leaks in the structure.
2. Check for sufficient ventilation and circulation of air in the building. Sufficient ventilation must be present to control moisture from condensation in heated areas of the building and to allow for circulation of clean air.
3. Select appropriate insulation material.
   a. Blanket insulation—laid in unfinished attic spaces, walls, and floors. Trim blanket to fit snugly in space.
   b. Loose-fill particles—blown into attic spaces or other unfinished, accessible building openings. Adhesive solutions may also be applied to help particles hold together if necessary.
   c. Spray foams—sprayed into hard-to-reach areas or between framing timbers. Must be applied with care, because the foam will expand to 30 times its original volume.
   d. Rigid insulation—used as exterior or interior protection. Some types may include foil layer to prevent moisture buildup.
   e. Foil insulation—applied before finishing ceilings, walls, or floors. Good at shielding against extreme summer heat and preventing winter heat loss.

1. Which would be the best insulation to put behind an existing interior brick wall?
   (1) blanket insulation
   (2) loose-fill particles
   (3) spray foam
   (4) rigid insulation
   (5) foil insulation

2. Which of the following would be an effective insulation material for homes in desert environments?
   (1) blanket insulation
   (2) loose-fill particles
   (3) spray foam
   (4) rigid insulation
   (5) foil insulation

3. Heat loss occurs when warm air moves from heated sections of a home to unheated sections. Using a separate piece of paper, explain why it would be important for the contractor to install insulation material under the floor of a room located above the home's garage.

Check your answers on page 249.

UNIT 4

Unit 4 Review
Physics

The Inclined Plane

A **simple machine** is a device used to do work. An inclined plane is one type of simple machine. An **inclined plane** is a long, sloping surface that helps raise an object that cannot be easily lifted. A ramp is an example of an inclined plane. Imagine trying to get a person in a wheelchair onto a porch that is one foot above the ground. Lifting the person and the wheelchair straight up would be difficult. You may not be able to exert a large enough force to do this. However, if the porch had a four-foot-long ramp, you could more easily get the person and the wheelchair onto the porch.

The amount of work done depends on the force needed and the distance moved. You would need less force to move the person up the ramp than to lift her straight up. However, you would have to move the person a longer distance, four feet instead of one. Therefore, it takes about the same amount of work to push the person up the four-foot ramp as it does to lift the person one foot straight up.

Friction is a force between surfaces that rub against each other. Friction makes it harder to use an inclined plane. It is easy to use an inclined plane to move a person in a wheelchair because the wheels have little friction. But if you had to push a box up the same ramp, you would need a large force just to overcome the friction.

Write the word or words that best complete each statement.

1. A(n) ____________________ is a long, sloping surface that helps raise an object that cannot be lifted.

2. ____________________ is a force between surfaces that rub against each other.

Circle the number of the best answer.

3. In which situation would you need to exert the least force?
   (1) lifting a 75-pound box to a height of one foot
   (2) lifting a 120-pound box to a height of one foot
   (3) pushing a 75-pound box up a ramp three feet long
   (4) pushing a wheeled 75-pound cart up a ramp three feet long
   (5) lifting a wheeled 75-pound cart up to a height of one foot

Momentum

If an object is moving, it has momentum. The object's **momentum** depends on its weight and speed. The faster an object moves and the heavier it is, the more momentum it has. If an object is not moving, it has no momentum.

An object's **momentum** depends on its weight and speed. Momentum is involved in the game of pool, which is played with balls on a large table. All the balls weigh the same. Players use a heavy stick, called a cue, to hit a white ball, called the cue ball. When the cue collides with the cue ball, momentum is transferred to the cue ball. The cue ball rolls along the table until it collides with one or more of the other balls.

If the cue ball hits one other ball dead on, the cue ball will stop and transfer all of its momentum to the other ball. The other ball will move away as fast as the cue ball was moving before the collision. If the cue ball hits two other balls at the same time, both of the other balls will move after the collision. Part of the cue ball's momentum will be transferred to each of the other balls.

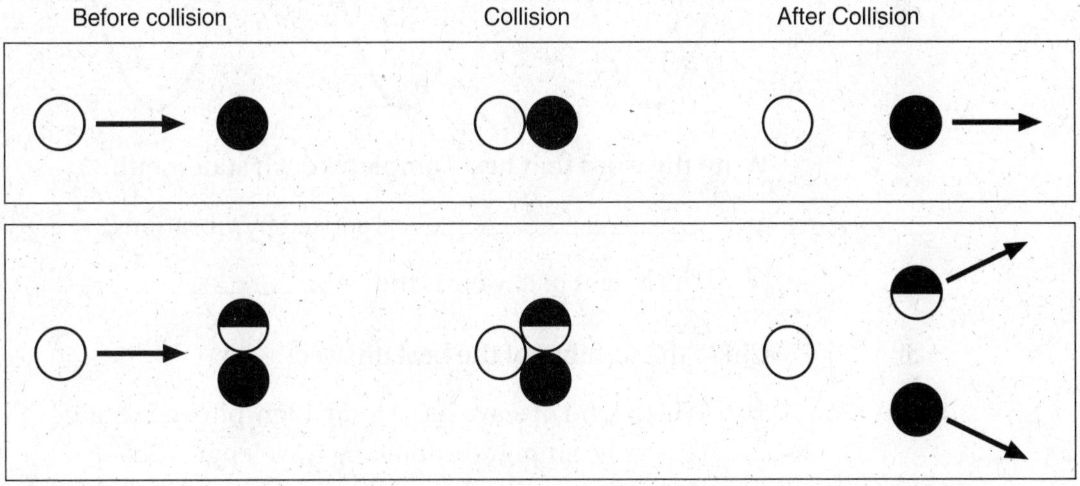

Write the words that best complete the sentence.

4. Two factors that help determine an object's momentum are

_________________ and _________________.

Circle the number of the best answer.

5. Which statement about the situation shown in the bottom diagram is correct?
   (1) The cue ball has more momentum before the collision than after.
   (2) The other balls have more momentum before the collision than after.
   (3) The other balls have the same momentum before and after the collision.
   (4) The cue ball moves at the same speed before and after the collision.
   (5) The other balls move faster before the collision than after.

Go on to the next page.

Sound Waves

Sound is caused by vibrations. If you pluck a stretched rubber band, you can see it vibrate, or move back and forth. The rubber band makes the air near it vibrate. These vibrations move through the air like ripples in a pond. Each ripple is a wave.

If you look at water waves, you can see the distance from the top of one wave to the top of the next. This distance is the **wavelength.** Each wavelength in music makes a sound of a different pitch. Short wavelengths are high sounds, like those made by a flute. Long wavelengths are low sounds, like those made by a tuba.

The height of a wave is the **amplitude.** The amplitude of a sound wave is the loudness of the sound. The larger the amplitude, the louder the sound.

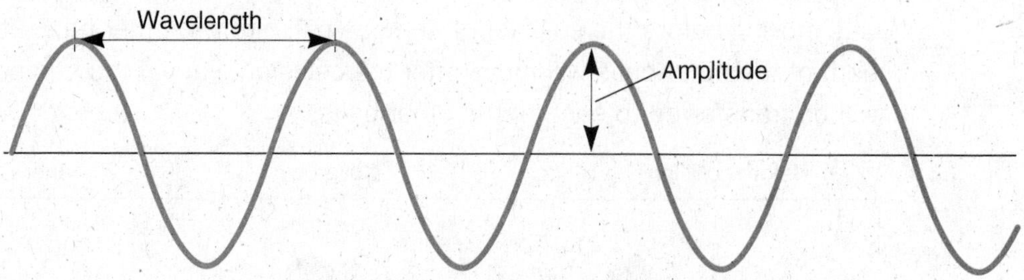

Write the word that best completes each statement.

6. ______________________ is caused by vibrations.

7. The height of a wave is the ______________________.

Circle the number of the best answer.

8. Which kind of wave has a loud, high-pitched sound?
   (1) large amplitude and long wavelength
   (2) large amplitude and short wavelength
   (3) small amplitude and long wavelength
   (4) small amplitude and short wavelength
   (5) small amplitude and medium wavelength

9. What will happen to the wave in the diagram if the sound gets softer and lower in pitch?
   (1) The wavelength will be longer and the amplitude larger.
   (2) The wavelength will be shorter and the amplitude larger.
   (3) The wavelength will be longer and the amplitude smaller.
   (4) The wavelength will be shorter and the amplitude smaller.
   (5) Nothing will happen to the wave.

Electromagnetic Fields

Any device that uses electricity has an energy field around it. The field caused by an electric current is called an **electromagnetic field,** or **EM field.** The EM field has properties of electricity and magnetism. For example, the EM field of a TV can turn the needle of a compass, just as a magnet can. An EM field is produced only while the electric current is flowing. When the TV is turned off, there is no EM field.

An EM field can ruin a video- or audiotape. The tape contains metal particles lined up in a pattern. This pattern is read when you play the tape. Because it is magnetic, an EM field can move the metal particles in the tape. When you play the tape, the picture or sound will be scrambled. Computer diskettes and video game cartridges work in the same way as tapes. They all should be kept away from EM fields. Compact discs and digital video discs (DVDs) do not have a magnetic pattern, so they are not damaged by EM fields.

The metal detector at an airport has an EM field. When you walk through the EM field, metal objects you are carrying affect it. If the field detects enough metal, an alarm sounds. After removing keys, coins, and jewelry, people can usually walk through the metal detector without affecting the EM field. The alarm does not ring.

Fill in the blank with the word or words that best complete the statement.

10. An EM field can affect metal because the field acts like a

_______________________.

Circle the number of the best answer.

11. Which of the following can be safely carried through an airport metal detector without damage?
    (1) an audiotape
    (2) a videotape
    (3) a computer diskette
    (4) a video game cartridge
    (5) a compact disc

Science Extension

Simple machines are all around us. Look in your home for examples of simple machines. (They may be part of a compound machine.) Make a table. In one column list these simple machines: inclined plane (ramp or wedge), lever, wheel and axle, gears. In the second column list all the examples you find. Here's one to get you started: Lever: bottle opener.

Check your answers on pages 249–250.

Mini-Test • Unit 4

GED PRACTICE

This is a 15-minute practice test. After 15 minutes, mark the last number you finished. Then complete the test and check your answers. If most of your answers were correct but you did not finish, try to work faster next time.

Directions: Choose the one best answer to each question.

Questions 1 through 2 refer to the following diagram.

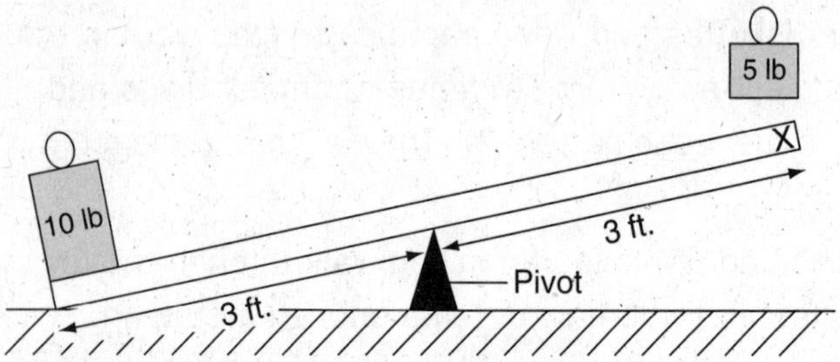

1. What will be the effect of placing the 5-pound weight at point X on the lever?
   (1) The right half of the lever will rise quickly and then fall.
   (2) The pivot will move closer to point X.
   (3) The lever will rotate around the pivot.
   (4) The lever will come to rest with both ends off the ground.
   (5) The lever will end up in its starting position, shown in the diagram.

2. Which of the following devices is a technological application of the simple machine shown in the diagram?
   (1) an axe
   (2) a shovel
   (3) a loading ramp
   (4) an automobile gearbox
   (5) a volume-control dial on a radio

3. Humans can detect sounds because of specialized cells in the inner ear that sense the vibrations produced by sound waves. All of these cells are made before birth. Loud sounds can damage or kill some of the cells. The cells that die cannot be replaced.

   Which statement supports the conclusion that ear plugs should be worn in noisy places?
   (1) Sound waves produce vibrations.
   (2) Humans can hear well before birth.
   (3) Specialized cells in the ear aid hearing.
   (4) Loud sounds kill cells in the inner ear.
   (5) Wearing earplugs is uncomfortable.

4. The compact disc (CD) is a plastic disc on which music, images, or other information can be stored in digital format. CD players read the stored information by scanning the surface of a CD with a low-intensity laser. The laser beam reflects off the surface. Electronic circuitry in the CD player converts the reflected laser beam into an electrical signal. The signal is then sent to a stereo amplifier or a computer.

   Which statement about CDs or CD players is an opinion rather than a fact?
   (1) The best use for CDs is recording music.
   (2) CDs store digital information.
   (3) A laser is an essential part of a CD player.
   (4) CD players include electronic circuitry.
   (5) CD players produce an electrical signal.

5. The law of conservation of momentum states that the total momentum of a system does not change. For example, imagine a bowling ball rolling toward bowling pins. The ball has momentum because it is moving. The pins have no momentum because they are stationary. If the ball strikes some of the pins, it will slow slightly, losing some of its momentum. The pins will move, gaining momentum. The total momentum of the ball and the pins does not change.

   Which sentence below restates information in the paragraph above?

   (1) Bowling pins and bowling balls have the same momentum.
   (2) A bowling ball gains momentum when it strikes some of the pins.
   (3) Bowling pins do not have momentum unless they are moving.
   (4) Momentum is conserved by bowling pins but not by bowling balls.
   (5) Momentum is not conserved if a bowling ball misses all of the pins.

6. The flow of electrons through a wire is called an electric current. For electrons to flow, there must be a continuous path, or circuit, from and to a power source. Almost anything placed in a circuit resists and slows the electronic current. The more resistance there is in the circuit, the smaller the current is.

   Think about how a light switch works. Which action is most similar to that of the switch?

   (1) a lead apron absorbing X rays
   (2) a prism splitting white light into its colors
   (3) a pump pushing water through pipes
   (4) a dam controlling the flow of a river
   (5) a furnace filter reducing airflow

Question 7 refers to the following information and graph.

A company that manufactures windows tested different window designs to determine which design was best at reducing the transmission of sound. The results of the testing are graphed below.

Sound Transmission Through Windows

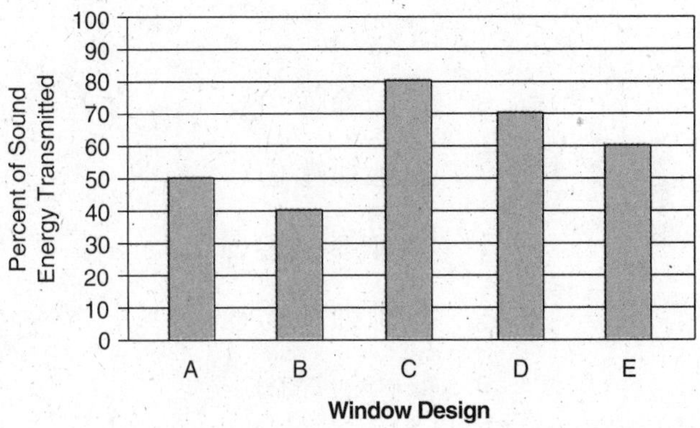

7. Which of the following conclusions is supported by the information presented in the graph?

   (1) Design C blocks more outside noise than any of the other designs.
   (2) All five designs are equally good at blocking noise.
   (3) Design B is the best choice for buildings in noisy neighborhoods.
   (4) Design E is the most expensive of the windows.
   (5) Design A allows the most light to pass through.

Check your answers on pages 250–251.

ANSWER SHEET

Posttest
Science

Name: ______________________ **Class:** ______________ **Date:** ________

1 ① ② ③ ④ ⑤
2 ① ② ③ ④ ⑤
3 ① ② ③ ④ ⑤
4 ① ② ③ ④ ⑤
5 ① ② ③ ④ ⑤
6 ① ② ③ ④ ⑤
7 ① ② ③ ④ ⑤
8 ① ② ③ ④ ⑤
9 ① ② ③ ④ ⑤
10 ① ② ③ ④ ⑤
11 ① ② ③ ④ ⑤
12 ① ② ③ ④ ⑤
13 ① ② ③ ④ ⑤
14 ① ② ③ ④ ⑤
15 ① ② ③ ④ ⑤
16 ① ② ③ ④ ⑤
17 ① ② ③ ④ ⑤
18 ① ② ③ ④ ⑤
19 ① ② ③ ④ ⑤
20 ① ② ③ ④ ⑤
21 ① ② ③ ④ ⑤
22 ① ② ③ ④ ⑤
23 ① ② ③ ④ ⑤
24 ① ② ③ ④ ⑤
25 ① ② ③ ④ ⑤

Directions

GED PRACTICE

This is a 40-minute practice test. After 40 minutes, mark the last number you finished. Then complete the test and check your answers. If most of your answers were correct but you did not finish, try to work faster next time.

The PreGED Science Posttest consists of multiple-choice questions that measure general science concepts. The questions are based on short readings and/or illustrations, including maps, graphs, charts, diagrams, or other figures. Study the information given and then answer the question(s) following it. Refer to the information as often as necessary in answering the questions.

Record your answers on the answer sheet on page 216. You may make a photocopy of this page. To record your answer, fill in the numbered circle on the answer sheet that corresponds to the answer you select for each question in the Posttest.

After you complete the Posttest, check your answers on pages 251–253. Then use the chart on page 227 to identify the science skills and content areas that you need to practice more.

EXAMPLE

Which object in the solar system has the greatest mass?

(1) the sun
(2) Earth
(3) the moon
(4) an asteroid
(5) a comet

(On Answer Sheet)

● ② ③ ④ ⑤

The correct answer is "the sun"; therefore, answer space 1 would be marked on the answer sheet.

If you do not use the answer sheet provided, mark your answers on each test page by circling or writing the correct answer for each question.

Directions: Choose the one best answer to each question.

Questions 1 and 2 refer to the following information and diagram.

There are three types of ants involved in an ant colony: workers, males, and the queen. Workers take care of the anthill and its queen. In the spring, newly hatched males and queens fly out of the anthill and mate. The new queens fly away, to set up new colonies.

1. What is one of the main differences between a male ant and a worker ant?
   (1) A male ant has wings and a worker ant does not.
   (2) A male ant has antennae and a worker ant does not.
   (3) A male ant has an abdomen and a worker ant does not.
   (4) A male ant has six legs and a worker ant has four legs.
   (5) A male ant is smaller than a worker ant.

2. After the mating flight, a queen loses her wings.

   Which of the following can you infer from this information?
   (1) The males lose their wings, too.
   (2) The workers grow wings instead.
   (3) The workers travel far from the anthill to find food.
   (4) The queen lays fertilized eggs under the wings.
   (5) The queen does not mate again.

Question 3 refers to the following chart.

Maximum Safe Load on a Frozen Lake

Ice Thickness (Inches)	Maximum Weight (Tons)	Example
2	<1	One person
3	<1	A few people
7.5	2	Car or snowmobile
8	2.5	Light truck
10	3.5	Medium truck
12	9	Heavy truck

3. Shawn is head of the parks department in Northern City. He must decide when the lakes are safe for ice-skating. What is the minimum ice thickness at which Shawn can safely post an "Ice Skating Permitted" sign on the lakes?

The ice must be at least
(1) 2 inches thick
(2) 3 inches thick
(3) 7.5 inches thick
(4) 8 inches thick
(5) 10 inches thick

4. In the 1890s, Wilhelm Roentgen studied light and other rays produced when electricity passes through a glass vacuum tube. One day he covered the tube with cardboard, yet a screen glowed 9 feet away. After more tests, Roentgen concluded that the glow was caused by invisible "X rays" from the tube. These rays can pass through cardboard, most substances, and soft body tissues. However, they can not pass through bones or metal. One of his first X-ray photographs showed his wife's hand with a ring.

Which of the following was evidence that X rays cannot pass through metal?
(1) The X rays passed through cardboard.
(2) The X-ray photo showed his wife's hand.
(3) The X-ray photo showed his wife's bones.
(4) The X-ray photo showed his wife's ring.
(5) The screen glowed nine feet away.

Question 5 refers to the following bar graph.

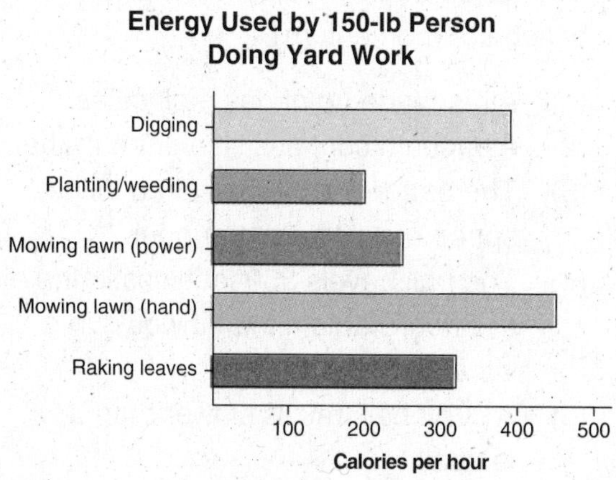

5. Althea needs to do yard work, but she wants to take it easy. Which task should she do?
(1) digging
(2) planting or weeding
(3) mowing grass with a power mower
(4) mowing grass with a hand mower
(5) raking leaves

Questions 6 and 7 refer to the following graph.

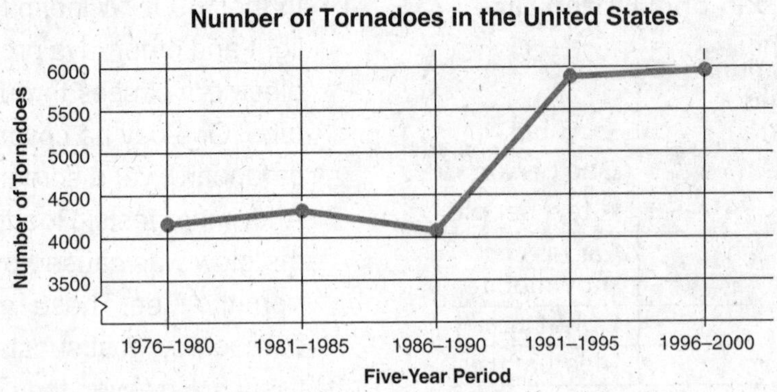

6. Approximately how many tornadoes occurred between1986 and1990?

(1) 3,500
(2) 4,100
(3) 4,700
(4) 5,300
(5) 5,900

7. Which generalization is best supported by the information in the graph?

(1) The number of tornadoes has increased during every five-year period since 1976.
(2) The number of tornadoes has decreased during every five-year period since 1976.
(3) Tornadoes have become more destructive over the past three decades.
(4) There were more tornadoes during the 1970s than during the 1980s.
(5) There were more tornadoes during the 1990s than during the 1980s.

Question 8 refers to the following information.

The momentum of a baseball is affected by air resistance. As the ball travels through the air, it must push the molecules of gas aside. Thus, the ball loses energy and speed. A ball batted at 110 miles per hour would travel 750 feet in a vacuum before falling to the ground. At Shea Stadium in New York, it would go about 400 feet.

8. Which of the following facts supports the conclusion that air resistance slows a baseball's momentum?

(1) Air is made up of gas molecules.
(2) A vacuum contains little or no matter.
(3) The batter hits the ball at an initial speed of 110 miles per hour.
(4) The ball travels 350 feet less in the air at Shea Stadium than it would in a vacuum.
(5) A curveball travels slower than a fastball.

9. Electricity needs a complete path, called a circuit, in order to flow. For example, when you flip a switch, you are completing a circuit. In the "on" position, the switch connects two wires, a source of electricity, and an electric device such as a doorbell or a light bulb.

A

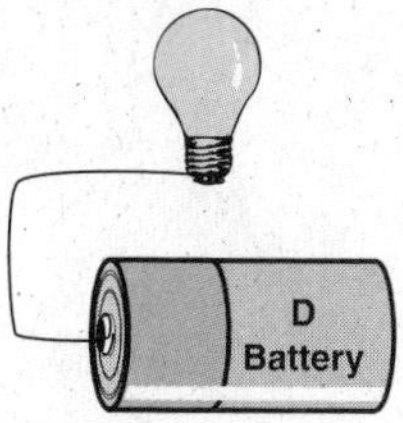

B

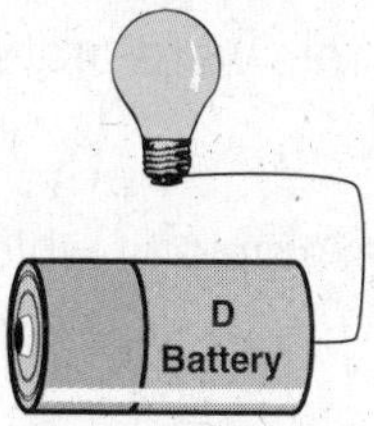

C

D

E

In which of the above diagrams is a complete circuit formed and the bulb lit?

(1) A
(2) B
(3) C
(4) D
(5) E

10. Each year, collisions between deer and vehicles cause more than 100 human deaths and more than $1 billion in damage. Deer destroy gardens, trees, and crops. In addition, deer carry ticks infected with Lyme disease; deer also carry diseases that infect farm animals.

Efforts to control the deer population include increased hunting and sterilizing females with a contraceptive dart gun. Still, some people still think of deer as welcome visitors. They put out feed to attract them to their yards.

Which of the following statements expresses an opinion rather than a fact?

(1) People die in car collisions with deer.
(2) Deer cause about $1 billion dollars in damage to vehicles every year.
(3) Deer aid the spread of Lyme disease.
(4) Hunting and sterilization are methods used to control the number of deer.
(5) Deer are attractive animals that are nice to see in a backyard.

11. Matter cannot be destroyed or created. When you burn something, however, you may notice there is usually less solid matter afterwards. For example, a piece of wood weighs more before burning than the resulting ash does. Which of the following would be evidence that no matter has been destroyed during combustion?

(1) Oxygen is required for combustion to occur.
(2) Wood smells pleasant when it's burning.
(3) Dryness of the wood effects how quickly it burns.
(4) Wood tends to turn black during combustion due to oxidation.
(5) Combustion changes some solid matter to gas and energy.

Questions 12 through 14 refer to the following information.

Conventional farming uses chemical fertilizers and pesticides, while organic farming does not. Ruth wanted to test the difference in taste between organically grown vegetables and conventionally grown vegetables. She set up an experiment by placing two groups of tomatoes, carrots, and broccoli, and a questionnaire on a table. Group A was the conventionally grown vegetables, and Group B was the organically grown ones. Ruth's questionnaire asked whether the taster liked Group A or B best. Ruth put the results from 25 tasters in the following chart:

Taste Test Results

Vegetable	Number who Preferred Group A	Number who Preferred Group B
Tomatoes	7	18
Carrots	4	21
Broccoli	10	15

Ruth decided that organically grown vegetables do taste better than conventionally grown vegetables.

The three questions in the next column ask you to classify statements about the experiment based on the following categories:

- the problem—the question being tested in the study
- the hypothesis—a testable statement that explains something related to the problem
- the experiment—a way of testing whether the hypothesis is correct
- data—information gathered through testing and/or observation during the experiment
- conclusion—a summary statement supported by the data from the experiment

12. Ruth organized a taste test of organically grown and conventionally grown vegetables.

This statement is an example of which category?

(1) problem
(2) hypothesis
(3) experiment
(4) data
(5) conclusion

13. Organically grown carrots were preferred by 21 people.

This statement is an example of which category?

(1) problem
(2) hypothesis
(3) experiment
(4) data
(5) conclusion

14. Based on the taste-test results, organically grown vegetables taste better than conventionally grown vegetables.

This statement is an example of which category?

(1) problem
(2) hypothesis
(3) experiment
(4) data
(5) conclusion

Question 15 refers to the following graph.

Location of Bones in an Adult Human

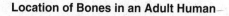

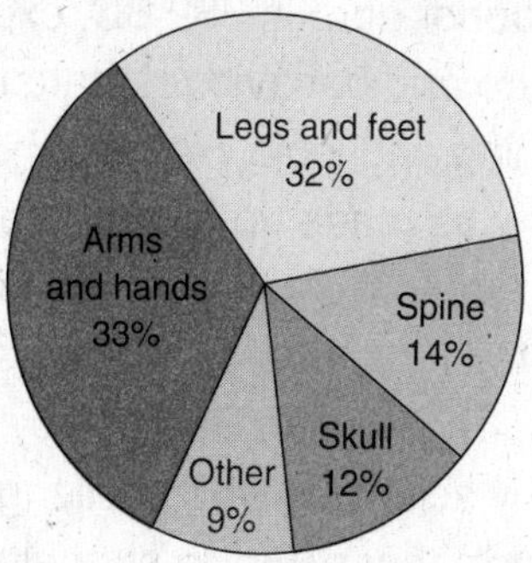

15. How does the number of bones in the arms and hands compare with the number of bones in the legs and feet?

    (1) There are three times as many bones in the arms and hands as in the legs and feet.
    (2) There are twice as many bones in the arms and hands as in the legs and feet.
    (3) There are about the same number of bones in the arms and hands as in the legs and feet.
    (4) There are half as many bones in the arms and hands as in the legs and feet.
    (5) There are one-third as many bones in the arms and hands as in the legs and feet.

Question 16 refers to the following diagram.

A Yeast Cell Budding

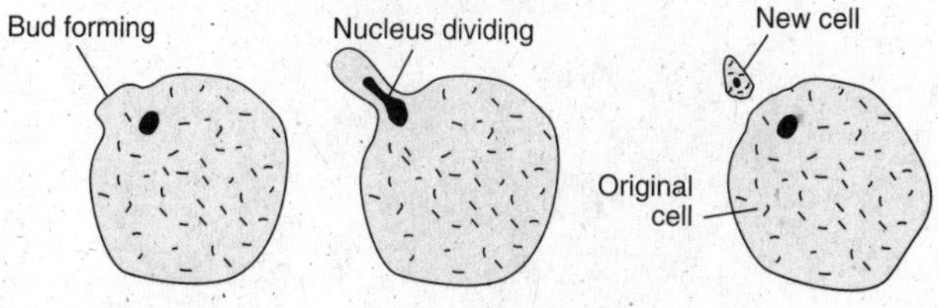

16. Which of the following best summarizes what is shown in the diagram?

    (1) Yeast cells reproduce by growing a bud that splits off the parent cell.
    (2) The original cell bulges outward, producing a small bud.
    (3) The nucleus of a yeast cell divides during budding.
    (4) Each yeast cell contains a nucleus.
    (5) Right after budding, the new cell is smaller than the original cell.

17. Some DNA paternity tests are done with samples of cells from the child and the alleged father. A cell sample from the mother is not necessary. Other DNA paternity tests are done with cells from the child, the mother, and the parents of the alleged father.

    What conclusion can you draw from this information?

    (1) A child and his or her parents have identical DNA.
    (2) A child and its grandparents have a identical DNA.
    (3) The mother's cells are always needed for DNA paternity tests.
    (4) DNA paternity tests can be done with or without cells from the alleged father.
    (5) DNA paternity tests are 100% accurate.

Question 18 refers to the following map.

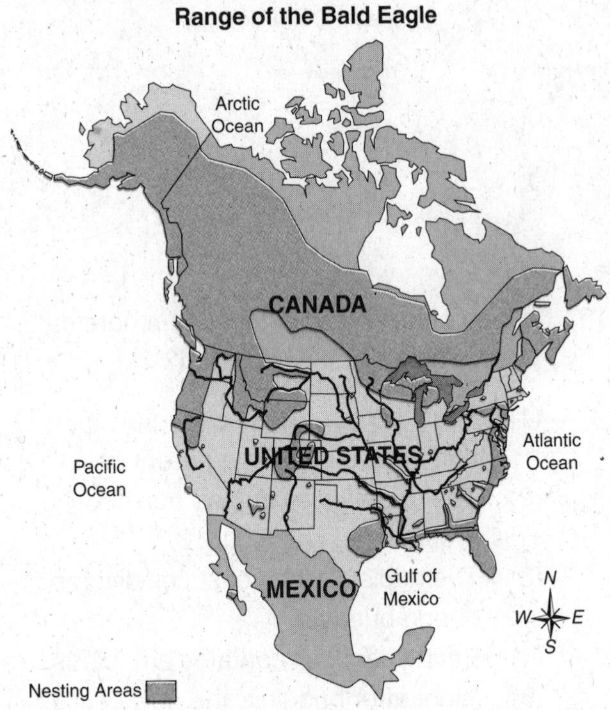

18. Based on the map, which could cause the most harm to bald eagles nesting in the United States?
    (1) increased pollution of arctic islands
    (2) increased pollution of the Mississippi River basin and the Great Lakes
    (3) increased farm size in the Midwest
    (4) decreased forestland in New England
    (5) decreased rainfall along the coast of California

19. Ancient people cooked food and worked metal without understanding these processes scientifically. Aristotle, a Greek philosopher born in 382 BC, explained the structure and behavior of matter through reasoning and logic. He thought that all matter was made up of four "elements": earth, water, fire, and air. This idea was accepted for almost 2,000 years. In the 1600s, Englishman Robert Boyle was one of many scientists who challenged Aristotle's theory. Boyle strongly promoted the use of experimentation to test ideas. He sought to identify elements—the building blocks of matter—through experiment rather than solely through logic.

    Which sentence best summarizes one of Boyle's main contributions to science?
    (1) Boyle invented processes for working metals.
    (2) Boyle showed that there are four basic elements.
    (3) Boyle said that scientific knowledge could be gained solely through logic.
    (4) Boyle encouraged experimentation to test scientific ideas.
    (5) Boyle promoted Aristotle's ideas.

Question 20 refers to the following chart.

Common Air Pollutants

Pollutant	Source
Carbon monoxide	Burning fuel in motor vehicles
Lead	Smelting and manufacturing plants
Nitrogen oxides	Burning fuel in power plants, boilers, and motor vehicles
Particulate matter	Solid particles in smoke, dust, vehicle exhaust
Sulfur oxides	Emissions from factories, power plants, and refineries

20. Which statement best summarizes the chart?
    (1) Air pollution comes from transportation and industry.
    (2) Lead is a byproduct of smelting.
    (3) Burning fuel releases nitrogen oxides.
    (4) Sulfur oxides are industrial emissions.
    (5) Some air pollution consists of particulate matter.

Question 21 refers to the following diagram.

A Homemade Electromagnet

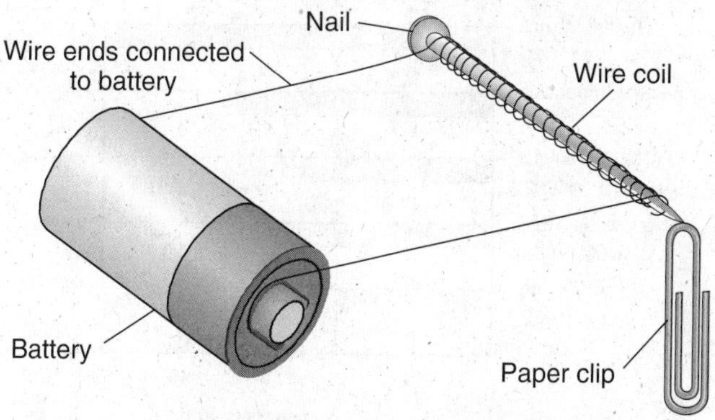

21. The battery and nail in the diagram are on the edge of a table. What would happen if the wire between the battery and the nail were cut?
    (1) The wire coil would wind tighter.
    (2) The nail would fall.
    (3) The paper clip would fall.
    (4) The magnetic force would increase.
    (5) The nail would become magnetic.

Question 22 refers to the following diagrams.

Partial solar eclipse

Total solar eclipse

22. A solar eclipse occurs when the moon passes in front of the sun, blocking it. What is the difference between a total solar eclipse and a partial solar eclipse?

    In a total eclipse of the sun, the moon
    (1) blocks the sun except for a rim of light
    (2) blocks half of the sun
    (3) is larger than in a partial eclipse
    (4) is farther away than in a partial eclipse
    (5) is on the far side of the sun

Go on to the next page.

Question 23 refers to the following graph.

Some Deadly Volcanic Eruptions

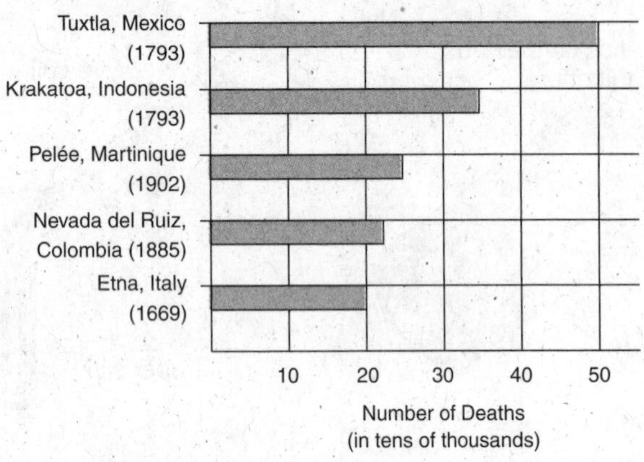

23. What can you conclude based on the information in the graph?

    (1) Volcanic eruptions can be predicted.
    (2) The first volcanic eruption causing more than 1,000 deaths occurred in Italy in 1669.
    (3) Of the volcanic eruptions listed in the graph, Tuxtla, in Mexico, caused the most known deaths.
    (4) More people died in volcanic eruptions in prehistoric times than in ancient or modern times.
    (5) Deadly eruptions occur every 100 years.

Question 24 refers to the following chart.

Common Acids and Bases

Substance	Acid or Base	Uses
Vinegar	Acid	Cooking; cleaning glass
Muriatic acid	Acid	Cleaning concrete, cleaning toilets
Phosphoric acid	Acid	Improving taste of cola drinks
Baking soda	Base	Cooking; cleaning
Washing soda	Base	Boosting the power of laundry detergent

24. What do vinegar and baking soda have in common?

    (1) Both are acids.
    (2) Both are bases.
    (3) Both are used for cooking only.
    (4) Both are used for cleaning only.
    (5) Both can be used for cooking and cleaning.

Question 25 refers to the following graph.

Federal Funding for Research by Field of Science, 2000

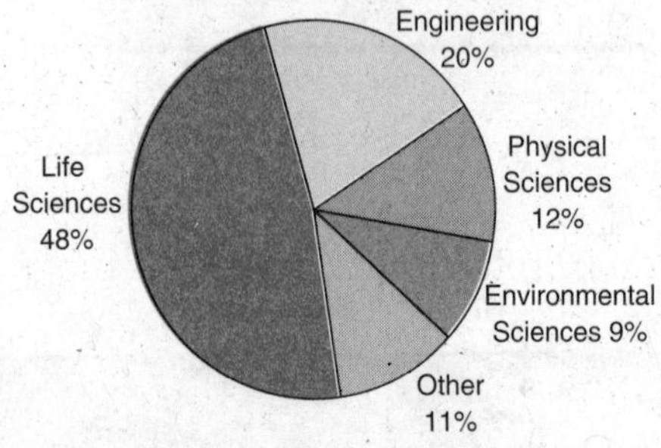

25. Which most likely accounts for this division of federal funding for the sciences?

    Americans place the highest value on

    (1) privately funded scientific research
    (2) the benefits of life science research
    (3) knowledge of the physical sciences
    (4) road construction techniques
    (5) computer hardware development

Posttest Evaluation Chart

The chart will help you determine your strengths and weaknesses in science content and thinking skills.

Directions

Check your answers on pages 251–253. In the first box below, circle the number of each item that you answered correctly on the Posttest. Count and write the number of items you answered correctly in each row. For example, in the Life Science row, write the number correct in the blank before */12,* which means *out of 12.*

Complete this process for the remaining rows. Then add the 3 totals to get your *Total Correct* for the whole Posttest.

- If you answered fewer than 20 items correct, determine the areas in which you need more practice. Go back and review the content in those areas. Page numbers for specific instruction appear in the left-hand column.
- If you answered 20 or more items correctly, your teacher may decide that you are ready to go on to Steck-Vaughn's *GED Science* book.

Thinking Skill/ Content Area	**Comprehension**	**Application**	**Analysis**	**Evaluation**	**Total Correct**
Life Science (Pages 14–101)	2, **16**	**5**, 12, **13**, 14	**1**, 10, **15**, 17, **18**	**25**	______/12
Earth and Space Science (Pages 102–141)	**6**, **20**		**22**, **23**	**7**	______/5
Physical Science (Pages 142–215)	19	**3**, **9**	**21**, **24**	4, 8, 11	______/8

Total Correct for Posttest ______ out of 25

National Science Education Standard	**Question**
Unifying Concepts & Processes	2, 8
Science as Inquiry	12, **13**, 14
Scientific Understanding & Skills	**1**, 4, **6**, **7**, 10, 11, **15**, **16**, 17, **18**, **20**, **23**, **24**
Science & Technology	**9**, **22**
Science in Social & Personal Perspectives	**3**, **21**, **25**
History & Nature of Science	**5**, 19

Boldfaced numbers indicate questions based on charts, diagrams, graphs, and maps.

PRETEST

PAGES 3–12

1. nucleus
2. cell wall
3. **(3) vacuole is empty** According to the diagram, the vacuole stores water and minerals, so the plant would need more water if the vacuole were empty. Options 1, 2, 4, and 5 are incorrect because these structures have functions other than storing water.
4. contracts
5. relaxing
6. **(2) at the front of the thigh** According to the diagram, the paired muscles in the arm are on opposite sides of the arm. From this, you can infer that muscles that do opposite jobs are in opposite positions. If the muscles at the back of the thigh bend the knee, muscles at the front of the thigh would straighten the knee. Option 1 is incorrect because these muscles bend the knee. Options 3 and 4 are incorrect because these muscles move the ankle joint. Option 5 is incorrect because muscles around the hip bend the hip joint.
7. Lactic acid
8. bacteria
9. **(1) Pasteurizing kills bacteria with high temperatures.** According to the article, pasteurizing involves heating and then quickly cooling the milk. The heat kills the bacteria. Option 2 does not kill the bacteria. Options 3 and 4 are incorrect because the bacteria are killed by pasteurization, not slowed. Option 5 is incorrect because no chemicals are involved in pasteurization.

10. insects   11. insects

12. wind   13. insects

14. **(5) anthers and ovary** According to the article, these structures make the sperm and egg, which are needed for reproduction. Options 1 and 4 are incorrect because petals are not necessary for reproduction. The article states that some flowers have no petals. Options 2 and 3 are incorrect because both parts are necessary for reproduction.

15. forest   16. grassland   17. cactus

18. **(2) drier** The article states that the grassland is drier than the forest, and the desert is drier than the grassland. Options 1, 3, and 4 are incorrect because the article does not indicate a pattern in these conditions. Option 5 is incorrect because the desert and grassland biomes are drier, not wetter, than the forest biome.

19. c   20. e   21. b

22. a   23. d

24. sedimentary rocks
25. metamorphic rocks
26. **(1) granite** According to the article, granite is an igneous rock. Options 2, 4, and 5 are incorrect because limestone, sandstone, and shale are sedimentary rocks. Option 3 is incorrect because marble is a metamorphic rock.
27. **(4) volcanoes** According to the article, volcanoes contain melted rock. When melted rock hardens, igneous rocks form. From this, you can infer that an area with many igneous rocks once had volcanoes. Options 1 and 2 are incorrect because rivers and sediment are associated with the formation of sedimentary rocks. Option 3 is incorrect because pressure is associated with the formation of metamorphic rocks. Option 5 is incorrect because earthquakes are not associated with the formation of rocks.

28. b   29. c   30. a

31. c   32. a

33. **(4) solid and liquid only** These states of matter have a definite volume that does not change. Options 1 and 2 are incorrect because they list only one of the states with a definite volume. Options 3 and 5 are incorrect because the volume of a gas changes as the gas expands to fill its container.

34. **(1) Its shape changes from not definite to definite.** According to the table, a liquid does not have a definite shape, but a solid does. Option 2 is incorrect because it is the opposite of what happens. Option 3 is incorrect because both solid and liquid have definite volumes. Option 4 is incorrect because the change is to the lowest temperature range. Option 5 is incorrect because there is a change in a property.
35. force
36. acceleration
37. **(1) acceleration** According to the article, when an unbalanced force acts on an object, the movement of the object changes. This is acceleration. All other options are examples of forces, not effects of forces.

UNIT 1: LIFE SCIENCE

LESSON 1

PAGE 16

Relate to the Topic

Many answers are possible. Answers should reflect the learner's personal experience.

Reading Strategy

1. an experiment in space
2. observation, hypothesis, experiment, and conclusion

PAGE 18

a

PAGE 19

1. c 2. a 3. b

PAGES 20–21

1. scientific methods
2. observation
3. hypothesis
4. experiment
5. conclusion
6. a 7. b 8. b 9. a
10. **(5) a possible explanation for something observed** According to the glossary, a hypothesis is a guess about the answer to a question based on observations.
11. **(1) proposing how weightlessness would affect embryos** Making a hypothesis is giving a possible explanation for how something works.
12. **(2) The eggs that were fertilized nine days before the launch would hatch.** This is the best prediction because it is the most similar to the results of the chicken embryo experiment.
13. Experimenting helps you gather evidence to support or disprove the hypothesis. Without experimenting, you cannot tell whether the hypothesis will be supported by facts.
14. Many answers are possible. Sample answer: No, because the risk to the unborn child is too great. We don't know enough about the effect of weightlessness to take chances with a human embryo.

LESSON 2

PAGE 22

Relate to the Topic

Many answers are possible. Sample answer: I got a sunburn at the beach. Now I wear sunscreen and a hat when I'm in the sun.

Reading Strategy

1. a type of light given off by the sun and tanning lamps
2. basal cell skin cancer, squamous cell skin cancer

PAGE 24

a

PAGE 25

b

PAGES 26–27

1. a 2. d 3. c
4. b 5. f 6. e

7. Basal cell skin cancer looks like an open sore, mole, or shiny bump; this type of cancer rarely spreads to other parts of the body and usually can be cured. Squamous cell skin cancer looks like raised pink spots; it grows faster and can spread to other parts of the body. Melanomas are oddly shaped blotches that can grow and spread quickly.
8. b 9. a
10. Any three of the following: stay out of the sun from 10 A.M. to 4 P.M.; wear a hat and long sleeves; use sunscreen with an SPF of 15 or more; avoid tanning parlors; check your skin regularly
11. (3) **Sunlight can cause skin cancer.** This sentence sums up the main point of the paragraph.
12 (3) **in the cytoplasm** The diagram on page 24 shows the mitochondria in the cytoplasm.
13. (5) **Preventing Skin Cancer** This section deals with ways to avoid getting skin cancer.
14. The doctor can check the moles for changes in size or color that might indicate skin cancer.
15. Many answers are possible. Sample answer: I will sit in the shade, wear sunscreen, and avoid the midday sun.

LESSON 3

PAGE 28

Relate to the Topic

Many answers are possible. Sample answer: I like chips, chocolate, and ice cream. These foods probably aren't good for my heart because they have a lot of fat and calories.

Reading Strategy

1. the percent of total calories provided by various nutrients in tortilla chips
2. left graph: nutrient percentages for regular tortilla chips; right graph: nutrient percentages for low-fat tortilla chips

PAGE 30

page 35

PAGE 31

1. a 2. three

PAGES 32–33

1. d 2. b 3. a
4. e 5. c 6. a
7. Extra cholesterol is deposited on the inside walls of arteries and clogs them.
8. a 9. b, c, d, e
10. **(2) 34–35** If you look up *heart* in the index, you will find an entry that says "heart, exercise and, 34–35."
11. (2) **saturated fat.** There is no wedge representing saturated fat in the circle graph for low-fat tortilla chips.
12. (5) **You cannot tell because the graphs do not show the salt content.** The graphs only show fat, carbohydrates, and protein, so you cannot tell how much salt is in either type of chip.
13. This is surprising because large amounts of saturated fat are usually found in animal products, not in fruit or vegetables.
14. Many answers are possible. Sample answer: It would be easiest to give up butter, cheese, and eggs. It would be hardest to give up ice cream and potato chips. I would eat more fruits, vegetables, and whole grains instead.

LESSON 4

PAGE 34

Relate to the Topic

Many answers are possible. Sample answer: I would recommend walking because it's safe, easy, and cheap. It's important to exercise regularly to stay healthy, keep weight down, and look good.

Reading Strategy

1. how muscles work in pairs
2. the joints of the body

PAGE 36

b

PAGE 37

b

PAGES 38–39

1. joint
2. ligament
3. aerobic
4. osteoporosis
5. sprain
6. healthier lungs and heart, stronger muscles, stronger bones
7. When one muscle contracts, the bone moves one way. When the other muscle in the pair contracts, the bone moves the other way.
8. Your heart should be beating faster.
9. (2) **It takes longer to walk a mile than to jog one.** The other comparisons, while true, do not answer the question.
10. (3) **Walking does not put a lot of stress on joints.** According to the paragraph, joggers get stress injuries more than walkers do, and that implies that walking does not put a lot of stress on joints.
11. (2) **The calf muscles are contracted.** In the diagram, only the calf muscles are contracted in the leg on the left.
12. Many answers are possible. Sample answer: A hinge joint works like a door hinge.
13. Many answers are possible. Sample answer: I would choose walking because it would place less stress on my joints and ligaments.

LESSON 5

PAGE 40

Relate to the Topic

Many answers are possible. Sample answers: Alcohol, tobacco, and cocaine. I would tell her not to drink alcohol at all, because it could harm her developing baby.

Reading Strategy

1. Answers will vary. Sample answer: What types of things are hereditary?
2. Answers will vary. Sample answer: How do a mother's activities affect an unborn child's health?

PAGE 42

a

PAGE 43

a, c, d

PAGES 44–45

1. zygote, uterus
2. embryo
3. placenta
4. fetus
5. Thalidomide and DES
6. zygote, embryo, fetus
7. embryo
8. any three of the following: Thalidomide, DES, cocaine, nicotine (cigarettes), alcohol
9. a, b, d
10. (3) **the embryo is connected to the placenta, which is connected to the mother** The left side of the diagram gives you a view of the embryo, placenta, and mother's uterus and shows how they are connected to one another.
11. (1) **all of the body organs have formed** After the body organs have formed, any damage that occurs is more likely to be minor.
12. (5) **do all of the above** Diet, medical care, and no smoking or drinking will give a pregnant woman the best chance of having a healthy baby.
13. Many answers are possible. Sample answer: It is a good law because some women may not know that alcohol is dangerous and this would warn them.
14. Many answers are possible. Sample answer: I would tell her that she should not smoke because it is bad for her baby.

LESSON 6

PAGE 46

Relate to the Topic

Many answers are possible. Sample answer: Diabetes; I would take such a test so that I could prepare myself and my family, should I test positive for getting the disease.

Reading Strategy

1. Answers will vary. Sample answer: I have my mother's nose and cheekbones and my father's build.
2. Answers will vary. Sample answer: I have my grandfather's curly hair.

PAGE 48

1. no 2. yes

PAGE 49

1. fact
2. opinion; circle the word *feel*

PAGES 50–51

1. dominant trait
2. Traits
3. Genetics
4. heredity
5. recessive trait
6. a
7. dark hair; dark eyes
8. sickle cell anemia
9. Down syndrome
10. to help parents deal with possible inherited diseases and problems in their prospective children
11. **(2) amniocentesis** According to the article, this is a test performed during pregnancy.
12. **(3) two out of four** Two of the four boxes contain the dominant trait (H) for Huntington's.
13. **(3) Some young people think it is better to be tested and know whether they will develop Huntington's in middle age.** The word *think* signals an opinion.
14. three out of four, because three combinations would include the dominant Huntington's trait, and one would not
15. Many answers are possible. Sample answer: Yes, because then we could prepare for any problems before the baby is born.

LESSON 7

PAGE 52

Relate to the Topic

Many answers are possible. Sample answer: I caught a bad cold from my son. My head was congested, my nose was running, and I had a headache. I took decongestants and rested.

Reading Strategy

1. germs
2. colds, flu, tonsillitis, chicken pox

PAGE 54

cell wall, cell membrane, genetic material, cytoplasm

PAGE 55

a

PAGES 56–57

1. e 2. c 3. b
4. a 5. d 6. b
7. a. virus
   b. virus
   c. virus, bacteria
8. b
9. a dose of a dead or weakened disease-causing agent that causes the body to form antibodies against the disease
10. a substance the body makes to fight disease
11. **(4) genetic material** According to the diagrams on pages 54 and 55, both a bacterial cell and a virus contain genetic material.

12. **(3) Avoid people with colds.** Since it's possible that colds are spread both by touch and by breathing air near people with colds, the best way to avoid colds is to avoid sick people.
13. **(1) Antibiotics do not fight viruses.** According to the article, antibiotics fight bacteria, not viruses, and colds and the flu are caused by viruses.
14. During the winter, people spend more time in small spaces indoors where it is easy to catch a cold or the flu from others.
15. Many answers are possible. Sample answer: Try to stay away from people who are sick; wash hands frequently; avoid touching the face; eat well and exercise to improve fitness; get flu shots for older people in the family.

LESSON 8

PAGE 58

Relate to the Topic

Many answers are possible. Sample answer: I eat apples and tomatoes. Pine trees, oak trees, and bamboo are used to build homes and furniture. I use herbs and spices when I cook.

Reading Strategy

1. medicines and their plant sources
2. the names, plant sources, and uses of different plant-based medicines

PAGE 60

a

PAGE 61

a

PAGES 62–63

1. f	2. a	3. d
4. b	5. e	6. c

7. by affecting the body's chemistry and by affecting disease-causing bacteria and viruses
8. a, c, d
9. to find out what they know about medicinal tropical plants
10. a, b
11. **(2) type of organism** Plant species are described as kinds of plants, so species must be kinds of organisms in general.
12. **(3) the chemical that works as a medicine** The paragraph contains the clue that the active chemical comes from the plant and that it has an effect on the cancer cells, bacteria, or viruses.
13. **(4) wintergreen** By looking at the "Use" column, you can find "soothe muscle aches". By reading across the row to the middle column, you can see that wintergreen is the plant source.
14. Many young people of the tropical rain forests are interested in modern culture, so they don't learn about rain forest plants. Also, the rain forest is being destroyed, which destroys plant species.
15. Many answers are possible. Sample answer: I used menthol in cough drops to relieve a cough.

LESSON 9

PAGE 64

Relate to the Topic

Many answers are possible. Sample answer: I saw dolphins perform at an aquarium show. They did tricks like jumping through hoops, and they made clicking sounds.

Reading Strategy

1. What are signature whistles?
2. How does echolocation work?

PAGE 66

a

PAGE 67

a

PAGES 68–69

1. mammals, language
2. sound waves

3. echolocation
4. density
5. Tyack invented the vocalight, a device that lights up when a dolphin makes a sound.
6. a unique sound that identifies that particular dolphin
7. a 8. a
9. **(3) as mammals** According to the article, dolphins are mammals, not fish.
10. **(4) They are a form of social communication** Tyack inferred that Scotty had become quieter because Spray was no longer there.
11. **(2) in their lower jaw** According to the diagram on page 66, dolphins receive sound waves in their lower jaw.
12. Many answers are possible. Sample answer: Even though dolphins behave differently in tanks than they do in the wild, we can still learn a lot about dolphins from studying them in captivity.
13. Many answers are possible. Sample answer: I trained a dog to come, stay, and fetch a ball or stick by repeating the command and rewarding the dog when she obeyed it correctly. This shows that some animals can recognize words that refer to specific things.

LESSON 10

PAGE 70

Relate to the Topic

Many answers are possible. Sample answer: Baby: helpless, learned to walk and talk; child: learned a lot, played a lot; adolescent: grew up, understood more about the world; adult: became responsible for myself.

Reading Strategy

1. the gypsy moth's life cycle
2. egg, caterpillar, pupa, adult

PAGE 72

1. pupa
2. egg, caterpillar, pupa

PAGE 73

1. about a month and a half
2. in late June or early July

PAGES 74–75

1. egg
2. pupa
3. caterpillar
4. adult
5. life cycle
6. A Frenchman brought gypsy moth eggs to the United States to use in the silk industry, and a few moths escaped.
7. It eats the leaves of certain trees, such as oak.
8. b 9. a 10. d 11. c
12. **(5) egg, caterpillar, pupa, adult** According to the life cycle diagram and the article, this is the order in which the stages of the life cycle take place.
13. **(1) egg** The longest segment on the timeline is that of the egg stage.
14. **(5) Soak the egg masses in kerosene, bleach, or ammonia.** According to the timeline, in March the gypsy moths are in the egg stage. Soaking them in a toxic substance destroys them at that stage.
15. Many answers are possible. Some animals that look different at different stages of the life cycle include butterflies, mosquitoes, mayflies, frogs, and toads.
16. Many answers are possible. Sample answer: When we had ants in the house, we put an insecticide powder along doors and windows and in cupboards.

LESSON 11

PAGE 76

Relate to the Topic

Many answers are possible. Sample answer: Yes, newspapers, glass and plastic bottles, and metal cans are collected weekly. I try to recycle, but sometimes I don't have the time. It can be a messy job.

Reading Strategy

1. Many answers are possible. Sample answer: Recycling involves processing used items for reuse.
2. Many answers are possible. Sample answer: paper, cardboard, aluminum, glass, and plastic

PAGE 78

1. car batteries
2. glass bottles and jars

PAGE 79

a

PAGES 80–81

1. pollute
2. landfill
3. natural resources
4. internal recycling
5. external recycling
6. raw material
7. Most garbage in the U.S. goes to landfills.
8. Newspapers, magazines, paper, cardboard, plastic, glass, aluminum and other metals
9. Reasons for recycling should include two of the following: keeping materials out of landfills; helping the economy; creating jobs; saving natural resources, money, energy; reducing pollution.
10. **(3) Recycling costs more in these cities than landfill disposal does.** According to the article, some cities would save money by disposing of garbage in landfills.
11. **(4) plastic soft-drink bottles** According to the graph, about 35% of plastic soft-drink bottles were recycled in 2000.
12. **(5) donating used clothing to a charity** When you donate used clothing to charity, the clothes can be used again by others.
13. It takes time to rinse and sort materials that are to be recycled. Taking the items to a recycling drop-off center can be inconvenient.
14. Many answers are possible. Sample answer: I think cities should continue recycling even if the costs are high. Recycling saves natural resources and creates jobs, which is important. Eventually, I think recycling will save money as well as resources.

LESSON 12

PAGE 82

Relate to the Topic

Many answers are possible. Sample answer: Tropical rain forests are green, wet, and full of plants and animals. If I were in a tropical rain forest, I might see many colorful plants, feel warm and sweaty, and hear birds calling.

Reading Strategy

1. the world's tropical rain forests
2. Dark gray represents the area covered by rain forests today. Dark orange represents rain forests that have been damaged or destroyed.

PAGE 84

a

PAGE 85

a

PAGES 86–87

1. ecosystem
2. Respiration
3. carbon dioxide–oxygen cycle
4. Photosynthesis
5. tropical rain forests
6. Rice, bananas, coffee, and sugar first came from the rain forests.
7. a
8. Farming, ranching, and logging; all three involve cutting down rain forest trees, which destroys the ecosystem.
9. **(1) increased** According to the article, burning fuel gives off carbon dioxide. So the increase in burning fuel has increased the amount of carbon dioxide in the air.

10. **(5) an increase in the amount of carbon dioxide in the atmosphere** According to the article, global warming may result from increased carbon dioxide in the atmosphere.
11. **(3) Most tropical rain forests are located near the equator.** According to the map, tropical rain forests are near the equator.
12. Any three of the following reasons: Tropical rain forests have a wealth of plant and animal life. Tropical rain forests are the source of many medicines. Tropical rain forests are the source of many foods. Tropical rain forests help control the temperature of Earth. Tropical rain forests help add oxygen to the atmosphere.
13. Many answers are possible. Sample answer: I can buy rain forest products that are harvested without damaging the forest. I can refuse to buy furniture made from tropical woods.

LESSON 13

PAGE 88

Relate to the Topic

Many answers are possible. Sample answer: Birds have wings, feathers, beaks and claws. I recognize birds by their feathers and wings.

Reading Strategy

1. a model of a feathered dinosaur called *Caudipteryx*
2. how birds might have evolved from dinosaurs

PAGE 90

b

PAGE 91

a

PAGES 92–93

1. mutation
2. adaptation
3. Convergence
4. Natural selection
5. evolution
6. They all had feathers.
7. insulation; to attract females
8. a
9. **(2) are very different types of animals** Birds have feathers and lay eggs, bats are mammals and have fur, and butterflies are insects, so you can infer they are not closely related.
10. **(3) adaptation** According to the article, an adaptation is a change that permits an organism to better survive in its environment. Bacteria that are resistant to antibiotics have a better chance of surviving.
11. **(2) Humans would develop stronger legs.** Through adaptation, as legs were used more, over generations of offspring they would become more important as a body part.
12. Many answers are possible. Sample answer: I think birds evolved from dinosaurs because there are so many structural similarities between them, including feathers, flexible wrists, wishbones, and air-filled skulls.
13. Many answers are possible. Sample answer: Before I read this article, I thought of dinosaurs as slow, heavy creatures; now I realize that some were light and some may have been very fast and even able to fly.

SCIENCE AT WORK

PAGE 95

1. **(4) hand weights**
2. **(2) He might get hurt from too much exercising.**
3. **c, a, b**

UNIT 1 REVIEW

PAGES 96–99

1. DNA

2. mitosis
3. **(4) An X-shaped chromosome consists of two copies of a parent chromosome.** According to the diagram, the DNA doubles in the parent cell before cell division. The X-shaped chromosomes appear in the diagram just after the doubling. Later in the diagram, the chromosomes split and each new cell gets only one-half of each X-shaped chromosome.
4. artery
5. left atrium
6. **(1) right atrium, right ventricle, lungs, left atrium, left ventricle** According to the arrows and labels in the diagram, the blood moves from the right atrium to the right ventricle. Then, the blood moves through an artery to the lungs. Next it flows to the left atrium of the heart through a vein. It moves from the left atrium to the left ventricle, which pumps the blood throughout the body.
7. b 8. c 9. a
10. nitrogen-fixing bacteria
11. food, shelter
12. protection
13. scavengers
14. **(1) A bird eats ticks that are on the back of an ox.** The bird gets food from this relationship, and the ox gets rid of parasites. Options 2 and 3 are incorrect because the only living species involved is the ant. Option 4 is incorrect because the lions don't get anything from the wild dog. Option 5 is incorrect because the two animals in the relationship are the same species, and mutualism is a relationship between two different species.

Mini-Test Unit 1

PAGES 100–101

1. **(3) The bird gets infected with the virus.** *(Unifying Concepts and Processes: Life Science: Analysis)* According to the diagram, infected mosquitoes can infect birds with the virus.
2. **(5) West Nile virus is a major health concern.** *(Unifying Concepts and Processes: Life Science: Analysis)* This statement is an opinion, because it expresses the idea that one health concern, West Nile virus, is more serious than other health concerns.
3. **(2) not producing enough antibodies** *(History and Nature of Science: Life Science: Comprehension)* The white blood cells of a healthy person make enough antibodies to kill invading germs. So the person stays healthy. Therefore, you can infer that when someone gets an infection, his or her white blood cells are not producing enough antibodies to fight off invading germs.
4. **(4) White blood cells protect the body.** *(History and Nature of Science: Life Science: Comprehension)* According to the information, white blood cells protect people from the numerous germs in the environment by producing germ-killing antibodies.
5. **(3) Yes, if both parents have recessive genetic material for the handedness trait.** *(Scientific Understanding & Skills: Life Science: Application)* If both parents are right-handed, you can conclude that each parent has dominant genetic material for the trait of handedness. Each parent may also have recessive genetic material for the trait. In this case, the recessive form does not show up in the parents. However, both parents can pass recessive genetic material to their child, who would then be left-handed.

6. **(1) not actively dividing** *(Science as Inquiry: Life Science: Evaluation)* According to the graph, about 75% of the cells are in between cell divisions, and thus not actively dividing.
7. **(3) more time in Phase 1 than in Phase 2** *(Science as Inquiry: Life Science: Analysis)* According to the graph, Phase 1 is much longer than Phase 2.

UNIT 2: EARTH AND SPACE SCIENCE

LESSON 14

PAGE 104

Relate to the Topic

Many answers are possible. Sample answer: Yes, I heard about it on the radio. An ice storm covered everything with a layer of ice. The weight of the ice broke tree branches and brought down power lines.

Reading Strategy

1. high temperatures and precipitation for the continental United States on June 28
2. a cold front

PAGE 106

1. a 2. a 3. b

PAGE 107

1. b 2. a

PAGES 108–109

1. air mass 2. front
3. forecast 4. meteorologists
5. weather map 6. stationary front
7. precipitation
8. a, c 9. b, c 10. a, d 11. b, d
12. from west to east
13. There are too many factors affecting the weather over a long period of time for accurate predictions to be possible.
14. **(3) stationary front** The map key shows that alternating triangles and half circles pointing in opposite directions are the symbols for a stationary front.
15. **(4) New York** Of all these cities, New York has the hottest weather with temperatures in the 100s—definitely a beach day.
16. **(1) occasional showers, high temperature in the 60s** In Salt Lake City, temperatures are in the 60s and 70s and there are showers. Even as the cold front moves to the east, Salt Lake City is likely to have this weather the next day.
17. The cold air mass in the west is probably a maritime polar air mass. It is cool, indicating polar. And it is moist (showers), indicating maritime origins.
18. Many answers are possible. Sample answer: The weather is cold and clear, so there is probably a continental polar air mass over the area.

LESSON 15

PAGE 110

Relate to the Topic

Many answers are possible. Sample answer: We use oil to heat the house; gas to cook; and gasoline in the car. We can turn the thermostat down in winter and carpool.

Reading Strategy

1. Answers will vary. Sample answer: I watched a television program about how scientists use computer models to learn about global warming.
2. Answers will vary. Sample answer: More snow in the mountains and more ice at the poles might melt, raising water levels in rivers, lakes, and the oceans, and increasing the risk of severe floods.

PAGE 112

1. a 2. a

PAGE 113

1. all over the world
2. a building (house) with plants (green)

PAGES 114–115

1. atmosphere
2. global warming

3. infrared radiation
4. greenhouse effect
5. fossil fuels
6. Radiant energy warms you when you sit out in the sun.
7. The greenhouse effect traps heat in the atmosphere the way a blanket traps heat.
8. carbon dioxide, ozone, chlorofluorocarbons (CFCs), methane, and nitrogen oxide
9. to reduce emissions of greenhouse gases
10. **(2) using light to combine substances into food** During photosynthesis, plants use light energy to combine carbon dioxide and water to produce food.
11. **(1) Trees take in carbon dioxide during the process of photosynthesis.** This statement explains how planting trees could reduce levels of greenhouse gases. Options 2, 3, and 5 are true, but do not link the statements. Option 4 is not true.
12. **(3) The ice caps at the North and South poles would melt.** More water in the oceans would raise sea level.
13. Industrialized nations have more factories, trucks, cars, and power plants, all of which produce greenhouse gases.
14. Many answers are possible. Sample answer: Reduce energy consumption in the home and car. Recycle as much as possible. Plant some trees.

LESSON 16

PAGE 116

Relate to the Topic

Many answers are possible. Sample answer: My tap water comes from a reservoir. If I had no tap water, I would buy bottled water from a supermarket.

Reading Strategy

1. Glaciers are large masses of ice that form where more snow falls than melts.
2. reservoir

PAGE 118

a

PAGE 119

b

PAGES 120–121

1. renewable resource
2. groundwater
3. resource
4. Glaciers
5. water cycle
6. from the mountains in the northern part of the state and from other states
7. rivers, lakes, precipitation, and groundwater
8. Not enough precipitation falls on an area.
9. Any two of the following: take shorter showers; fix leaky faucets; install low-flow toilets; run the washing machine and dishwasher only with full loads; if doing dishes by hand, don't run the water continuously; turn off water when brushing teeth
10. **(1) There is too little precipitation in the northern part of the state.** Since California gets most of its water from the northern mountains, dry weather there will result in a statewide drought.
11. **(4) Some areas get too much precipitation, while others do not get enough.** According to the article, water shortages are caused by the uneven distribution of rainfall in the United States. Even though there may be plenty of water on average, there is not enough in specific areas, depending in part on their population and water use.
12. **(2) It carries water from the Owens River to Los Angeles.** The map shows that the Los Angeles Aqueduct carries water from the southern end of the Owens River to Los Angeles.
13. Many answers are possible. Sample answer: Taking the salt out of seawater is one alternative.

14. Many answers are possible. Sample answer: I turn off the water when brushing my teeth and I water the grass only once a week.

LESSON 17

PAGE 122

Relate to the Topic

Many answers are possible. Sample answer: Yes, I would go because I enjoy having new experiences. I would hope to learn whether there is life on the planet.

Reading Strategy

1. Many answers are possible. Sample answer: When was the first space probe to an outer planet launched?
2. under the heading "Uranus and Neptune"

PAGE 124

1. 39 2. 84 years

PAGE 125

a

PAGES 126–127

1. outer planets 2. Space probes
3. solar system 4. inner planets
5. c 6. b 7. e 8. a 9. d
10. Mercury, Venus, Earth, Mars, Jupiter, Saturn, Uranus, Neptune, and Pluto
11. The mission was to send photos and information about the outer planets and their moons.
12. its rings
13. (3) **Uranus** According to the table, Saturn is 892 million miles from the sun. Uranus is 1,790 million miles from the sun. This distance is about twice as far from the sun as Saturn's distance.
14. (2) **Jupiter** According to the table, Jupiter has 39 known moons, which is more than the other planets listed in the table.
15. (5) **The cameras could be pointed at specific objects.** This is the only option that follows logically from the fact that the camera platforms were movable.
16. Many answers are possible. Sample answer: It is not practical because of the distances involved, the length of time required, and the hostile environments of the outer planets.
17. Many answers are possible. Sample answer: Yes, because eventually we may need to use resources found in other parts of the solar system.

LESSON 18

PAGE 128

Relate to the Topic

Many answers are possible. Sample answer: I need food to eat, water to drink, and air to breathe. When I am far from home, I eat and drink at a restaurant. I breathe just as I would at home.

Reading Strategy

1. what it would be like to carry out experiments while traveling at 17,500 miles per hour
2. what it is like to be in freefall

PAGE 130

a

PAGE 131

b

PAGES 132–133

1. e 2. a 3. f
4. b 5. c 6. d
7. to allow scientists to perform experiments in space that cannot be done on Earth
8. b
9. wastewater from the sinks and showers, excess humidity in the air, and water in crewmembers' urine
10. a 11. a
12. (5) **carbon dioxide and hydrogen** Two arrows labeled "Carbon dioxide" and "Hydrogen" point to the box labeled "Release into space."

13. **(4) filtration and purification** The box labeled *Filtration and purification* has arrows labeled *Wastewater from sinks and showers* pointing to it and *Pure water* pointing away from it.
14. **(3) The ISS recycles water and oxygen, but early spacecraft did not.** Both early spacecraft and the ISS carried a supply of water and oxygen from Earth. However, recycling water and oxygen on the ISS helps conserve these necessities so that the ISS does not have to be resupplied with water and oxygen from Earth.
15. On the ISS, everything appears to be weightless because it is in freefall. In a long, steep drop on a roller-coaster, you briefly feel nearly weightless because you are almost in freefall.
16. Many answers are possible. Sample answer: Yes, it is a good idea because it promotes cooperation between nations.

SCIENCE AT WORK

PAGE 135

1. **(4) sand and rock dust**
2. **(3) to make sure rain and splash water don't collect around the pool**
3. Many answers are possible. Sample answer: We have a new apartment building going up in my neighborhood. There are construction workers there all the time. First they leveled the ground and then dug a hole for the foundation. Now they are nailing lumber to form the skeleton for the building. There have been many safety issues for them to consider. At the beginning of the project they used huge, noisy machines to do most of the work. They had to be careful that nobody was in the way of the machines, and they wore ear muffs. Now, they must also be careful when using hammers and nail guns.

UNIT 2 REVIEW

PAGES 136–139

1. 90s 2. showers
3. **(2) hot, with showers** The map shows diagonal lines along the stationary front. According to the key, these lines indicate showers. The map also shows temperatures in the 80s, which is hot.
4. oxygen
5. Ultraviolet
6. **(3) skin cancer** According to the article, more ultraviolet rays reach Earth as CFCs destroy the ozone layer. These rays cause skin cancer. Options 1 and 2 are incorrect because poisoning is not part of the problem caused by CFCs. Option 4 is incorrect because ultraviolet rays do cause sunburn, but people do not usually die of sunburn. Option 5 is incorrect because only Option 3 is correct.
7. **(4) Its thickness decreased most rapidly between 1978 and 1989.** The graph shows a general decline in the thickness of the ozone layer between 1956 and 2000. To find the years when the thickness of the ozone layer decreased most rapidly, you have to find the portion of the graph with the steepest downward slope. The graph shows it was from 1978 to 1989.
8. continental shelf
9. **(4) waters of the continental-shelf region** According to the article, these waters have the richest fishing.
10. **(5) continental shelf, continental slope, ocean basin.** The continental shelf is where the oceans meet the continents. The continental slope lies between the continental shelf and the ocean basin.
11. **(4) Shellfish are harvested from the continental shelf.** Because we get shellfish from the continental shelf, you can conclude that polluting the water in this area will hurt the shellfish industry.
12. sun
13. core

14. **(4) the surface** Since Altair and the sun are similar in size and age, they have a similar structure. The diagram shows that the coolest part of the sun is the surface; applying this information to Altair, you can see that the surface would be the coolest part of this star as well.

Science Extension

Many answers are possible. Sample answer for a hurricane: Bring outdoor furniture and objects indoors. Tape up windows to prevent breakage. Stock up on food and water for a few days. Stock up on flashlights, batteries, and candles in case of power outage. Follow instructions if evacuating is recommended.

Unit 2 Mini-Test

PAGES 140–141

1. **(2) greater in the western half of Oregon than in the eastern half of Oregon** ***(Unifying Concepts & Processes: Earth & Space Science: Analysis)*** The map shows that most of the western half of Oregon receives more than 20 inches of precipitation in an average year. Most of the eastern half receives less.
2. **(3) Desert plants are found mostly in the eastern half of Oregon.** ***(Scientific Understanding & Skills: Earth & Space Science: Comprehension)*** The map shows that most of the eastern half of Oregon receives less than 20 inches of rain annually, meaning that this region is relatively dry; the western half of Oregon, on the other hand, generally receives 20 or more inches of rain per year, with large portions receiving more than 60 inches of rain. Therefore, you can infer that desert plants would be found mostly in eastern Oregon. The other options are contradicted by information on the map.
3. **(2) Every year Saudi Arabia removes about one-ninetieth of its petroleum reserves.** ***(Science in Social & Personal Perspectives: Earth & Space Science: Evaluation)*** If Saudi Arabia removes one-ninetieth of its petroleum from the ground each year, it will take less than 100 years to deplete its known reserves.
4. **(4) the formation of limestone from remains of coral and plankton that are cemented together on the ocean floor** ***(Scientific Understanding & Skills: Earth & Space Science: Application)*** Like sandstone, limestone is formed by small parts that are bound or cemented together.
5. **(5) 32 °F at 1,000 feet, 29 °F at 2,000 feet, and 25 °F at 3,000 feet** ***(Science as Inquiry: Earth & Space Science: Evaluation)*** Option 5 is the only option that shows a decrease in temperatures as altitude increases.
6. **(3) Earth is the most beautiful planet.** ***(Scientific Understanding & Skills: Earth & Space Science: Analysis)*** Option 3 is a belief that cannot be proved true or false.
7. **(2) Venus** ***(Unifying Concepts & Processes: Earth & Space Science: Application)*** It takes 243 Earth days for Venus to rotate on its axis. This means that a day-night cycle on Venus is many Earth months long.

UNIT 3: CHEMISTRY

LESSON 19

PAGE 144

Relate to the Topic

Many answers are possible. Sample answer: We have hand soap, dish detergent, spot removers, laundry detergent, bleach, glass cleaners, tile cleaners, toilet-bowl cleaners, abrasive cleaners for the sinks, and floor polish. We have special cleaners for the kitchen, clothes, bathrooms, windows, and floors.

Reading Strategy

1. different forms of matter
2. mixtures, compounds, and elements

PAGE 146

1. nitrogen and hydrogen
2. one nitrogen atom and three hydrogen atoms

PAGE 147

1. a, c 2. b, c, d 3. four 4. c

PAGES 148–149

1. element
2. mixture
3. chemical reaction
4. substance
5. atom
6. compound
7. b 8. a 9. b
10. a 11. b
12. (4) **hydrogen and oxygen** H is the chemical symbol for the element hydrogen and O is the chemical symbol for the element oxygen.
13. (2) **magnesium sulfide** When a compound is made of just two elements, the suffix *-ide* is added to the root of the second element.
14. (4) **oxygen** The suffix *-ate* means that the compound has oxygen.
15. Paint prevents the oxygen in the air from reacting with the iron in the steel.
16. Many answers are possible. Sample answer: chlorine bleach (NaOCl), to brighten white fabrics; ammonia (NH_3), to wash floors; baking soda ($NaHCO_3$), to clean porcelain surfaces (stovetop, sink)

LESSON 20

PAGE 150

Relate to the Topic

Many answers are possible. Sample answer: My favorite cooked food is mashed potatoes. When the potatoes are raw, they are very firm solids. After you boil them, they soften and become hot. Mashing breaks them down into smaller particles and makes them even softer.

Reading Strategy

1. one shows ice cubes melting; the other shows water boiling
2. hotdogs and hamburgers being grilled

PAGE 152

a

PAGE 153

1. chemical change
2. physical change

PAGES 154–155

1. solid
2. liquid
3. gas
4. physical change
5. chemical change
6. solid—ice; liquid—water; gas—water vapor or steam
7. b 8. d 9. a 10. c
11. physical change
12. chemical change
13. (4) **Chemical and Physical Changes in Cooking** This title covers all the topics discussed in the article. Options 1–3 and 5 are too specific. They cover only parts of the article, so they are incorrect.
14. (4) **a physical change** The chocolate melted, a physical change from solid to liquid.
15. (4) **baking a cake** Baking a cake involves chemical changes in the liquid batter as it sets. Options 1–3 and 5 are all physical changes, so they are incorrect.
16. Many answers are possible. Sample answers: freezing leftovers, boiling water, melting chocolate, defrosting a turkey, melting snow, dew
17. Many answers are possible. Sample answer: I made pancake batter and cooked the pancakes on a griddle. A chemical change took place as the batter set into solid pancakes. I put butter on top and it melted, a physical change.

LESSON 21

PAGE 156

Relate to the Topic

Many answers are possible. Sample answer: orange juice, hot cocoa; I think they are mixtures because I mix the ingredients together when I make them.

Reading Strategy

1. the solubility of some solids in water
2. solubility and temperature

PAGE 158

1. b 2. b

PAGE 159

1. a 2. b

PAGES 160–161

1. solution
2. Distillation
3. solubility
4. solute
5. solvent
6. hot chocolate
7. instant coffee
8. brass
9. a 10. b
11. **(4) A solvent is present in a greater amount in a solution, and a solute in a lesser amount.** When two substances are mixed together in a solution, the solvent is the substance of which there is more.
12. **(3) They are all mixtures.** Even though these substances are in different states of matter, they all consist of mixtures of various substances.
13. **(4) 6 ounces** The answer can be found by reading the solubility curve of sucrose (sugar) on the graph on page 159.
14. The water is the solvent, and the grape powder and sugar are the solutes. When I added water to the solutes, very little dissolved at first. Stirring for a few minutes made the grape powder and sugar mix evenly throughout the water.
15. Many answers are possible. Sample answer: I left a soft drink out on the counter and when I returned for it a few hours later, all the fizz was gone. The carbon dioxide gas that had been in solution had escaped.

LESSON 22

PAGE 162

Relate to the Topic

Many answers are possible. Sample answer: Once a potholder I was using caught fire on the stove. I put out the fire by dropping it in the sink and turning on the water.

Reading Strategy

1. hydrogen and carbon
2. the temperature needed for a substance to burn

PAGE 164

b

PAGE 165

a

PAGES 166–167

1. combustion
2. hydrocarbon
3. activation energy
4. kindling temperature
5. oxygen
6. a 7. b, c, e, f 8. a
9. **(4) More fires are caused by small heaters than by built-in heating systems.** Small portable heaters are more likely to be placed near flammable objects or knocked over. In both cases, a fire is possible. Built-in heaters do not get as hot and can't be knocked over.
10. **(2) The pollutants released by incomplete combustion would eventually overcome the people in the room.** Combustion uses oxygen. When the oxygen in the room gets low, people will have trouble breathing. In addition, combustion will be incomplete,

producing deadly carbon monoxide and other pollutants.

11. (2) **Over time, people have burned fuels for many purposes.** The first paragraph gives an overview of people's use of combustion over the course of history. The other options are too specific.
12. Many answers are possible. Sample answers: Heaters should be placed out of traffic and away from anything that might catch fire. Keep a door or window open when using a combustion heater. Use high-quality kerosene in a portable heater.
13. Many answers are possible. Sample answer: Our car has a combustion engine that uses gasoline as fuel, and it produces pollutants.

SCIENCE AT WORK

PAGE 169

1. (3) **Body Plus**
2. (4) **Free and Clean**
3. (5) **Hair Today, Hair Dew, Wind Blown, Free and Clean, Body Plus**

UNIT 3 REVIEW

PAGES 170–173

1. mixture
2. graphite, clay
3. (3) **The 9H lead contains more clay.** The passage states that adding clay to graphite makes the pencil lead harder. The diagram shows that 9H is the hardest kind of lead. Therefore, you can infer that 9H lead contains more clay than 9B lead.
4. exothermic reaction
5. endothermic reaction
6. chemical reaction
7. combustion
8. (4) **The reaction in instant cold packs is endothermic.** The passage states that the pack feels cold after the chemical reaction takes place. Thus, the reaction takes in heat. A reaction that takes in heat is an endothermic reaction
9. (2) **combustion** A gas heater works by burning gas. The passage states that combustion is another name for burning.
10. (2) **The burning candle has used up all of the oxygen in the jar.** The passage states that fuel, heat, and oxygen are needed for fire. Heat and fuel are still in the jar, so the fire must have consumed all of the oxygen.
11. (2) **removing oxygen** According to the article, small fires can be smothered. Throwing a heavy blanket on a fire would smother it.
12. nuclear fusion
13. sun
14. helium

Science Extension

Many answers are possible. Sample answer: Mixtures: pudding, stew, chili, salsa, mustard, salad dressing; Solutions: iced tea, soda, popsicles, kids' fruit drink

Mini-Test Unit 3

PAGES 174–175

1. (1) **distilled water** *(Unifying Concepts & Processes: Physical Science: Analysis)* The graph shows that of the four samples, distilled water contains the water contains the lowest concentration of minerals, with close to 0 ppm.
2. (3) **decreases as mineral content increases** *(Science as Inquiry: Physical Science: Comprehension)* The line on the graph shows that as the mineral content in the water increases, the amount of water absorbed by 0.1 g of sodium polyacrylate decreases.

3. (2) **absorbs 50 mL of this water** *(Science as Inquiry: Physical Science: Evaluation)* The graph shows the amount of water of different types that is absorbed by 0.1 gram of sodium polyacrylate. By looking at the reading for tap water, you can see that 0.1 gram of sodium polyacrylate absorbed 50 mL of tap water. So if 0.1 gram of sodium polyacrylate absorbed 50 mL of the unknown sample of water, this would be strong evidence that the unknown sample consisted of tap water.
4. (4) **to soak up urine in disposable diapers** *(Science & Technology: Physical Science: Application)* The paragraph states that sodium polyacrylate absorbs water; urine is mostly water. Therefore, sodium polyacrylate might function well in disposable diapers to absorb urine.
5. (4) **The test tube cooled off after the reaction.** *(Science as Inquiry: Physical Science: Evaluation)* The paragraph states that the test tube felt cold after the chemical reaction. This supports the conclusion that the reaction took in heat.
6. (5) **The amount of heat produced by burning food is used to calculate calories.** *(Scientific Understanding & Skills: Physical Science: Comprehension)* The first part of the paragraph states that calories tell us how much energy is in food and that calories are measured using a calorimeter. The last sentence says that the increase in temperature of the water in the calorimeter indicates how much energy the burning food contains. You have to infer that the increase in water temperature that occurs when the food is burned indicates a release of a specific amount of heat, which is used to calculate the calories in the burned food.
7. (2) **the igniter** *(Scientific Understanding & Skills: Physical Science: Analysis)* The diagram shows that the food is in close contact with the hot igniter; the igniter raises the temperature of the food to its kindling temperature, at which point it catches fire.
8. (3) **a nutritionist** *(Scientific Understanding & Skills: Physical Science: Application)* Nutritionists analyze foods and help plan healthful meals and snacks in part based on the calorie content of the food. They might use the data collected from a calorimeter to compare the calorie content of different brands of prepared foods or snacks.
9. (5) **They will cause a greater temperature change than will low-calorie foods.** *(Science as Inquiry: Physical Science: Analysis)* The paragraph states calories are a measure of food energy; from this you can infer that a high-calorie food contains more energy than does a low-calorie food. The paragraph also states that the increase in water temperature in a calorimeter is used to calculate the amount of energy (calories) in food. Thus, you can conclude that a high-calorie food, which has more energy, will cause a greater change in the water temperature than will a low-calorie food.

UNIT 4: PHYSICS

LESSON 23

PAGE 178

Relate to the Topic

Many answers are possible. Sample answer: I rode the bicycle to get some exercise. The bicycle had ten speeds.

Reading Strategy

1. Many answers are possible. Sample answer: when I needed to pry something open or lift something heavy
2. Many answers are possible. Sample answer: in a bicycle or the inside of a machine

PAGE 180

1. b 2. b

PAGE 181

a

PAGES 182–183

1. force
2. simple machine
3. compound machine
4. mechanical advantage
5. work
6. a 7. a 8. a
9. b 10. a 11. c
12. **(2) The wheel and the axle turn in the same direction.** The arrows next to the word *Wheel* and *Axle* both point in the counterclockwise direction.
13. **(1) friction** According to the article, friction is a force between surfaces that touch. To overcome friction, you must use extra effort.
14. **(5) no work will be done** If the resistance is larger than the effort, there will be no motion, and in physics, no motion means no work.
15. Standing on the pedals adds to your effort force because you can use your weight—the downward pull of gravity—to help move the pedal.
16. Many answers are possible. Sample answer: I went bike riding in the neighborhood and when I hit a bump in the street, the chain slipped off the gears. I had to stop and put it back on before I could go on.

LESSON 24

PAGE 184

Relate to the Topic

In golf, momentum is transferred when the club hits the ball. In bowling, momentum is transferred when the ball hits the pins.

Reading Strategy

1. Howard Johnson
2. Corking bats affects momentum.

PAGE 186

a

PAGE 187

1. fact 2. opinion

PAGES 188–189

1. collision 2. momentum
3. elastic 4. Energy
5. a 6. a, b, c 7. a
8. b 9. a, b, c
10. **(5) A standing object will move if enough momentum is transferred.** This is the only conclusion supported by the facts in the article.
11. **(3) A corked bat is lighter than a solid bat.** This statement represents a measurement, which is a fact. The other options are statements of what people believe, think, or feel. These words indicate opinions.
12. **(4) Cars are not very elastic.** If cars were elastic, they would spring back into shape after a collision. Instead, they remain crumpled and dented.
13. The sport utility vehicle has more momentum because it is much heavier than the compact car.
14. Many answers are possible. Sample answer: I was in a car on a snowy day, going very slowly around a corner, when the car in front of me braked sharply. I braked, too, but the snowplow behind me did not stop in time. The blade of the plow hit the trunk lid of my car, denting it. Luckily, we were all going so slowly that not much momentum was involved and no one was hurt.

LESSON 25

PAGE 190

Relate to the Topic

Many answers are possible. Sample answer: The device was a TV remote control. It allowed me to change the volume on the TV without going over to the TV set.

Reading Strategy

1. tiny particles of matter with a negative electrical charge
2. a diode

PAGE 192

a

PAGE 193

a

PAGES 194–195

1. e 2. d 3. b
4. a 5. c 6. a
7. a device that controls the flow of electricity, for example, a transistor
8. a 9. b 10. b
11. (4) **No machine had beaten a reigning chess champion until Deep Blue did it.** This sentence is the only one that has the same meaning as the last sentence of the first paragraph on page 191.
12. (5) **became much smaller** The microprocessor was able to fit the complex circuits of a central processing unit on a single chip. This decreased the size of the computer dramatically.
13. (3) **It enabled Deep Blue's playing to be adjusted between games.** That was what the software was designed to do, and in fact the Deep Blue team changed its playing between games 1 and 2.
14. Many answers are possible. Sample answers: microwave oven, remote control, TV, CD player, computer, car, stereo system
15. Many answers are possible. Sample answer: No, because Deep Blue was basically an enormous calculator. The ability it had to evaluate chess moves was designed into its system by human beings.

LESSON 26

PAGE 196

Relate to the Topic

Many answers are possible. Sample answer: I would have a surgical scar removed because I think it is unattractive.

Reading Strategy

1. how a laser produces light
2. Energy is applied from an outside source.

PAGE 198

1. b 2. a

PAGE 199

a

PAGES 200–201

1. Light
2. frequency
3. wavelength
4. laser
5. b
6. They are all forms of energy that travel in waves.
7. a 8. a 9. a
10. (4) **distance between the top of one wave and the top of the next** The label *Wavelength* indicates the distance between the tops of two waves.
11. (1) **The atoms in the tube absorb the energy.** The diagram on page 199 and the description of how a laser works tell you that the next step after the application of energy is its absorption by the atoms in the tube.
12. (3) **reflect the light back and forth** The arrows in the tube show the light reflecting back and forth, and label 3 describes this as well.
13. Two treatments for the dyes in the tattoo, one for the blue and one for the red.

14. Many answers are possible. Sample answer: Yes, I would try the laser, because I don't like the idea of chemicals eating into my skin.

LESSON 27

PAGE 202

Relate to the Topic

Many answers are possible. Sample answer: I enjoy listening to rock music and R & B. The instruments are usually a guitar, a bass, and drums.

Reading Strategy

1. The sound of a foghorn is much lower than the sound of a referee's whistle.
2. The sound of an exploding firecracker is much louder than the sound of a snapping twig.

PAGE 204

a

PAGE 205

b

PAGE 206

1. b 2. f 3. e
4. a 5. c 6. d
7. vibration that creates alternating regions of compression and decompression traveling through air
8. b 9. a 10. b
11. amplitude
12. **(3) Pitch depends on the amount of tension in the part that vibrates.** Stretching a rubber band increases the tension in it, raising the pitch when the rubber band vibrates.
13. **(1) resonance** When the music box is held in the air, only the box vibrates. But when it is placed on a table, it causes the table to vibrate at the same frequency through resonance. That makes the sound louder.
14. **(5) rustling leaves and conversation** The sound of a hair dryer has a loudness of 75 decibels. Rustling leaves (40 decibels) and conversation (60 decibels) are both quieter because those decibel levels are lower than 75.
15. Most men are larger than most women, so most men have larger vocal cords than most women have. As with musical instruments, larger size correlates with the ability to produce lower-pitched sounds.
16. Many answers are possible. Sample answer: I can turn down the volume when I listen to music.

SCIENCE AT WORK

PAGE 209

1. **(3) spray foam**
2. **(5) foil insulation**
3. Sample answer: It would be a good idea to install insulation material under the floor of the room above the garage because garages are not usually heated. So, when the outside temperature is cold and you want the room to stay warm, the insulation material would limit the amount of heated air escaping through the floor into the garage. If the room were being cooled by air conditioning, the insulation material would block the passage of warm air from the garage into the air-conditioned room.

UNIT 4 REVIEW

PAGES 210–213

1. inclined plane or ramp
2. Friction
3. **(4) pushing a wheeled 75-pound cart up a ramp three feet long** Options 1, 2, and 5 are incorrect because they involve lifting, which takes more force than using an inclined plane. Option 3 is incorrect because friction adds resistance; thus you

need more force to push a box than a wheeled cart.

4. weight, speed (in either order)
5. (1) **The cue ball has more momentum before the collision than after.** The arrow near the cue ball shows that the cue ball is moving before the collision but not after. Since an object that is not moving has no momentum, the cue ball has more momentum before the collision. Option 4 is incorrect because the cue ball has no speed after the collision.
6. Sound   7. amplitude
8. **(2) large amplitude and short wavelength** The amplitude determines the loudness of the sound. The larger the amplitude, the louder the sound. The wavelength determines if the sound is high or low in pitch. The shorter the wavelength, the higher the pitch.
9. **(3) The wavelength will be longer and the amplitude smaller.** The article says that lower pitches have longer wavelengths. Also, as sounds get softer, the amplitude of their waves gets smaller.
10. magnet
11. **(5) a compact disc** According to the article, a compact disc does not have a magnetic pattern, so it will not be damaged by the EM field of the metal detector. All other options have magnetic patterns and could be damaged.

Science Extension

Many answers are possible. Sample answers:
Inclined plane: driveway, door stop, ax
Lever: bottle opener, hammer, tweezers, nutcracker, crowbar, balance
Wheel and axle: screwdriver, steering wheel, car wheel, wrench, faucet
Gears: can opener, bicycle gears, salad spinner, mechanical clock, egg beater

Unit 4 Mini-Test

PAGES 214–215

1. **(5)The lever will end up in its starting position, shown in the diagram.** ***(Scientific Understanding & Skills: Physical Science: Analysis)*** When the pivot is in the middle of a lever, the mechanical advantage of both sides is equal. Therefore, the lever will change its final position only if the effort is greater than or equal to the resistance. In the diagram, the effort is 5 lbs. but the resistance is 10 lbs., so the lever, if it moves at all, will return to its starting position.
2. **(2) a shovel** ***(Science & Technology: Physical Science: Application)*** A shovel is a lever with the pivot point at the ground. Effort is applied at the handle, and resistance is provided by the material being lifted. An axe is an example of a wedge. A loading ramp is an example of an inclined plane. An automobile gearbox and dials on a radio are examples of gears.
3. **(4) Loud sounds kill cells in the inner ear.** ***(Science in Social & Personal Perspectives: Physical Science: Evaluation)*** Ear plugs reduce the volume of sounds that reach the inner ear, so wearing ear plugs in noisy places can protect the specialized cells in the inner ear and preserve hearing.
4. **(1) The best use for CDs is recording music.** ***(Scientific Understanding & Skills: Physical Science: Analysis)*** Recording music is only one of the uses of CDs. Whether it is the best use depends on what someone believes, so it is an opinion.
5. **(3) Bowling pins do not have momentum unless they are moving.** ***(Scientific Understanding & Skills: Physical Science: Comprehension)*** The paragraph explains that bowling pins have no momentum

when they are stationary and gain momentum when they move.

6. **(4) a dam controlling the flow of a river** ***(Scientific Understanding & Skills: Physical Science: Application)*** A dam controls whether water in a river flows downstream or is stopped. A light switch completes or interrupts an electric circuit, and so controls the flow of electrons in the circuit. None of the other options illustrate this kind of relationship.
7. **(3) Design B is the best choice for buildings in noisy neighborhoods.** ***(Unifying Concepts and Processes: Physical Science: Evaluation)*** According to the information in the graph, Design B transmits the lowest percentage of sound. In a building with these windows, less outside noise would be transmitted into the building.

POSTTEST

PAGES 217–225

1. **(1) A male ant has wings and a worker ant does not.** ***(Scientific Understanding & Skills: Life Science: Analysis)*** The drawings show two main differences between male and worker ants. First, male ants have wings and workers do not. Second, male ants are larger than worker ants. The second difference is not listed among the choices; therefore, the correct answer is option 1.
2. **(5) The queen does not mate again.** ***(Unifying Concepts & Processes: Life Science: Comprehension)*** The males and queen mate during a flight they take outside the anthill. After that, the queen loses her wings. Since the queen can no longer fly, she cannot go on a mating flight again.
3. **(3) 7.5 inches thick** ***(Science in Personal and Social Perspectives: Physical Science: Application)*** Although 3 inches of ice can support a few people, there are likely to be many people on the ice. To be safe, Shawn should wait until the ice is 7.5 inches thick. At that point, it can support a car, so it would also be able to support a larger group of people.
4. **(4) The X-ray photo showed his wife's ring.** ***(History and Nature of Science: Physical Science: Evaluation)*** Evidence that X rays cannot pass through metals would be an image of a metal object on an X-ray photo. The fact that her ring appeared in Roentgen's X-ray photo of his wife's hand provides this evidence.
5. **(2) planting or weeding** ***(Scientific Understanding & Skills: Life Science: Application)*** The bar graph shows the amount of energy, measured in calories, that a person uses when performing different yardwork chores. The task that requires the least energy (the fewest calories per hour) is planting or weeding.
6. **(2) 4,100** ***(Scientific Understanding & Skills: Earth and Space Science: Comprehension)*** First find the years 1986–1990 on the horizontal axis. Then moving straight up from there, find the point on the trend line that represents those years. Read across to the vertical axis to see how many tornadoes occurred during that period.
7. **(5) There were more tornadoes during the 1990s than during the 1980s.** ***(Scientific Understanding & Skills: Earth and Space Science: Evaluation)*** In general the trend line slopes upward. For the periods 1991–1995 and 1996–2000, there were far more tornadoes than during the periods 1981–1985 and 1986–1990.

8. **(4) The ball travels 350 feet less in the air at Shea Stadium than it would in a vacuum.** *(Unifying Concepts & Processes: Physical Science: Evaluation)* Although options 1, 2, and 5 are all true statements, only option 4 provides evidence to support the conclusion that air resistance affects a baseball.
9. **(4) D** *(Science & Technology: Physical Science: Application)* According to the information, electricity flows only when it has a complete path, or circuit, between the energy source and the device being powered. Diagram D is the only one showing wires that make a complete path between the energy source (the battery) and the device being powered (the light bulb).
10. **(5) Deer are attractive animals that are nice to see in a backyard.** *(Scientific Understanding & Skills: Life Science: Analysis)* An opinion states a belief rather than a provable fact. Only option 5 is an opinion. The other options are facts stated or implied in the passage.
11. **(5) Combustion changes some solid matter to gas and energy.** *(Scientific Understanding & Skills: Physical Science: Evaluation)* Option 5 explains that matter changes state during combustion, and is changed without being destroyed. Options 1, 3, and 4 are true statements, but do not say anything about the amount of matter involved before or after combustion. Option 2 expresses an opinion, not a scientific fact.
12. **(3) experiment** *(Science as Inquiry: Life Science: Application)* The taste test that Ruth set up is an experiment, or a method of testing her hypothesis that organically grown vegetables taste better than conventionally grown vegetables.
13. **(4) data** *(Science as Inquiry: Life Science: Application)* When the tasters filled out the questionnaires, they provided Ruth with information about their preferences.
14. **(5) conclusion** *(Science as Inquiry: Life Science: Application)* Based on the questionnaire results, Ruth concluded that organically grown vegetables do taste better than conventionally grown vegetables. She had thought so before the experiment; but she had no data to support the idea. Once Ruth collected data about the preferences of a group of people, she could draw a valid conclusion.
15. **(3) There are about the same number of bones in the arms and hands as in the legs and feet.** *(Scientific Understanding & Skills: Life Science: Analysis)* The wedge that represents the percentage of bones in the arms and hands and the wedge that represents the percentage of bones in the legs and feet are about the same size and the percentages are very close. This means that there are about the same number of bones in the arms and hands as in the legs and feet.
16. **(1) Yeast cells reproduce by growing a bud that splits off the parent cell.** *(Scientific Understanding & Skills: Life Science: Comprehension)* The diagram shows the budding process of a yeast cell. This process results in two cells—the original cell and the new cell. Option 1 summarizes the process shown in the diagram. The remaining options describe details of the budding process.
17. **(4) DNA paternity tests can be done with or without cells from the alleged father.** *(Scientific Understanding & Skills: Life Science: Analysis)* According to the information, some DNA paternity tests are done with the alleged father's cell samples. However, if the alleged father is not available, then the test can be done with the alleged father's parents' cell samples.
18. **(2) increased pollution of the Mississippi River basin and the Great Lakes** *(Scientific Understanding & Skills: Life Science: Analysis)* The map shows eagle

nesting sites along the shores of the Great Lakes and along the banks of rivers that make up the Mississippi River system. Pollution to these bodies of water could harm the bald eagles nesting in these extensive areas. The other options are incorrect because the map indicates that few bald eagles nest in these regions.

19. **(4) Boyle encouraged experimentation to test scientific ideas.** ***(History & Nature of Science: Physical Science: Comprehension)*** Boyle was one scientist who suggested that only thinking about nature was not the best way to understand the world. Instead, he thought that scientific ideas needed to be tested by experiments that would provide data to support or reject the ideas.

20. **(1) Air pollution comes from transportation and industry.** ***(Science in Personal & Social Perspectives: Earth and Space Science: Comprehension)*** The chart shows five air pollutants and their sources, all from transportation (motor vehicles) or industry (smelting, manufacturing plants, power plants, refineries, etc.). The other options all provide details about particular pollutants.

21. **(3) The paper clip would fall.** ***(Science & Technology: Physical Science: Analysis)*** If the wire were cut, no electricity would flow around the nail. Therefore, no magnetic field would be created, and the paper clip would fall.

22. **(1) blocks the sun except for a rim of light** ***(Scientific Understanding & Skills: Earth and Space Science: Analysis)*** According to the two diagrams, the main difference between a total solar eclipse and a partial solar eclipse is the amount of sun blocked by the moon. In a total eclipse the moon almost entirely blocks the sun, but in a partial eclipse the moon blocks only a portion of the sun.

23. **(3) Of the volcanic eruptions listed in the graph, Tuxtla, in Mexico, caused the most known deaths.** ***(Scientific Understanding & Skills: Earth and Space Science: Analysis)*** According to the graph, about 50,000 people died when Tuxtla erupted—the highest number of known deaths given on this graph.

24. **(5) Both can be used for cooking and cleaning.** ***(Scientific Understanding & Skills: Physical Science: Analysis)*** According to the chart, vinegar can be used for cooking or cleaning glass. Baking soda can also be used for cooking or cleaning.

25. **(2) the benefits of life science research** ***(Science in Personal & Social Perspectives: Life Science: Evaluation)*** According to the circle graph, the largest amount (almost half) of all federal funding for scientific research goes to the life sciences. This suggests that Americans place the most value on such research. Option 1 does not apply to the topic of the circle graph. Options 3, 4, and 5 are related to areas of scientific research that get less funding than life sciences.

activation energy the energy necessary to start a chemical reaction

adaptation a trait that makes a plant or an animal better able to live in its environment

adult the stage of an organism's life cycle in which it is fully grown and developed

aerobic needing oxygen to live

air mass a large body of air with certain temperature and moisture

amniocentesis a test performed on pregnant women that detects certain birth disorders

amplitude the height of a wave

antibiotic a drug that fights bacteria

antibody a protein made by white blood cells that attacks and kills invading germs

antigen a foreign protein

aqueduct a pipe or concrete channel that carries water from a reservoir

artery a large blood vessel that carries blood away from the heart to parts of the body

asphalt a black substance that is used for paving roads

atmosphere the air surrounding a planet

atom the smallest particle of an element

bacteria simple one-celled organisms

bar graph a type of illustration that is used to compare sets of information

bark the woody outer part of a plant stem

basal cell skin cancer a type of slow-growing cancer that often appears on the hands or face as an open sore, reddish patch, mole, or scar

biome a large region with a certain climate and certain living things

boiling the rapid change of matter from a liquid to a gas

bud on a plant, areas of growth that develop into leaves and flowers

caption a short passage that accompanies a photograph or illustration

carbon dioxide–oxygen cycle a process in which plants use carbon dioxide given off by other living things and make oxygen, which is in turn used by the other living things

caterpillar the wormlike stage in the life cycle of a butterfly or moth

cause something that makes another thing happen

cell the smallest unit of a living thing that can carry on life processes

cell membrane a layer around the cell that controls what can enter or leave the cell

chart an organized list that gives information in a form that is easy to read

chemical change a change in the property of matter; a chemical change makes new substances

chemical equation a statement that shows the reactants and products of a reaction

chemical formula a group of symbols used to describe a compound (example: H_2O is the chemical formula for water)

chemical reaction a process in which elements or compounds are changed into other substances

chemical symbol a kind of shorthand that chemists use in which one or two letters stand for an element

chemistry the study of matter and its changes

cholesterol a fatlike substance found in all animals

chromosome a strand of genetic material, or DNA

circle graph a graph used to show parts of a whole; also known as a pie chart

classifying grouping things that are similar to help understand how they work

collision the result of a moving object striking another object

colloid a mixture of fine particles suspended in another substance, usually a liquid

combustion the chemical change also known as burning, in which oxygen reacts with fuel to create light and heat

compare to tell how things are alike

composting the breaking down of organic material in the soil by aerobic bacteria, fungi, insects, and worms

compound two or more elements combined chemically

compound machine a machine made up of two or more simple machines

conclusion a logical judgment based on facts

condensation the change from a gas to a liquid

conglomerate a type of sedimentary rock formed from large pebbles and stones

context surrounding material; you can often figure out the meaning of an unknown word by looking at its context—the rest of the words in the sentence

continental polar air mass a cold, dry air mass; for example, one that forms over Canada and the northern United States

continental shelf the nearly flat area of the ocean bottom where the ocean meets the continent

continental slope the sloping area that extends from the edge of the continental shelf to the ocean basin

continental tropical air mass a warm, dry air mass; for example, one that forms over the southwestern United States

contrast to tell how things are different

control group in an experiment, a group that is similar to the experimental group except for one feature

convergence the independent evolution of similar parts of unrelated organisms as adaptations to the environment (example: wings in bats, birds, and butterflies)

core the center of something such as the sun or Earth

cytoplasm a jellylike material that makes up most of a cell

density the quantity of matter in a given unit of volume

details small pieces of information that explain or support a main idea

diagram a picture that explains what something looks like or how it works

diode an electronic device that allows current to flow in one direction only

distillation the process for separating liquid mixtures

DNA the genetic material found in chromosomes

dominant trait a trait that can override a recessive trait

Down syndrome a disorder caused by an extra chromosome; children born with Down syndrome are mildly to severely mentally retarded and may also have other health problems

Earth and space science the study of Earth and the universe

echolocation a system in which sound waves are sent out and their echoes interpreted to determine the direction and distance of objects; certain animals, such as dolphins and bats, use this

ecosystem an area in which living and nonliving things interact

effect something that happens as a result of a cause

effort the force that is being used to do work

egg in animals, the female reproductive cell

egg mass a clump of eggs

elastic able to be stretched or compressed and then returned to the original shape

electrolysis the process of using electricity to produce chemical changes; water can be split into hydrogen and oxygen using electrolysis

electromagnetic field (EM field) the energy field surrounding and created by an electric current

electron a particle in atoms that has a negative electrical charge

electronics a branch of engineering concerned with devices that use electric current

element a substance that cannot be broken down into other substances by ordinary means, such as heating or crushing

embryo an organism in the early stages of development; a developing baby from the third to eighth week in the mother's womb

EM field *see* electromagnetic field

endothermic reaction a process in which heat is taken in (example: photosynthesis)

energy the ability of matter to do work

equator the imaginary circle around Earth halfway between the North and South Poles

erode to wear away

evaporation the slow change of a liquid to a gas

evolution the gradual change in a species over time

exothermic reaction a process in which heat is produced (example: combustion)

experiment a procedure used to test a hypothesis

experimental group in an experiment, the group being tested

external recycling the process in which individuals process waste materials so they can be made into new things

fact a statement about something that actually happened or actually exists

fat a substance that provides energy and building material for the body

fetal alcohol syndrome (FAS) a group of birth defects that can occur when a pregnant woman drinks alcohol

fetus a developing baby from the third to ninth month

filtration the process of separating substances by passing a mixture through a screen or similar material

flower in a plant, the reproductive organ that produces seeds and pollen

flu *see* influenza

force a push or a pull

forecast a prediction, as of the weather

fossil the remains or imprint of a long-dead organism

fossil fuel a fuel, such as coal, oil, or natural gas, that is formed from the remains of plants or animals that lived hundreds of millions of years ago

freefall a condition in which an object is falling back to Earth

freezing the change in matter from a liquid to a solid

frequency the number of waves that pass a point in a certain amount of time

friction a force between surfaces that touch

front the leading edge of a moving air mass

fuel a source of energy

fusion *see* nuclear fusion

gas a state of matter that does not have a definite size or shape and expands to fill its container

gear a wheel with teeth; each gear turns on its own center

genetics the study of how traits are inherited

genetic screening tests that can tell if certain disorders are likely to be inherited

glacier a mass of ice that forms when more snow falls than melts

global warming a worldwide increase in average temperature

glossary an alphabetical listing of important words and their definitions, located at the end of a text

gravity the natural force of attraction between two objects (example: the pull of Earth on humans)

greenhouse effect the warming of Earth caused by the absorption of infrared radiation into gases in the atmosphere

groundwater water that is found underground (examples: springs and wells)

heading the name of an article section that tells the topic or main idea of the text that follows

hereditary capable of being passed from a parent to an offspring through a father's sperm or a mother's egg

heredity the passing of traits from parents to their young

humidity water vapor in the air

hydrocarbon a compound made only of hydrogen and carbon

hypothesis an explanation of how something works, based on many observations

igneous rock rock formed when molten rock hardens

implied not stated

inclined plane a simple machine with a long, sloping surface that helps move an object (example: ramp)

inference the use of information to figure out things that are not actually stated

influenza (flu) an illness caused by a virus

infrared radiation the energy Earth radiates back into the atmosphere

inherit to acquire a trait or disease that is passed on from one's parents (examples: hair color, Huntington's disease)

inner planets the four planets closest to the sun: Mercury, Venus, Earth, and Mars

integrated circuit tiny electronic components linked together to form a circuit

internal recycling the process in which manufacturing businesses reuse their own waste materials

ion an atom with a positive or negative electric charge

joint the place where two or more bones come together

key something that explains the symbols on a map or a graph

kindling temperature the temperature at which a substance will burn

landfill an area of open land that is filled with layers of garbage

language a system of signs or sounds that refer to objects or ideas and that can be combined in different ways to produce different meanings

laser a tool that produces a narrow, strong beam of light in which all the waves have the same frequency and wavelength and are in phase

leaf the part of a plant that produces food from water, carbon dioxide, and sunlight

lever a bar that turns on a pivot

life cycle the series of changes an animal goes through in its life

life science the study of living things and how they affect one another

ligament a strong band of tissue that connects bones at joints

light a form of energy that travels in waves and makes vision possible

line graph a graph that shows how one thing changes as a second thing changes

liquid a state of matter that takes up a definite amount of space but does not have a definite shape

main idea the topic of a paragraph, passage, or diagram

mammal an animal with a backbone, hair or fur, and milk-producing glands to feed its young

map a drawing that shows places or features on Earth

maritime polar air mass a cold, moist air mass; for example, one that forms over the northern Atlantic Ocean and northern Pacific Ocean

maritime tropical air mass a warm, moist air mass; for example, one that forms over the Caribbean Sea, the middle of the Atlantic Ocean, or the middle of the Pacific Ocean

mechanical advantage the number of times a machine multiplies your effort to do work

melanoma a fast-growing skin cancer that may appear as oddly shaped blotches

melting the change in matter from a solid to a liquid

metamorphic rock rock formed in conditions of great heat and pressure

meteorologist a scientist who studies changes in Earth's atmosphere to forecast the weather

microgravity apparent weightlessness experienced by objects that are falling or are in orbit around a body in space

microprocessor an integrated circuit that functions as a computer's central processing unit

mitochondria the parts of a cell that give the cell the energy it needs to grow and reproduce

mitosis the process by which a cell's nucleus divides and therefore reproduces

mixture a combination of two or more kinds of matter that can be separated by physical means

molecule the smallest particle of a compound

momentum the property of a moving object that is a product of its mass and velocity

monounsaturated fat a type of fat found in some vegetable products

mutation a change in a gene

mutualism a relationship in which two species help each other

natural resource a natural material or space that humans need and use

natural selection the survival of organisms best suited to their environment

neutron a particle found in the nucleus of an atom that has no electrical charge

nitrate a substance made by soil-dwelling bacteria using nitrogen from the air

nuclear fusion the reaction in which two nuclei combine

nuclear reaction changes in the nucleus, or center, of an atom

nucleus in life science, a cell's control center, which contains genetic material; in chemistry and physics, the protons and neutrons forming the core of an atom

observation the act of watching or using other senses to gather information

ocean basin the bottom of the sea

opinion a statement that expresses what a person or group of people think, feel, or believe about a fact

ore a rock or earth from which minerals are extracted

osteoporosis a condition of brittle bones common to older people, especially women

outer planets the five planets farthest from the sun: Jupiter, Saturn, Uranus, Neptune, and Pluto

oxidation the process in which a substance reacts with oxygen, causing the formation of a new compound called an oxide

overtone a frequency of sound that is an exact multiple of another frequency produced at the same time

ozone a form of oxygen

paleontologist a scientist who studies ancient forms of life

paraphrase to restate information in a different way that keeps the original meaning

parasite an organism that lives on or in another organism and harms it

photosynthesis the process by which plants use carbon dioxide, energy from sunlight, and water to make food

pH scale a measurement from 0 to 14 of the strength of an acid or a base

physical change a change in the appearance of matter without a change in its properties (example: the dissolving of sugar in water)

physics the study of energy and forces and their effect on matter

pitch the perceived frequency of a sound

pivot the point around which an object turns

placenta a structure that attaches the embryo/fetus to the uterus and allows substances to pass between the embryo/fetus and the mother

plaque deposits of cholesterol on the inside walls of arteries

pneumonia an infection of the lungs caused by viruses or bacteria

pollute to make dirty or contaminate

polyunsaturated fat a type of fat found in some vegetable foods and fish

precipitation water falling from the atmosphere in the form of rain, snow, or sleet

prediction a guess about what may happen

printed circuit board a board to which electronic components that form circuits are attached

process diagram a type of drawing that shows steps in a process, often with arrows showing how one step leads to another

product a substance that forms in a chemical reaction

proton a positively charged particle in the nucleus of an atom

Punnett square a diagram used to show all possible combinations of a trait among offspring of two parents

pupa the nonfeeding stage in the life cycle of some insects when their adult tissues are formed

pure tone a sound made up of a single frequency

radiant energy energy that exists in the form of waves, such as light waves or radio waves

raw material an unprocessed natural material or other material used to make something new

reactant a substance that reacts in a chemical reaction

recessive trait a trait that will not appear if it is paired with a dominant trait

recycle to collect and process waste materials so they can be used again

renewable resource a resource that does not get used up (example: water)

reservoir a lake created by a dam

resistance a force that must be overcome to do work

resonance the process in which a vibrating object causes another object to vibrate at the same frequency

resource a material that people need from Earth

respiration the process by which living things take in oxygen and release carbon dioxide to obtain energy

rhinovirus a virus that causes certain types of colds

ribosome a part of a cell that makes the proteins the cell needs in order to grow

root the part of a plant that holds it in the ground and absorbs water and nutrients from the soil

saturated fat a type of fat that is solid at room temperature

scan to look over something quickly to find details

scientific methods organized ways of solving problems; the processes scientists use for getting information and testing ideas

sedimentary rock rock formed when particles are deposited and then harden over time

sequence the order in which things happen

silicon the most common element in Earth's crust

simple machine a device to do work (example: lever)

skim to look over something quickly to get the main ideas

software instructions that tell a computer how to perform a task

solar cell a device that converts sunlight into electricity

solar system a sun and the objects that revolve around it, such as planets and their moons

solid a state of matter that has a definite shape and takes up a definite amount of space

solubility the amount of a solute that will dissolve in a given amount of solvent at a given temperature and pressure

solute the substance in a solution that is present in the smaller amount

solution a type of mixture in which the ingredients are distributed evenly throughout

solvent the substance in a solution that is present in the greater amount

sound a sensation caused by vibrations and perceived by hearing

sound waves vibrations transmitted through substances in waves with frequencies that can be heard

space probe unmanned spacecraft used for the exploration of space

species a group of organisms with similar characteristics that can interbreed to produce fertile offspring

spectrometer a device used to analyze what things are made of

sprain a joint injury in which the ligaments are stretched or torn

squamous cell skin cancer a type of cancer that looks like raised, pink spots or growths that may be open in the center

stationary front the zone between two air masses, caused when the masses stop moving

stem the part of a plant that provides support and transports substances

substance matter that is of one particular type

summarize to condense or shorten a larger amount of information into a few sentences

table a type of chart that organizes information in rows and columns

timbre the quality of a sound, which depends on the number and strength of overtones

timeline an illustration that shows when a series of events took place and the order in which they occurred

topic sentence the sentence that contains the main idea in a paragraph

trait an inherited characteristic such as hair color or blood type

transistor an electronic device used to amplify, detect, or switch electric current

tropical rain forest dense forest found near the equator where the climate is hot and wet

ultraviolet light a type of light with wavelengths too short to be visible to the human eye; also known as black light

ultraviolet rays a type of harmful energy in sunlight

uterus a woman's womb, in which an unborn baby develops

vaccination an injected dose of dead or weakened disease-causing agent; the body reacts to a vaccination by forming antibodies to fight the disease

virus a tiny particle of genetic material with a protein covering

water cycle the circulation of water on Earth through evaporation from the surface into the atmosphere and back to the surface as precipitation

wavelength the distance from the top of one wave to the top of the next wave

weather map a map showing where cold, warm, and stationary fronts are, as well as areas of high and low pressure

wheel and axle a simple machine composed of two objects that turn in a circular motion on the same center, multiplying both force and speed

work the process of using force to cause an object to move

zygote a fertilized egg resulting when the sperm from the father joins with the egg produced by the mother

A

B

C